Bank-Industry versus Stock Market-Industry Relationships

This book focuses on a variety of themes concerning the relationship between financial systems in a broader sense and firms' growth in historical perspective in some European countries. Financial systems are nowadays largely acknowledged to be a crucial element in determining economic growth. In modern economies, they play a key role by mobilizing savings, pricing risks, and allocating capital to firms. Following a consolidated taxonomy focusing on the historical perspective, countries have been conventionally divided into bank-oriented (Continental Europe countries and Japan) and market-oriented systems (Anglo-Saxon countries).

The chapters in this book present case studies on Belgium, Great Britain, France, and Italy and show that financial systems do not trigger growth processes and industrialization, but they are essential to sustain them over time. Each society has the financial system that fits with its historical trajectory, without any being better or worse than others. The important thing is to have a financial system that is sophisticated and stable, and that evolves according to the demand forces of the moment. History matters.

Bank-Industry versus Stock Market-Industry Relationships will be a beneficial read for students interested in economics and business history. The chapters in this book were originally published as a special issue of *Business History.*

José L. García-Ruiz is Professor of Economic History at the Complutense University of Madrid (Spain). His lines of research are business history, financial history and industrial history. Between 2015 and 2019 he was Editor-in-chief of *Investigaciones de Historia Económica-Economic History Research* (IHE-HER), the academic journal of the Spanish Economic History Association.

Michelangelo Vasta is Professor of Economic History at the University of Siena (Italy). He received his D.Phil at University of Oxford. His main fields of interest are economics of innovation in the long run perspective, institutions and economic performance, the economic history of living standard, entrepreneurship and trade. He pays particular attention to historical datasets and quantitative methods. He has published extensively in the major economic history and business history journals.

Bank-Industry versus Stock Market-Industry Relationships

Edited by
José L. García-Ruiz and Michelangelo Vasta

Routledge
Taylor & Francis Group
LONDON AND NEW YORK

First published 2023
by Routledge
4 Park Square, Milton Park, Abingdon, Oxon OX14 4RN

and by Routledge
605 Third Avenue, New York, NY 10158

Routledge is an imprint of the Taylor & Francis Group, an informa business

British Library Cataloguing in Publication Data
A catalogue record for this book is available from the British Library

ISBN13: 978-1-032-43742-2 (hbk)
ISBN13: 978-1-032-43743-9 (pbk)
ISBN13: 978-1-003-36867-0 (ebk)

DOI: 10.4324/9781003368670

Typeset in Myriad Pro
by Newgen Publishing UK

Publisher's Note
The publisher accepts responsibility for any inconsistencies that may have arisen during the conversion of this book from journal articles to book chapters, namely the inclusion of journal terminology.

Contents

Citation Information

The chapters in this book were originally published in the journal *Business History*, volume 63, issue 6 (2021). When citing this material, please use the original page numbering for each article, as follows:

Introduction

Financing firms: Beyond the dichotomy between banks and markets
José L. García-Ruiz and Michelangelo Vasta
Business History, volume 63, issue 6 (2021), pp. 877–891

Chapter 1

The coevolution of banks and corporate securities markets: The financing of Belgium's industrial take-off in the 1830s
Stefano Ugolini
Business History, volume 63, issue 6 (2021), pp. 892–913

Chapter 2

Did French stock markets support firms of the Second Industrial Revolution?
Emilie Bonhoure and David Le Bris
Business History, volume 63, issue 6 (2021), pp. 914–943

Chapter 3

Debating banking in Britain: The Colwyn committee, 1918
Mark Billings, Simon Mollan and Philip Garnett
Business History, volume 63, issue 6 (2021), pp. 944–965

Chapter 4

Corporate networks in post-war Britain: Do finance–industry relationships matter for corporate borrowing?
Philipp Kern and Gerhard Schnyder
Business History, volume 63, issue 6 (2021), pp. 966–987

Chapter 5

The banking-industry relationship in Italy: large national banks and small local banks compared (1913–1936)
Alberto Rinaldi and Anna Spadavecchia
Business History, volume 63, issue 6 (2021), pp. 988–1006

Notes on Contributors

Mark Billings is Senior Lecturer in Accounting and Business History at the University of Exeter Business School, UK. His research interests are in banking, financial and accounting history.

Emilie Bonhoure is Assistant Professor at the Finance-Accounting-Economics department, Kedge Business School, France. Her research relates to several topics: financial history (particularly dividends, governance, and profit allocation within the listed firms of the beginning of the 20th century; venality and the financial system of the French early modern period), governance, and banks and other financial or banking institutions.

José L. García-Ruiz is Professor of Economic History at the Complutense University of Madrid (Spain). His lines of research are Business History, Financial History and Industrial History. Between 2015 and 2019 he was the Editor-in-chief of *Investigaciones de Historia Económica-Economic History Research* (IHE-HER), the academic journal of the Spanish Economic History Association.

Philip Garnett is a Lecturer at the York Management School, University of York where he is also a member of the York Centre for Complex Systems. His research is broadly focused on modelling organisational structure and interactions between organisations and their environment; and understanding the flow of information through organizations.

Philipp Kern is Lecturer in International Management at Loughborough University London, UK. His research focuses on comparative management at the intersection of institutions and firms.

David Le Bris is Associate Professor at Toulouse Business School, Department of Finance, University of Toulouse Capitole, France. His research is published in specialized reviews (*Business History, Financial History Review*) as well as in general reviews (*Revue d'Economie Politique, Bankers, Markets and Investors, Revue Economique*).

Simon Mollan is Senior Lecturer at the School for Business and Society, University of York. His research interests include international development, international management and organizational strategy, financialisation and the social studies of finance, imperialism, organisational modelling and complexity, business/management history, international business theory, and research methods.

Alberto Rinaldi is Associate Professor of Economic History at the University of Modena and Reggio Emilia, Italy. He has researched extensively on the history of industrial districts and local production systems in Italy with special reference to the case of the Emilia-Romagna region.

Gerhard Schnyder is Professor of International Management and Political Economy at Loughborough University London, UK. His research adopts an interdisciplinary and comparative approach to investigate the institutional and political determinants of economic activity.

Anna Spadavecchia is Reader in the Hunter Centre for Entrepreneurship at the University of Strathclyde (Glasgow, UK). She completed her PhD in the Department of Economic History at the London School of Economics and Political Science. Her research interests are in the fields of Innovation and patent management in an international perspective, and the role of institutions in the development of industry clusters in Italy in the second half of the 20th century. Her research has been published in Business and Economic History journals, as well as journals in the broad fields of Innovation and Business.

Stefano Ugolini is Associate Professor of Economics at Sciences Po Toulouse and a Researcher at LEREPS, University of Toulouse, France. He has published extensively on the history of international finance, banking, and money. He is the author of *The Evolution of Central Banking: Theory and History* (Palgrave Macmillan, 2017).

Michelangelo Vasta is Professor of Economic History at the University of Siena (Italy). He received his D.Phil at University of Oxford. His main fields of interest are economic of innovation in the long run perspective, institutions and economic performance, the economic history of living standard, entrepreneurship, and trade. He pays particular attention to historical datasets and quantitative methods. He has published extensively in the major economic history and business history journals.

Introduction—Financing firms: Beyond the dichotomy between banks and markets

José L. García-Ruiz and Michelangelo Vasta

ABSTRACT

This article provides a review of the different streams of literature that have contributed, since the seminal work by Alexander Gerschenkron, to the issue on firms' financing. We show that, although the traditional dichotomy between bank and stock market is out of date, the Gerschenkronian thesis is still debated. We find that many microeconomic issues have yet to be explored. In particular, the interaction between bank and stock market in financing firms merits further attention. Finally, we show that the combinations of several approaches and the use of new techniques, such as the network analysis, can contribute to provide further results on this topic.

Financial systems are nowadays largely acknowledged to be a crucial element in determining economic growth. In modern economies, they play a key role by mobilising savings, pricing risks and allocating capital to firms. The two main components of financial systems are financial institutions and financial markets. Financial institutions, being mainly different kinds of banks but also insurances, act as intermediaries by channelling resources from the suppliers of funds to the users. Conversely, financial markets allow buyers and sellers of securities to trade directly.

Following a consolidated taxonomy focussing on the historical perspective, countries have been conventionally divided in bank-oriented (Continental Europe countries and Japan) and in market-oriented systems (Anglo-Saxon countries). In the former, financial institutions that bear risks and lend resources through close relationship with their clients prevails. In the latter, savings are mainly channelling through markets, where equity and debt securities are traded. One of the most important issues in the functioning of the financial systems is how resources are allocated to industrial firms. The way in which firms are financed affects many elements of a country such as the industrial structure, its specialisation, the corporate governance and, ultimately, the pace of economic growth.

Traditionally, the historical literature has mainly focussed on the role played by banks following the seminal contribution by Alexander Gerschenkron (1962). Indeed, in his very influential essay *Economic Backwardness in Historical Perspective*, Gerschenkron maintained that banks, particularly the long term financing universal ones, are the major drivers of industrial spurts of latecomer countries, such as Germany and Italy, in the pre-World War I years. In his view, this typology of banks functioned as a 'substitutive factor' for otherwise missing prerequisites of industrialisation, i.e., the substantial capital accumulation and the willingness to invest it in the industries related to the technologies of the Second Industrial Revolution. The creation of a bank system to stabilise the currency and, particularly, to provide capital to business has been still considered by Robert Allen in his recent survey of global economic history, as one of the pillars of the 'standard model' of industrialisation adopted by the Western countries (Allen, 2011).[1] In his model, Allen has acknowledged the crucial role played by the investment banks, which did not have a role in British industrialisation, in Continental Europe, especially in Germany.

Indeed, the nexus between banks and the successful catching up of the German economy during the Second Industrial Revolution is a classical topic in economic history. The idea of a positive impact of large German joint stock credit banks dates back to the traditional contribution by Otto Jeidels in 1905 and Rudolf Hilferding in 1910, but has been systematised by Gerschenkron in 1962 in his original model of 'conditional convergence' based on the adoption of new technologies of latecomer countries (Hilferding, 1910; Jeidels 1905). According to Gerschenkron, the German investment banks are a so crucial invention to be comparable to that of the steam engine.

The main idea of the Gerschenkron thesis has been analysed by several empirical researches not only mainly focussed on the German case. In his influential book *Scale and Scope*, Alfred Chandler gave support to the Gerschenkronian thesis suggesting that German universal banks provided capital for new industries and contributed to guide industrial firms in the initial stage of their growth (Chandler, 1990). In the same vein, Jürgen Kocka maintained that the joint stock companies, closely linked with the universal banks, played a major role in the big rise of the German industry (Kocka, 1978). The combination of joint stock companies and the investment banks would have provided savings to the new industrial investment necessary for the sectors of the Second Industrial Revolution.

1. Gerschenkron hypothesis is still alive?

The Gerschenkronian thesis on the crucial role of the universal banks has been reviewed and tested by many contributions. Jeremy Edwards and Sheilagh Ogilvie found that the claim that universal banks played a crucial role in German industrialisation is not confirmed for at least three reasons (Edwards & Ogilvie, 1996). First, universal banks accounted for a small proportion of the total assets of financial institutions before World War I. Second, they did not support the increase in concentration in German industry. Third, their contribution to coordinate the system exploiting the information flows they got via supervisory boards was over evaluated. Finally, they claim that other type of banks (savings banks, mortgage banks, and credit cooperatives) were also important for financing the German industrial system. Successively, in a series of empirical research, Caroline Fohlin found evidence that universal banks had a limited impact on capital mobilisation, industrial investment, and economic growth since firms connected to universal banks performed similarly to 'unattached' ones (Fohlin, 1999a). Carsten Burhop, in an empirical exercise, provided a nuanced view of the Gershenkronian thesis, by suggesting that the universal banks played an important role in the early phases of German industrialisation (1851–1882), while their role faded away later on (Burhop, 2006).

The Gerschenkronian hypothesis has been largely tested also for other countries (Cameron, 1967, 1972).[2] It is not possible to mention all the related studies in this context, but two cases are worth noting. The first refers to Italy, a country directly analysed by Gerschenkron in 1962. Fohlin showed formalised relationships with universal banks had limited impact on firms' investment, while Michelangelo Vasta, Carlo Drago, Roberto Ricciuti and Alberto Rinaldi reconsidering the centrality of the universal banks suggested that also local banks played a role in funding new industries (Fohlin, 1998, 1999b; Vasta et al., 2017). The second concerns the United States, the country which shares with Germany, great success during the rise of the Second Industrial Revolution. In a kind of counterfactual exercise, Charles Calomiris found that, at the turn of the twentieth century, American firms paid more for financing their investment than German firms, and attributed this gap to the lack of universal banks in the United States (Calomiris, 1995).

Although, the Gerschenkronian thesis dates back more than half century, it continues to be tested also by following the new theoretical approaches developed by the economic literature. However, the first criticism of the Gerschenkronian thesis came, at least implicitly, from Raymond Goldsmith in his seminal contribution *Finance Structure and Development* (Goldsmith, 1969).[3] In his quantitative survey, Goldsmith provided a large amount of data on the historical evolution of financial systems in a large sample of countries, developed and less developed. Although the work is by and large a vast collection of data, it casts doubts about the critical role played by banks and emphasised the crucial contribution of markets in financing of industrial firms and in determining economic growth.

Since the Goldsmith contribution, a growing stream of literature has emphasised, both theoretically and with a series of empirical studies, the great importance of financial markets for economic growth (Allen & Gale, 2000; Demirgüç-Kunt & Maksimovic, 2002; King & Levine, 1993). All these contributions generated a large amount of literature which overcame the traditional dichotomy between bank-oriented vs market-oriented financial system by emphasising that banks and markets must be seen as complementary rather than substitutes in financing industrial firms. In the same context, it has been highlighted that both, bank and markets, have an empirical connection with long run growth rates (Allen & Gale, 2000; Boot & Thakor, 2010; Levine & Zervos, 1998).

Following this stream of literature, new research offered further analysis of the Gerschenkron hypothesis. Fohlin provided new insights into the structure of the German financial system (Fohlin, 2007). Her results showed that key characteristics of universal banking emerged late in the industrialisation process and their influence came from something other than the formalised control relationship over firms. The importance of universality—the combination of investment and commercial banking—appears mostly in the support that universal banks gave to the development of active securities markets, not in the domination of industry nor in the dramatic alteration of firm behaviour or performance. In a recent study, Sibylle Lehmann, acknowledging the importance of the large universal German banks, modified the Gerschenkronian hypothesis by showing that these banks played an important role in fostering the development of the stock market, which increasingly replaced loans as a major source of capital for industrial firms (Lehmann, 2014).

2. Bank-based vs market-based financial systems?

Following the stream of theoretical and empirical literature which has been developed since the late 1990s, Fohlin provided a reappraisal of the dichotomy bank-based vs market-based by adopting a historical perspective (Fohlin, 2012, 2016). She showed most financial systems have a mix of characteristics and do not fit into a clear-cut taxonomy. In a nutshell, she suggested that the historical perspective helps to understand that a well-functioning financial system is crucial for economic growth, beyond the specific type it has developed.

Although some scholars continued to maintain the peculiarities of the firms' financing patterns in the two systems, the dichotomy between bank-based and market-based financial systems seems to be overcome (Lescure, 2007).[4] Indeed, many studies have tried to understand the determinants of the structure of financial systems. For instance, the crucial role played by the legal origin in determining the level of financial development of different countries has been highlighted, in some seminal contributions, by Rafael La Porta, Florencio Lopez-de-Silanes, Andrei Shleifer and Robert Vishny (La Porta et al., 1997, 1998).[5] This approach, labelled as 'Law and Finance', maintained that the efficiency of the legal system is positively related to economic growth via financial development. In a nutshell, they suggested that countries with a civil law system (France, Germany, Italy, etc.) have both a weak investor protection and least developed capital markets. In contrast, common law countries (United Kingdom and United States) have led to market-oriented financial systems. Furthermore, they also reconsidered the dichotomy of bank-based vs market-based systems arguing that it is the financial development and not the financial structure which are crucial for supporting firms' investments. In contrast with this hypothesis, Raghuram Rajan and Luigi Zingales, by adopting a comparative perspective, maintained that the driving force of the development of financial institutions is the political context. Indeed, they showed that, at the eve of World War I, the most developed countries had similar levels of financial development, regardless of the legal system they have (Rajan & Zingales, 2003).

The Law and Finance approach has been tested and discussed even in further contributions which have adopted a historical perspective. Most of the various works have not found much evidence in support of this hypothesis. For instance, Timothy Guinnane, Ron Harris, Naomi Lamoreaux and Jean-Laurent Rosenthal challenged the idea that the Anglo-Saxon common law is supporting economic growth more strongly than the civil law systems diffused in Continental Europe (Guinnane et al., 2007). Within the business history, a recent issue of this journal has tackled the topic of the effectiveness of the Law and Finance hypothesis. These contributions have emphasised that legal origins do not matter that much in driving the financial development of a country.[6] Furthermore, in a recent contribution, Christopher Coyle, Aldo Musacchio and John Turner, looking at the capital market in the United Kingdom (the home of common law), in the early twentieth century, showed that both the size of the UK domestic capital market is not correlated with the investor protection laws and that UK legislation was so not different in comparison with those of the civil law countries (Coyle et al. 2019). Thus, they maintained that the divergence, if any, of the two different systems does not have its roots in the period before the World War I.

3. New approaches to the analysis of the financial systems

In recent times, many works have highlighted the complexity and the rich variety of the institutional set up of the financial systems which, to provide resource to industrial firms, have shown a vast heterogeneity of forms involving a plurality of actors. The growing interest in the analysis of the structure of financial systems and their determinants in economics have thus relaunched interest in the historical perspective.[7]

The field of the history of financial systems and, particularly, on the financing of industrial firms is nowadays characterised by a mix of epistemological approach and research subject (Colvin, 2017). It is not easy to provide an exhaustive survey of all studies in this field, but it is possible to emphasise the main general trends. First of all, it seems rather clear that both business historians and economic historians continue to contribute to the field, although, in recent times, business historians seem to be more active.[8] Second, most of the studies are still largely concentrated on the major European countries and on the United States, even if in the last few years some research has focussed on other cases. Third, if the economic historians use the nowadays traditional quantitative techniques, also in the field of business history these techniques are more diffused than in the past (de Jong et al. 2015; Eloranta et al., 2010). Indeed, in recent years, the network analysis has spread in business history and its use seems to be particularly concentrated in the reconstruction of corporate networks and in the relationships between industrial firms with banks and financial companies. Indeed, a stream of research focussing on corporate networks has used the network analysis to look at the dense relationship between different actors providing a detailed description of the structure of the corporate system.[9] Some works have investigated the structure of the national networks for different countries such as Germany (Fohlin, 1997, 1999a; Windolf, 2014), United Kingdom (Schnyder & Wilson, 2014), Italy (Rinaldi & Vasta, 2005, 2012; Vasta & Baccini, 1997; Vasta et al., 2017), Switzerland (Ginalski et al. 2014), Belgium (Deloof et al., 2010), Japan (Okazaki et al., 2005) and United States (Frydman & Hilt, 2017) for different periods. In all these works, the crucial role played by banks (but also financial companies) in monitoring and financing industrial firms is analysed in detail. In the same vein, other studies have investigated interlocking directorship, by adopting a qualitative approach, for single cases. For instance, the Rotterdamsche Bankvereeninging in the Netherlands and the J.P. Morgan in US (Colvin, 2014; Pak, 2013).

4. The content of this special issue

This special issue aims to contribute, by using different approaches, to the issue on how firms, particularly industrial ones, have been funded in different historical periods. The main aim is to look at the financial system as a whole, focussing on both financial institutions and financial markets and, particularly, on their interactions. The selected articles, although limited to Western-European case studies, contribute to that goal.

For the First Industrial Revolution, Stefano Ugolini focuses on the financing of the take-off of industry in Belgium, the first country to follow the path pioneered by Great Britain in the mid eighteenth century. Belgium's independence was recognised by the London Conference of 1830, although the decision was not accepted by the Dutch until 1839. Ugolini's article analyses that decade and demonstrates how financial markets and institutions worked together to consolidate the new country's economy. Far from having a conflictive relationship, the stock market and banks found a way to 'co-evolve', both for their mutual benefit and for that of the national economy.

The author investigates this co-evolution based on information provided by two databases: his own dataset and the SCOB Database. The starting point was an underdeveloped financial system, where the Société Générale (SG) (1822) played a prominent role. The SG was soon joined by the Banque de Belgique (BdB) (1835). Both were entities with strong state intervention. Ugolini illustrates the critical role played by the banking industry in the Belgian industrial take-off. SG and BdB acted as universal banks and did not hesitate to purchase a significant quantity of shares of the innovative companies that contributed to spread the Industrial Revolution to the Continent.

In a second phase, the banks then helped those companies to list on the Brussels Stock Exchange and proceeded to act as 'market makers' at all times. Thus, in Belgium, there was no conflict whatsoever between the banks and the stock exchange. In contrast, the banks viewed the Brussels Stock Exchange as an additional financial instrument. The 1839 crisis, which came about as a result of the final conflict with Netherlands, had a disastrous effect on BdB, which had to be rescued and converted into a commercial bank. However, SG and other banks continued to serve as universal banks without preventing Brussels from becoming an important international financial hub.

This special issue addresses the Second Industrial Revolution with a study undertaken by Emilie Bonhoure and David Le Bris. The study looks at the role played by the stock exchanges in France. Although the leaders of the Second Industrial Revolution were Germany and the United States, France also played a significant role, notably, for example, with its automobile industry, which continues to enjoy success today. The research question posed by Bonhoure and Le Bris is whether the Paris stock exchanges provided sufficient support to the successful firms that appeared during the Second Industrial Revolution. These firms were emerging businesses and, therefore, often lacked information. If the answer is yes, according to the authors, one might identify high Tobin's Q ratios even if dividends were meagre.

The authors work with their own database of around a thousand companies that, in 1907, were listed on the Paris stock exchanges (both the Parquet official exchange and the non-regulated Coulisse), as well as information provided by the new Data for Financial History Equipment of Excellence (DFIH Equipex). According to their findings, Second Industrial Revolution companies accounted for 9% of total market capitalisation in 1907 and 27% in 1929, so they had tripled their share. These data indicate that France's industrial efforts in new and upcoming sectors were well supported by the country's stock exchanges. The authors believe that in 1907 the trajectories of the Second Industrial Revolution had only just arrived on French shores. Funding during the first stage of the revolution would have primarily been provided by banks; however, in early twentieth-century the stock markets began to take centre stage in the United States, although much less so in Germany. France would follow the American model.

When comparing the sectors of the Second Industrial Revolution with others, Bonhoure and Le Bris found significant differences between Tobin's Q, which was higher for Second-Industrial-Revolution companies, and the dividend yield, which was somewhat lower for those same companies. The regression analyses of both variables controlling risk, liquidity, governance, and nationality only point towards a connection between the Second Industrial Revolution and Tobin's Q. Because Tobin's Q is a more definitive variable than dividend yield, the authors conclude that, despite information asymmetries, the French financial markets were indeed able to recognise the potential of some of the emerging companies that were poised to change the world.

With regard to Britain, the relationships between financial system and industrialisation have always been viewed critically. The qualitative study undertaken by Mark Billings, Simon Mollan, and Philip Garnet uses the work of the Colwyn Committee to review the state of that relationship at a crucial moment in time: the end of World War I in 1918. This was a banking system where the universal banking is not working, preferring to deal with customers through credit. According to the figures, the banks extended credit abundantly, but with significant aversion to doing so on a long-term basis. In any case, in the British financial system, the markets tended (and tend) to dominate the institutions. The British saw the commercial banks, the merchant banks, and the stock exchanges as completely disconnected from the industrialisation process. The problem became more serious with the advent of the Second Industrial Revolution, when the need for capital was clearly greater than in the First.

The Colwyn Committee, chaired by the entrepreneur and banker Lord Colwyn, was convened by the British Treasury to investigate the process of bank concentration which had led to the excessive weight of the well-known 'Big Five' in the City of London (Barclays, Lloyds, Midland, National Provincial, and Westminster). The committee was made up of 12 members—among them, the governor of the Bank of England—and compiled 280 pages of information obtained from 22 witnesses. The committee members and witnesses included many bankers, including representatives of the 'Big Five', except Barclays. For this reason, the Colwyn Committee report is often blamed for partiality and, according to the authors of the article, has not been received proper consideration.

In reality, the work of the Colwyn Committee constituted a vital step in the British banking industry's journey towards accepting regulation and supervision. The Committee had heated debates on issues that continue to be relevant, such as the rationality of using mergers as an expansion strategy, the need to have large institutions to compete with those in other countries (the United States or Germany), the structural weakness of local banks and their failure to capture savings in regions with surplus and invest it in regions with deficit, the debatable effect of mergers on competition (would a handful of entities be enough to maintain a sufficient level of competition?), the advantages and disadvantages of nationalising banks (which the Labour Party was proposing), the role of regulation now that liberal capitalism had come to an end (there was only agreement on promoting transparency), the desirability of reinforcing capital ratios, and the possibility of moving towards German-style universal banking as a mechanism for supporting industry more effectively.

The work of the Colwyn Committee may not have resulted in legal changes, but the authors of the article suggest it did bring about a more tentative approach towards bank mergers and greater acceptance of an increased degree of regulation. Far fewer mergers took place between 1924 and 1987 than between 1810 and 1924. The number increased again at the turn of the twenty-first century.

The trajectory of the British banking industry after World War II is addressed by an article written by Philipp Kern and Gerhard Schnyder. The authors claim that a fundamental issue in the relationship between financial institutions and companies is the power created by interlocking directorates, i.e., the coordinated actions made possible by common directorships. In a specialised banking system, such as the British in 1918, there was no place for interlocking directorates. As Sir Edward Holden, the Chairman of Midland Bank, stated forthrightly before the Colwyn Committee: 'Interlocking directors are unknown in our banking world' (see article by Billings, Mollan and Garnett in this issue). However, during the 1950–2010 period analysed by Kern and Schnyder, things had changed in line with the British bank's move towards universal banking. This move was broadly backed by the political authorities.

The ambitious approach by Kern and Schnyder attempts not only to identify British interlocking directorates and their evolution over time but also their influence on levels of corporate debt. They use an own dataset that includes information on the 50 largest financial companies and the 200 largest non-financial companies, in eight benchmark years (1950, 1958, 1976, 1983, 1993, 1997, 2003 and 2010). The theory identifies different reasons why bankers would want to be on the boards of companies, and why companies would want to be on the boards of banks. The authors suggest three hypotheses: (1) debt levels are greater in companies with more connections to financial institutions; (2) the debt level of a company increases if those connections occur throughout the company network; and (3) the influence of those connections on debt levels was greater before the stock market reforms of 1986—the 'Big Bang'—than afterwards.

Before World War II, the British financial system kept aside from universal banking because this was seen as a formula to keep funds inside the borders and a way to accelerate growth in countries lagging in industrialisation. The war changed everything. By the end of the 1940s, 90% of the stocks listed in the London Stock Exchange were domestic, compared to just 8% in 1913. The financial system concentrated its interest in the national economy and, between 1945 and 1979, banks reinforced their commitment to British industry by adopting universal banking practices. Everything changed again in 1979, when the Conservative leader Margaret Thatcher introduced a neoliberal program which, among other things, was intended to boost the London Stock Exchange. This was achieved by a package of measures introduced in 1986 known as the 'Big Bang'. In line with these reforms, deposit and merchant banks merged their activities to give birth to a new type of universal banking that focussed on globalisation and had little concern for domestic industry.

The interlocking directorates are subjected to network analysis in order to understand the resulting maps for each year and a regression analysis was conducted to test the three hypotheses on debt levels. It should be noted that the authors refer to financial institutions in the broadest sense of the term, with banks constituting 56% of the sample in 1950 but only 14% in 2010, and that debt is assumed to be anything that is not capital or self-financing. The results suggest that there was increasing integration between 1950 and 1976, with banks occupying a central role. This was in line with the proposed hypotheses. Since the late 1970s, the ties have loosened and financial institutions have lost centrality, which in turn, has brought about a change in the way companies are financed. The article ends by pointing out that, overall, the traditional view of the British financial system is upheld, because the links identified were weak, their impact on financing only lasted for a short period and industrial companies continued to have difficulties in obtaining long-term funding throughout. The networks that existed before Thatcher were due more to regulatory pressures than to the will of the financial institutions.

The last article in this special issue focuses on financing for small and medium-sized industrial firms. These were particularly significant in economies such as Italy's, which was analysed by Alberto Rinaldi and Anna Spadavecchia. The authors concentrate on the period 1913–1936, when universal banking still existed in Italy. In 1936, following the financial crisis that provoked a large state intervention in industry and in its funding channels, a new law prohibited universal banking. The analysis is based on interlocking directorates with information obtained from Imita.db (http://imitadb.unisi.it), the database on Italian joint stock companies. The research intends to further test the Gerschenkron hypothesis, which gave all the credit for the Italian industrial take-off to the large German-style universal banks and the large companies.

The largest nation-wide five universal banks are studied separately with the 20 most prominent local banks in three benchmark years (1913, 1927, and 1936). The common denominator is that they all have links to the more industrialised regions of Italy, in particular, Lombardy, which had more dealings with local banks. The larger banks tended to extend their reach throughout the country. The Great Depression would end up seriously affecting the large banks, and Banca Commerciale, Credito Italiano, and Banco di Roma had to be rescued by the Istituto per la Ricostruzione Industriale (IRI), while the local banks remained largely independent of the bigger banks throughout.

The interlocking directorates indicate a correlation in size: the large companies tended to work with the big banks and smaller companies preferred the smaller local banks. It was also the case that emerging companies began their financial dealings with local banks and then moved them to the larger banks. It seems, therefore, that local banks were less averse to risk and would have played a significant role in the country's industrial take-off, although this role seems to be mainly concentrated in the light sectors.

Importantly, the article also addresses the direction of causality in the interlocks. Based on the theory that the more powerful exerts an influence on the less powerful, it examines who would have been more important in the interlock relationship. If the bank influences the company, the relationship is described as 'outdegree', but if the company exerts influence on the bank, it is an 'indegree' relationship. By calculating the outdegree/indegree ratio one can deduce the directionality of a set of relationships. The results obtained are inconclusive, leading the authors to believe that in Italy the bank-industry relationship was one of mutual dependence, or leaned slightly towards industry exerting influence over the banks, but that in no case was industry completely subjected to the power of the banks as has sometimes been assumed. It could even be suggested that the problems experienced by the banking industry in the 1930s came as a result of pressure exerted by industry. In this sense, there were few similarities between the Italian situation and that of Germany or the United States.

The article concludes with two case studies: Banca Lombarda (1870) and Banca di Legnano (1887), two leading local banks. The interlocks they had reveal that both banks had a lot of involvement in the development of the textile and silk industries, but they also had some links with the sectors of the Second Industrial Revolution. For Rinaldi and Spadavecchia, these cases confirm the two main conclusions of their article: (1) local banks played an important role in supporting emerging firms in light-industry sectors; and (2) relationships between banks and industry were not always dictated by a hierarchical system where the banks held the most power. According to the authors, the Gerschenkron thesis is too simple to be applied to the complex realities behind the industrial take-off in Italy.[10]

5. Conclusion and further development

In the long review of the book that Rondo Cameron dedicated to challenging the Gerschenkron hypothesis, Raymond Goldsmith concluded that it was necessary to extend the sample to include more countries, adopt a 'common statistical framework', analyse more carefully the causal relationships and take 'the study of the relationship on a microeconomic level, i.e., from the point of view, and on the basis of the records, of selected individual financial institutions or of selected business firms' (Goldsmith, 1973). In the almost half a century that has elapsed since then, much progress has been mainly made in the macroeconomic aspects proposed by Goldsmith. The microeconomic issues have been analysed deeply only in more recent times. This special issue follows this recent pattern by adopting the more updated approaches developed within the business history.

From the theoretical point of view, it has been usual to distinguish between countries with financial systems based on banks and financial systems based on markets and, more recently, also between systems based on civil law (institutions) and systems based on common law (markets). It has even sought to contrast universal banking with specialised banking and relational banking with fully competitive banking. Historical research has concluded that 'setting up banks and markets as opposites misses the fundamental complementarities between them and ignores their complexity and heterogeneity' (Fohlin, 2012, p. 151, 2016). It also begins to become clear that financial systems do not trigger growth processes and industrialisation, but they are essential to sustain them over time. Each society has the financial system that fits with its historical trajectory, without any being better or worse than others. The important thing is to have a financial system sophisticated and stable and that evolves according to the demand forces of the moment. History matters.

The analysis of the Belgian case in the 1830s diminishes the role of the banks in order to stress the existence of a 'co-evolution' of banks and financial markets, even if the former were essential in the take-off of the first country in Continental Europe that catched up the trajectories of the First Industrial Revolution. For France in the early decades of the twentieth century, an analysis with new sources also revalued the role of financial markets in the Second Industrial Revolution. Both works contribute to a more balanced and nuanced image of the role of the components of the financial system in the industrialisation process.[11]

The difficulty of joining the Second Industrial Revolution by Great Britain is found in the reports of the Cowlyn Committee that met in 1918. The work of the Cowlyn Committee has been neglected because it was not translated into legal measures, but a rereading of the reports allows us to verify the frustration of British bankers in the face of the success of universal banking in Germany and the United States (closely linked to the stock market in this latter case and perhaps, as suggested by Sybille Lehmann (2014) even in the former) and their willingness to consider greater regulation inevitable, which was what followed the world wars of the twentieth century.

Finally, the modern network analysis, through interlocking directorates, proves its effectiveness in both the British case, for 1950–2010, and the Italian case, for 1913–1936. Ending a long tradition of pure commercial banking, British banks and companies were integrated into networks during the Golden Age, where banks took centre stage. In truth, it was a universal banking system forced by the authorities, which did not prevent the continuation of the industrial decline and that jumped through the air with the neoliberal revolution of Margaret Thatcher. In the Italian case, the study reveals the existence of networks segregated by size (large banks with large companies and local banks with small and medium-sized companies) and more complex than those derived from Gerschenkron thesis.

This special issue has focussed on a variety of themes concerning the relationship between financial systems in a broader sense and firms' growth. However, many research topics remain pending.

If, as said, the traditional dichotomy between banking system and stock market seems to be out of date, the interaction between these two elements seems to be under-researched. Thus, many aspects related to the regulation, both of the banking system and of the stock market, deserve to be further analysed. Indeed, financial regulation is a crucial element in the selection process of firms' investments. For instance, the existence of a self-regulation, able to provide some oversight, seems to have played a positive role to reduce the IPO failure even in the London stock exchange in the early 19th century (Burhop et al., 2014). We believe that both qualitative and quantitative studies can contribute to increase our knowledge on how regulation mechanisms have determined firms' investments and, ultimately, economic growth.

The second issue that merits much attention is related to the characteristics of the firms to be financed. Most of the literature has concentrated its attention to the firms lato sensu or, more often, to the archetypal firm associated to one single country. In our view, what we need is to have more analysis that take into account the vast heterogeneity of firms in different countries. First of all, as we have seen in this special issue, size matters. Thus, we believe that more attention should be paid to the different conditions to access to capital for firms of different size, also within the same country. Generally, small and medium-sized companies have to settle for self-financing their projects or resorting to bank credit by providing guarantees and compensation. In contrast, larger companies may face expensive but wider access to capital markets. However, these differences are crucial in order to understand whether there were factors that can favour (limit) firms' growth capacity. Second, it would be important to understand if sectoral and technological characteristics of the firms can have determined, in different context, their capacity to be funded. In particular, we would need to have more analysis—both as case studies on single firm and/or at more aggregate level—able to explore the capacity for a country to foster firms that are close to the technological frontier.

Last but not least, we would like to emphasise some methodological issues. First, much of the analysis is still focussed on a small number of European countries. Our knowledge has been often limited to the most successful countries, such as England or Germany, or to countries for which some general hypothesis was developed by some seminal studies (e.g. Gerschenkron for Italy). In this special issue, attention has been paid to Belgium and France, but many efforts must be made in order to study several other countries in Europe and also in other continents. Second, as showed in this special issue, the interaction between the tools of the business historians and those of the economic historians can provide fruitful results. If we still believe that qualitative sources can be used to validate theoretical and empirical hypotheses, in the last years, the quantitative methodologies have been largely used by business historians. In this perspective, network analysis seems to be one of the more promising approaches to develop our knowledge on the relationship between financial markets and industrial firms.

Notes

1. The other pillars of Allen's standard model are the creation of a 'mass education' system able to speed the adoption of modern industrial technologies, the construction of a national transport infrastructure for creating a large national market and an external tariff for protecting 'infant' industries.
2. Cameron (1967) and Cameron (1972) were the first attempts to contrast the Gerschenkron's thesis. Cameron and his collaborators studied 12 national cases (Austria, Belgium, England, France, Germany, Italy, Japan, Russia, Scotland, Serbia, Spain and the United States) with mixed results.
3. In his book, Goldsmith quoted Gerschenkron only once in a footnote (p. 402).
4. Lescure is an example of maintaining the dichotomy.
5. See La Porta et al. (2008) for a survey.
6. See Musacchio and Turner (2013) for a survey of these contributions.
7. For two recent surveys respectively on banking history and on stock market history, see Colvin (2014) and Smith and Tennent (2017).
8. However, it is worth noticing that, according to Cioni et al. (2020, Table 3), the studies on banking and financial systems have increased considerably their weight within the top five economic history journals in the last twenty years.
9. For a comparative long run studies on this issue, see David and Westerhuis (2014).
10. The article by Rinaldi and Spadavecchia in this issue follows the line opened by Rinaldi and Vasta (2005), which has inspired Rubio-Mondéjar and Garrués-Irurzun (2016). According to these authors, the Spanish networks were mere examples of crony capitalism, which is at odds with the Gerschenkronian interpretation of the role of the banks in the Spanish economic development by Tortella and García-Ruiz (2013).
11. In a recent work, Heblich and Trew (2019) have investigated the role of banks in the spreading of the Industrial Revolution in England since the early XIX century. They find that the presence of banks in a given area accelerated the industrialization process.

Disclosure statement

No potential conflict of interest was reported by the authors.

ORCID

José Luis García Ruiz https//doi.org/0000-0002-3612-6217
Michelangelo Vasta https//doi.org/0000-0002-8683-8095

References

Allen, F., & Gale, D. (2000). *Comparing financial systems*. The MIT Press.

Allen, R. C. (2011). *Global economic history. A very short introduction*. Oxford University Press.

Boot, A., & Thakor, A. V. (2010). The accelerating integration of banks and markets and its implications for regulation. In A. N. Berger, P. Molyneux, & J. O. S. Wilson (Eds.), *The Oxford handbook of banking* (pp. 58–90). Oxford University Press.

Burhop, C. (2006). Did banks cause the German industrialization?*Explorations in Economic History*, *43*(1), 39–63. https://doi.org/10.1016/j.eeh.2005.04.005

Burhop, C., Chambers, D., & Cheffins, B. (2014). Regulating IPOs: Evidence from going public in London, 1900–1913. *Explorations in Economic History*, *51*(1), 60–76. https://doi.org/10.1016/j.eeh.2013.07.003

Calomiris, C. W. (1995). The costs of rejecting universal banking: American finance in the German mirror, 1870-1914. In N. R. Lamoreaux & D. M. G. Raff (Eds.), *The coordination of economic activity within and between firms* (pp. 257–321). University of Chicago Press.

Cameron, R. (1967). *Banking in the early stages of industrialization: A study in comparative economic history*. Oxford University Press.

Cameron, R. (Ed.) (1972). *Banking and economic development: Some lessons of history*. Oxford University Press.

Chandler, A. D. (1990). *Scale and scope. The dynamic of industrial capitalism*. Harvard University Press.

Cioni, M., Federico, G., & Vasta, M. (2020). The long-term evolution of economic history: Evidence from the top five journals (1927-2017). *Cliometrica*, *14*(1), 1–39. https://doi.org/10.1007/s11698-019-00186-x

Colvin, C. L. (2014). Interlocking directorates and conflicts of interest: The Rotterdamsche Bankvereeniging, Müller & Co. and the Dutch financial crisis of the 1920s. *Business History*, *56*(2), 314–334. https://doi.org/10.1080/00076791.2013.771342

Colvin, C. L. (2017). The past, present and future of banking history. In J. F.Wilson, S.Toms, A.de Jong, & E.Buchnea (Eds.), *The Routledge companion to business history* (pp. 89–106). Routledge.

Coyle, C., Musacchio, A., & Turner, J. D. (2019). Law and finance in Britain c. 1900. *Financial History Review*, *26*(3), 267–293. https://doi.org/10.1017/S0968565019000179

David, T., & G. Westerhuis (Eds.) (2014). *The power of corporate networks: A comparative and historical perspective*. Routledge.

de Jong, A., Higgins, D. M., & van Driel, H. (2015). Towards a new business history? *Business History*, *57*(1), 5–29. https://doi.org/10.1080/00076791.2014.977869

Deloof, M., Roggeman, A., & van Overfelt, W. (2010). Bank affiliations and corporate dividend policy in pre-World War I Belgium. *Business History*, *52*(4), 590–616. https://doi.org/10.1080/00076791003753178

Demirgüç-Kunt, A., & Maksimovic, V. (2002). Funding growth in bank-based and market-based financial systems: Evidence from firm-level data. *Journal of Financial Economics*, *65*(3), 337–363. https://doi.org/10.1016/S0304-405X(02)00145-9

Edwards, J., & Ogilvie, S. (1996). Universal banks and German industrialization: A re-appraisal. *The Economic History Review*, *49*(3), 427–446. https://doi.org/10.2307/2597758

Eloranta, J., Ojala, J., & Valtonen, H. (2010). Quantitative methods in business history: An impossible equation? *Management & Organizational History*, *5*(1), 79–107. https://doi.org/10.1177/1744935909353837

Fohlin, C. (1997). Universal banking networks in pre-war Germany: New evidence from company financial data. *Research in Economics*, *51*(3), 201–225. https://doi.org/10.1006/reec.1997.0044

Fohlin, C. (1998). Fiduciari and firm liquidity constraint: The Italian experience with German-style universal banking. *Explorations in Economic History*, *35*(1), 83–107. https://doi.org/10.1006/exeh.1997.0690

Fohlin, C. (1999a). The rise of interlocking directorates in imperial Germany. *The Economic History Review*, *52*(2), 307–333. https://doi.org/10.1111/1468-0289.00127

Fohlin, C. (1999b). Capital mobilisation and utilisation in latecomer economies: Germany and Italy compared. *European Review of Economic History*, *3*(2), 139–174. https://doi.org/10.1017/S1361491699000088

Fohlin, C. (2007). *Finance capitalism and Germany's rise to industrial power*. Cambridge University Press.

Fohlin, C. (2012). *Mobilizing money: How the world's richest nations financed industrial growth*. Cambridge University Press.

Fohlin, C. (2016). Financial systems and economic development in historical perspective. In C. Diebolt & M. Haupert (Eds.), *Handbook of cliometrics* (pp. 393–430). Springer.

Frydman, C., & Hilt, E. (2017). Investment banks as corporate monitors in the early twentieth century United States. *American Economic Review, 107*(7), 1938–1970. https://doi.org/10.1257/aer.20150143

Gerschenkron, A. (1962). *Economic backwardness in historical perspective*. Belknap Press of Harvard University Press.

Ginalski, S., David, T., & Mach, A. (2014). From national cohesion to transnationalization: The changing role of banks in the Swiss Company Network, 1910-2010. In T. David & G. Westerhuis (Eds.), *The power of corporate networks: A comparative and historical perspective* (pp. 107–124). Routledge.

Goldsmith, R. W. (1969). *Financial structure and development*. Yale University Press.

Goldsmith, R. W. (1973). Review of Rondo Cameron (ed.), Banking and Economic Development: Some Lessons of History (Oxford University Press, 1972). *Journal of European Economic History*, 2(2): 497–501.

Guinnane, T., Harris, R., Lamoreaux, N. R., & Rosenthal, J.-L. (2007). Putting the corporation in its place. *Enterprise and Society, 8*(3), 687–729. https://doi.org/10.1093/es/khm067

Heblich, S., & Trew, A. (2019). Banking and industrialization. *Journal of the European Economic Association, 17*(6), 1753–1796. https://doi.org/10.1093/jeea/jvy037

Hilferding, R. (1910). *Das Finanzkapital. Eine Studie über die jüngste Entwicklung des Kapitalismus*. Wiener Volksbuchhandlung.

Jeidels, O. (1905). *Das Verhältnis der deutschen Grossbanken zur Industrie mit besonderer Berücksichtigung der Eisenindustrie*. Duncker & Humblot.

King, R. G., & Levine, R. (1993). Finance and growth: Schumpeter might be right. *The Quarterly Journal of Economics, 108*(3), 717–737. https://doi.org/10.2307/2118406

Kocka, J. (1978). Entrepreneurs and managers in German industrialization. In M. M. Postan, D. C. Coleman, & P. Mathias (Eds.), *The Cambridge economic history of Europe, Volume 7, Part 1, The industrial economies: Capital, labour, and enterprise* (pp. 492–589). Cambridge University Press.

La Porta, R., Lopez-de-Silanes, F., & Shleifer, A. (2008). The economic consequences of legal origins. *Journal of Economic Literature, 46*(2), 285–332. https://doi.org/10.1257/jel.46.2.285

La Porta, R., Lopez-de-Silanes, F., Shleifer, A., & Vishny, R. W. (1997). Legal determinants of external finance. *The Journal of Finance, 52*(3), 1131–1150. https://doi.org/10.1111/j.1540-6261.1997.tb02727.x

La Porta, R., Lopez-de-Silanes, F., Shleifer, A., & Vishny, R. W. (1998). Law and finance. *Journal of Political Economy, 106*(6), 1113–1155. https://doi.org/10.1086/250042

Lehmann, S. H. (2014). Taking firms to the stock market: IPOs and the importance of large banks in imperial Germany, 1896–1913. *The Economic History Review, 67*(1), 92–122. https://doi.org/10.1111/1468-0289.12016

Lescure, M. (2007). Banking and finance. In G. Jones & J. Zeitlin (Eds.), *The Oxford handbook of business history* (pp. 319–346). Oxford University Press.

Levine, R., & Zervos, S. (1998). Stock markets, banks, and economic growth. *The American Economic Review, 88*(3), 537–558.

Musacchio, A., & Turner, J. (2013). Does the law and finance hypothesis pass the test of history? *Business History, 55*(4), 524–542. https://doi.org/10.1080/00076791.2012.741976

Okazaki, T., Sawada, M., & Yokoyama, K. (2005). Measuring the extent and implications of director interlocking in the prewar Japanese banking industry. *Journal of Economic History, 65*(4), 1082–1115.

Pak, S. J. (2013). Reputation and social ties: J. P. Morgan & Co. and private investment banking. *Business History Review, 87*(4), 703–728.

Rajan, R. G., & Zingales, L. (2003). The great reversals: The politics of financial development in the twentieth century. *Journal of Financial Economics, 69*(1), 5–50. https://doi.org/10.1016/S0304-405X(03)00125-9

Rinaldi, A., & Vasta, M. (2005). The structure of Italian capitalism, 1952-1972: New evidence using the interlocking directorates technique. *Financial History Review, 12*(2), 173–198. https://doi.org/10.1017/S0968565005000090

Rinaldi, A., & Vasta, M. (2012). The Italian corporate network after the "golden age" (1972-1983): From centrality to marginalization of state-owned enterprises. *Enterprise and Society, 13*(2), 378–413. https://doi.org/10.1093/es/khr071

Rubio-Mondéjar, J. A., & Garrués-Irurzun, J. (2016). Economic and social power in Spain: Corporate networks of banks, utilities and other large companies (1917–2009). *Business History, 58*(6), 858–879. https://doi.org/10.1080/00076791.2015.1115483

Schnyder, G., & Wilson, J. F. (2014). The structure of networks: The transformation of UK business, 1904-2010. In T. David & G. Westerhuis (Eds.), *The power of corporate networks: A comparative and historical perspective* (pp. 48–65). Routledge.

Smith, A., & Tennent, K. D. (2017). Stock markets and financial capitalism. In J. F. Wilson, S. Toms, A. de Jong, & E. Buchnea (Eds.), *The Routledge companion to business history* (pp. 107–122). Routledge.

Tortella, G., & García-Ruiz, J. L. (2013). *Spanish money and banking. A history*. Palgrave Macmillan.

Vasta, M., & Baccini, A. (1997). Bank and industry in Italy 1911-1936: New evidence using the interlocking directorates technique. *Financial History Review, 4*(2), 139–159. https://doi.org/10.1017/S0968565000000937

Vasta, M., Drago, C., Ricciuti, R., & Rinaldi, A. (2017). Reassessing the bank industry relationship in Italy, 1913-1936: A counterfactual analysis. *Cliometrica, 11*(2), 183–216. https://doi.org/10.1007/s11698-016-0142-9

Windolf, P. (2014). The corporate network in Germany, 1896-2010. In T. David & G. Westerhuis (Eds.), *The power of corporate networks: A comparative and historical perspective* (pp. 66–85). Routledge.

The coevolution of banks and corporate securities markets: The financing of Belgium's industrial take-off in the 1830s

Stefano Ugolini

ABSTRACT
Recent developments in the literature on financial architecture suggest that banks and markets not only coexist, but also coevolve in ways that are non-neutral from the viewpoint of optimality. This article aims to analyse the concrete mechanisms of this coevolution by focussing on a very relevant case study: Belgium (the first Continental country to industrialise) at the time of the very first emergence of a modern financial system (the 1830s). The article shows that intermediaries played a crucial role in developing secondary securities markets (as banks acted as securitisers), but market conditions also had a strong feedback on banks' balance sheets and activities (as banks also acted as market-makers for the securities they had issued). The findings suggest that not only structural, but also cyclical factors can be important determinants of changes in financial architecture.

1. Introduction

Since the foundational contributions of Gurley and Shaw (1955), Gerschenkron (1962), and Goldsmith (1969), a massive body of research has been devoted to the understanding of financial architecture, and the pros and cons of allegedly market- or bank-based financial systems have been thoroughly investigated. Starting from the late 1990s, the relevance of the traditional 'banks vs. markets' dichotomy has been questioned theoretically (Allen & Gale, 2000), empirically (Levine, 2005), as well as historically (Fohlin, 2012). A new consensus appears to have emerged on the fact that banks and markets should no longer be seen as substitutes, but rather as complements (Boot & Thakor, 2010). As a result, the question of the interaction between banks and markets has started to raise increasing interest. While the earlier literature had considered the evolution of banks and markets as a 'zero-sum game' in which the ones only grow at the expense of the others and *vice-versa* (Baliga & Polak, 2004; Boot & Thakor, 1997; Boyd & Smith, 1998; Chakraborty & Ray, 2007; Da Rin, 1997; Greenwood & Smith, 1997), more recent contributions have underlined that this need not be the case (Allen & Gale, 2000; Deidda & Fattouh, 2008; Mattana & Panetti, 2014). Their conclusion is that banks and market not only coexist, but also coevolve in ways that are non-neutral in terms of welfare. Banks perform three fundamental functions (screening, qualitative asset transformation, and credit enhancement) whose implementation allows for the development of financial markets; securitisation puts in motion a virtuous cycle that is beneficial for the real economy, as it increases the efficiency of capital allocation (Song & Thakor, 2010).

Although economic historians have been paying increasing attention to the coexistence of banks and markets, the concrete mechanisms through which banks and markets coevolved in the past have not been specifically investigated to date. This article aims at filling this gap by studying the synchronous emergence of new intermediaries (universal banks) and new markets (secondary corporate stock markets) at the very time of the industrial take-off of a 'moderately backward' country (Belgium in the 1830s). The idea is to understand what factors drove the spectacular changes in financial architecture that allowed for the financing of growth in that national economic system, which was the first to follow Britain on the path to industrialisation. As 1830s Belgium was the context in which universal banks first appeared at all, this article is also *de facto* a study of the very origins of universal banking.

The remainder is organised as follows. Section 2 reviews the historical literature on financial architecture. Section 3 surveys available historical evidence on Belgium and presents my original database. Section 4 focusses on the impact of banks' actions on market evolution. It underscores the role of Belgian banks in fostering the emergence of the Brussels stock market through their securitisation of corporate assets. Section 5 focusses on the impact of market conditions on bank evolution. It shows that securitisation did not mean a total dismissal of such assets by banks: banks actually had to continue intervening on the stock market well beyond the underwriting process, and securities originated by them tended to reappear on their balance sheets in times of crisis. Finally, Section 6 draws some general conclusions on the determinants of banks' and markets' coevolution.

2. Literature review

The historical literature on financial architecture has long been dominated by an 'institutional' approach (Fohlin, 2016). On the one hand, Gerschenkron's (1962) highly influential contribution encouraged generations of historians to focus on the role of banks as drivers of industrialisation in moderately-backward countries. On the other hand, Goldsmith's (1969) criticism of Gerschenkron led other historians to insist on the contribution of markets to the financing of economic growth. Both strands of the historical literature thus tended to take a (more or less strict) dicothomical view on the subject: financial systems were generally categorised as being either bank- or market-based. Yet, as argued by Fohlin (2016), the traditional 'institutional' approach tends to obstruct a proper understanding of how financial systems actually worked, and should be replaced by a 'functional' one. Focussing *ex post* on the provision of financial functions (rather than on the action of some specific organisations whose characteristics are defined *ex ante*) actually allows to by-pass the sterile controversies on the preeminence of banks or markets that have long dominated the historical literature.[1] In a series of contributions, Fohlin (2007, 2012, 2016) showed convincingly that financial architecture at the time of industrialisation was far from being clearly bank- or market-based in any major country.

If recent contributions have substantially improved our understanding of how financial systems were structured at the time of industrialisation, the very mechanisms through which such structures actually emerged and evolved over time still remain to be clarified. For instance, the best available synthesis of recent scholarship (Fohlin, 2012) adopts a cross-sectional rather than a truly chronological view on the subject. Even more detailed single-country studies (esp. Fohlin, 2007) are rather descriptive in nature and do not really ask why the provision of financial functions was actually organised the way it was. Yet, anecdotal evidence on the emergence of modern financial systems at the time of industrial take-off is actually available. In particular, three cases have attracted more scholarly attention: Germany, Austria, and Italy – the three countries that were identified by Gerschenkron (1962, p. 14) as paradigms of 'moderately backward' countries having adopted universal banking as a 'facilitator' of industrialisation.

Germany has naturally attracted much scholarly attention, but most of the focus has been on the mature stages of the financial system after the 1870s rather than on its infancy in the 1850s (see e.g. Gerschenkron, 1962; Fohlin, 2007). Available studies of the earlier phase of financial development (see e.g. Riesser, 1911; Tilly, 1966) have nonetheless shown that early German joint-stock banks' main business consisted of the floatation of 'innovative' companies on previously inexistent secondary corporate securities market.

Austria has also been mostly studied in the more mature stages of financial development since the 1890s rather than in the early times preceding the *Gründerkrach* of 1873 (see e.g. Gerschenkron, 1977; Good, 1991). Recent studies of this 'formative' crisis have however revealed the overwhelming involvement of early Austrian joint-stock banks in the underwriting of 'innovative' equities and into the related repo market, suggesting that banks were a driving force of the emergence of a stock market (Rieder, 2017).

In the case of Italy, the formative years of the modern financial system (the 1890s) have actually been covered by most of the literature (see e.g. Federico & Toniolo, 1991; Fohlin, 2012). These studies have consistently pointed to the same results found for 1850s Germany or 1870s Austria: in 1890s Italy, banks were largely concerned with the floatation of 'innovative' equities on the new stock exchange and provided liquidity to the latter through the repo market (Brambilla, 2010; Confalonieri, 1974-6).

Thus, available evidence on the very origins of financial architecture seems to suggest that early universal banks were heavily involved in the securitisation of 'innovative' assets and played a crucial role in developing corporate securities markets. In what follows, this point will be thoroughly investigated through a case study on Belgium. Perhaps because of Gerschenkron's original oversight, this country has attracted comparatively little international attention. This lack of interest is unwarranted: Belgium was actually the first Continental country to experience, already in the 1830s, both an industrial take-off and the emergence of a modern financial system. More than that, 1830s Belgium was the place and time in which universal banking first emerged at all (Chlepner, 1943). The intermediaries that appeared in this context were very similar to the 'prototypical' universal bank: they extensively underwrote strictly industrial securities and collected deposits from the public (Ugolini, 2011). As Sylla (1991, p. 54) put it, 'Gerschenkron chose Germany as his example of a moderately backward country that employed dynamic banking to industrialise. He might better have chosen Belgium'.

3. Background and data

At the beginning of the nineteenth century, the financial capital of the Belgian region was still located in Antwerp. The seat of Belgium's rich aristocracy, Brussels just hosted a number of tradesmen and a few bankers specialised in wealth management (Ugolini, 2011). Yet when in 1822 William I of the Netherlands decided to found a chartered bank of issue (acting as Treasury's agent) in the southern part of his Kingdom, he chose to locate it in Brussels. Officially established to provide credit to infant industries (as suggested by its name: *Société Générale pour favoriser l'industrie nationale*, i.e. 'Financial Company for the Aid of the National Industry'), the bank was also intended for facilitating government borrowing in the South. The charter provided no restrictions on the financial operations the bank could implement, making it very different from the typical early-nineteenth-century bank of issue (Demoulin, 1938, pp. 49–70).

Société Générale (hereafter SG) was supposed to be a purely private joint-stock company, but its stock capital was mostly provided by the King himself, who swapped a vast real-estate endowment (Crown forestlands) for equity. The rest was intended for sale to the public, but the rights issue failed, and William I found himself with a larger stake than planned (83%). The largest part of the remaining capital (a mere 9% of the total) was held by a group of Brussels notables (landowners, retailers, and private bankers), from whom the members of the board came (Brion & Moreau, 1998, pp. 23–24). In 1830, the directors of SG took advantage of the opportunity offered by the Belgian revolt: the King's stake was frozen, and Crown forestlands were seized as private assets of the company. *De facto*, the bank came to be owned by itself.

During the first decades of the nineteenth century, Belgium's industrial potential (tied to the presence of coal and iron ore deposits) had become increasingly clear, and a number of partnerships had been created with the aim of developing mechanised plants (Briavoinne, 1839; Mokyr, 1976). The new firms, however, were faced with the typical difficulties inherent with infant 'high-tech' sectors: high growth potential was actually counterbalanced by large uncertainty and by the volatility of revenues, thus discouraging lenders from providing credit (Cameron, 1967; Lévy-Leboyer, 1964). In the 1820s, credit rationing had been partially alleviated by direct state aid and government-sponsored lending by SG (Demoulin, 1938), but the 1830 revolt led to a 'sudden stop'. The crisis had two important consequences for the newborn country's financial system. First, municipal savings banks, which were heavily invested in Dutch public debt, went bankrupt, and SG was called to the rescue by absorbing them: as a result, the bank assumed large deposit-taking activities (Ugolini, 2011). Secondly, growth perspectives were jeopardised, and many infant industries slid into insolvency. Facing difficulties in recovering industrial credits, from late 1834 SG started to negotiate their conversion into equity. Industrial partnerships were thus transformed into joint-stock companies and then floated on the stock market, although the bank kept a stake in them. As argued by Briavoinne (1839, p. 230), the bank ventured into incorporation with the aim of mobilising its own assets. The incorporation wave had started, and the first prototype of a universal bank was born.

In 1834, a conflict occurred between SG and the Belgian government, which was willing to seize the Dutch Crown's assets appropriated by the bank. In order to challenge SG's monopoly, in January 1835 a new joint-stock bank, called Banque de Belgique (hereafter BdB), was founded. The bank was intended to replace SG as the Treasury's agent, and therefore to become Belgium's main bank of issue – a step that the government did not eventually dare to take. BdB was designed along the model of SG in all details. This was due to the fact that, among its founders, there was a group of private bankers eyeing the possibility to restructure the underperforming debt of a number of firms to which they found themselves directly exposed (Chlepner, 1926, pp. 63–67). As a result, as SG began to float new companies on the Brussels stock exchange, BdB followed suit. In the space of a few months, their example was imitated by a number of private companies unconnected with banks.

The Belgian incorporation boom came to a sudden stop in December 1838, when an exogenous shock (fear of a new war with the Netherlands) triggered bank runs. SG held out, while BdB suspended payments and was bailed out by the government. The effects of the crisis were long-lasting, as the Brussels stock market did not recover until the 1850s (Ugolini, 2011).

In what follows, these 'formative' events will be analysed on the basis of an original database including all available information on both markets and banks during the 1830s. Table 1 provides details on the series included in the database, as well as the sources from which they are drawn. The analysis of quantitative data performed in the following sections also builds on insights from a rich historical literature, including above all Chlepner's (1926, 1943) contributions, based on an impressive collection of qualitative sources.

Table 1. Summary of series and sources in author's database.

Name of Series	Number of Series	Period of Coverage	Source
Market price of selected securities traded on the Brussels bourse (end-of-week)	48 industrial stocks; 2 government bonds	1835–1839	*Moniteur Belge*; *Journal du Commerce d'Anvers*
Number of securities traded on the Brussels bourse (end-of-year)	6 classes of securities	1834–1839	*L'Indépendance Belge*
Sector of activity of joint-stock companies founded in Belgium and amount of capital raised	151 companies	1831–1839	Briavoinne (1839)
Names and affiliation of leading administrators in Belgian joint-stock companies	149 companies	1833–1838	Briavoinne (1839); Laureyssens (1975)
IPO discounts on the Brussels bourse	4 companies	1835–1838	Chlepner (1926); Brion and Moreau (1998)
Dividends paid by companies listed on the Brussels bourse	10 companies	1835–1848	SCOB database (University of Antwerp)
Total amount of industrial securities held and total amount of loans on securities by Belgian banks (end-of-year)	2 banks	1835–1842	Chlepner (1926)
SG: Breakdown of corporate loans by region	1 bank	1830–1839	De Troyer (1974)
SG: Average amount lent on securities during the year	1 bank	1835–1842	Malou (1863)
SG: Breakdown of loans on securities by type of collateral	1 bank, 1 date	1848	Annales Parlementaires 1848, CdR n° 251 (28th April 1848)
BdB: Breakdown of loans on securities by type of collateral	1 bank, 1 date	1838	Archives Générales du Royaume (Brussels), Fonds Min. Finances, 307/1/15, A

4. From banks to markets

4.1. Banks as securitizers: conceptual framework

The literature on the industrial organisation of corporate finance generally maintains that banks are better positioned than markets for overcoming information asymmetries. This is due to the existence of economies of scope between lending and the provision of payment services, which allows a bank to access relevant information on borrowers (Goodfriend, 1991). This explains why bank loans are often the only source of external funding available to firms at non-prohibitive costs.

But lending is not banks' sole corporate finance activity. Innovative start-ups, whose cash flows are highly uncertain, may need subsidised lending in their early stages, yet intertemporal cross-subsidisation is only feasible if the lender-borrower relationship is durable (Petersen & Rajan, 1995). Lenders can solve this moral hazard problem by acquiring a stake in the borrowing firm and thus getting a say in future decision-making. Banks may hence behave as strategic investors in view of the synergies between venture capital investment and relationship lending (Hellmann, Lindsey, & Puri, 2008). Debt restructuring may be another reason for banks to acquire equity in start-ups. Firms with a higher probability of default are more likely to approach banks, because of the latter's superior ability to minimise inefficient liquidations (Chemmanur & Fulghieri, 1994). Banks will be willing to accept a conversion of debt into equity when the market value of their claim on the firm is significantly lower than its fundamental value, when the firm's growth opportunities are high, and when indebtedness to other lenders is low (James, 1995). This means that debt-for-equity swaps are more likely to occur between banks and start-ups.

While banks may have good reasons to acquire equity in innovative start-ups, this does not mean they will necessarily keep it for long. Equity in unlisted firms is an idiosyncratic and illiquid asset. To reduce their exposure to liquidity risk, banks can perform qualitative asset transformation and convert it into standardised exchange-traded securities (Loutskina, 2011): the bigger the investment, the stronger the incentive to put it off balance sheet (Ghent & Valkanov, 2016). Securitising past investments will allow banks to find new liquid resources for seizing new investing opportunities (Vargas-Martínez, 2010).

Empirical research has found a net certification effect by banks in the securitisation process. Shares in companies underwritten by banks perform better than others: the effect is stronger when the bank keeps a stake in the firm, and is increasing in the size of the stake (Puri, 1999). The originator's continued involvement in the floated company is equivalent to an IPO lockup (Brav & Gompers, 2003): as it is supposed to ensure high-quality monitoring, it works as a credit enhancement for issued securities (Boot, 2000).

Three of the literature's findings are relevant for understanding the role of banks in the very early stages of industrialisation. First, banks will have a predominant role in the funding of innovative start-ups both through lending (because of their privileged access to information on borrowers) and through capital venture investing (because of incentives to perform debt-for-equity swaps). Thus, banks can be expected to become the leading providers of capital to innovative firms in view of their superior screening technologies. Secondly, in order to continue profiting from their competitive advantage, banks will need to discharge part of the acquired equity by converting it into marketable securities. Thus, banks can be expected to promote the qualitative transformation of innovative corporate assets. Thirdly, banks have a positive certification effect for newly-floated corporate securities that is directly proportional to their subsequent involvement in the floated company. Thus, banks can be expected to maintain corporate control on the floated companies, and this will work as a credit enhancement in the eyes of investors. These three hypotheses will now be tested in the context of Belgium's industrial take-off.

4.2. Banks as securitizers: evidence from 1830s Belgium

At the time of Independence, the Belgian provinces possessed neither a developed capital market nor a sophisticated banking sector: the bourses of Antwerp and Brussels had thin trading activities in a handful of sovereign bonds, while the banking sector only consisted (if we exclude SG) of a bunch of small private banks unable to open sizeable credit lines to industrial firms (Ugolini, 2011). In the 1820s, the earliest attempts at industrialisation had thus been financed either through internal capital accumulation or through direct state aid (Mokyr, 1976). Tellingly, in the more than 250 pages dedicated by his treatise on Belgian industrialisation to the 'institutions fostering economic growth', Natalis Briavoinne referred to banks only as providers of means of payments or as underwriters, but not as lenders (Briavoinne, 1839). SG was an exception, but its intervention was seen as yet another form of state aid. In the 1820s, SG had been the one significant source of credit available to industrial concerns: as the Chamber of Commerce of Mons wrote in 1830, the local branch of SG had been 'the main, and we can now say it with certitude, in the last analysis the one and only foundation' to the development of the coal industry in the region (Demoulin, 1938, p. 100; Ugolini, 2016). When the 1830 crisis erupted, the bank thus found itself largely exposed to defaults in the corporate sector (Houtman-De Smedt, 1997). Table 2 shows that in 1830–1831, SG was indeed abnormally engaged in short-term lending in the Mons region, in order to meet the pressing demand of the corporate sector (especially coalmines). As soon as it became clear that loans would be unrecoverable, the bank started to negotiate debt-for-equity swaps with defaulting firms. The Mons region would thus become the heartland of SG's industrial empire (Brion & Moreau, 1998). Yet debt restructuring was not the main way in which banks took stakes in innovative firms. More typically, entrepreneurs approached their bank to request funds for the modernisation of their private partnership, and negotiations took place: then the firm was incorporated, a portion of the stock reserved for the entrepreneur, and the rest underwritten by the bank (Chlepner, 1943).

Table 2. Geographic breakdown of total amounts of new short-term corporate lending (i.e. discount of trade bills) accorded by SG, 1830–1839 (in million francs). Source: De Troyer (1974, p. 110).

	Mons	Brussels	Rest of Belgium	TOTAL
1830	63.3	27.3	13.7	*104.3*
1831	20.5	35.9	0.0	*56.4*
1832	8.9	24.6	1.3	*34.8*
1833	6.0	22.6	1.6	*30.2*
1834	5.9	22.5	5.5	*33.9*
1835	4.2	35.4	26.0	*65.6*
1836	5.0	27.3	25.4	*57.7*
1837	2.3	25.9	6.0	*34.2*
1838	0.8	24.1	7.3	*32.2*
1839	0.3	27.5	6.7	*34.5*

Following 1831, Belgium experienced a boom of incorporations. Under the aegis of the Napoleonic *Code de Commerce* (still in force in the country), three corporate forms were available at the time: 1) *société en nom collectif* (ordinary partnership with unlimited liability of all partners), 2) *société en commandite* (special partnership with unlimited liability of active partners and limited liability of silent partners), and 3) *société anonyme* (joint-stock company with limited liability of all shareholders). Because it provided an almost unchecked power to active partners and thus opened scope for abuses, *société en commandite* soon became a very unpopular corporate form. *Société anonyme* was considered as granting better protection to shareholders, but its creation had to be approved by decree, making it a hardly accessible corporate form for most industries (Freedeman, 1965). The text of the new Constitution of 1831, however, opened a juridical loophole with non-negligible consequences for the corporate sector. The establishment of 'unlimited freedom of association' as a constitutional right was actually interpreted by many as an abolition of the requirement of government approval for the incorporation of *sociétés anonymes*. The result was an unchecked boom of creations of joint-stock companies (Chlepner, 1926). Figure 1 shows that the peak of the phenomenon took place between 1835 and 1838. As illustrated by Table 3, almost two-thirds of the total amount of capital raised went to three specific sectors: financials, coalmines, and ironworks. The role played by banks is highlighted by Table 4: SG and BdB contributed to the incorporation of 37% of the companies created, and these very companies absorbed more than 60% of the total amount of capital raised. This means that banks acted as venture capital investors for more capital-intensive firms, whose growth prospects and cash flow volatility were highest at the time. On the whole, available evidence appears to be consistent with the first hypothesis: at the time of Belgium's industrial take-off, the provision of capital to innovative firms was actually dominated by banks.

Given the dearth of data concerning the Belgian capital market during the 1830s, the only available proxy for the width of this market consists of the number of securities exchanged at the bourse.[2] Table 5 describes the population of securities traded in Brussels by asset class. It shows that a Belgian stock market only emerged in 1835 (when universal banks entered the underwriting business), and continued to be dominated by banks

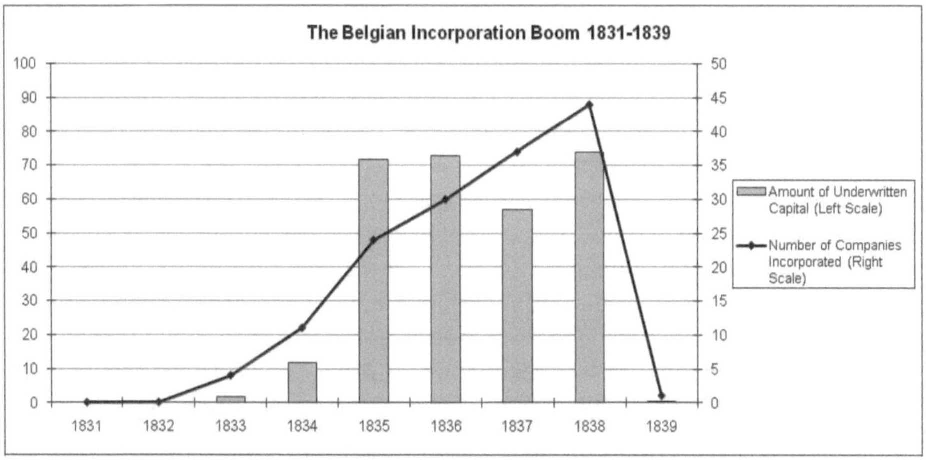

Figure 1. Total number of joint-stock companies founded (right scale) and total underwritten capital (in million francs, left scale), 1831–1839. Source: Briavoinne (1839, pp. 223–224).

Table 3. Breakdown per industrial sector of the total amount of capital raised, 1831–1839. Source: Author, from Briavoinne (1839, pp. 224–226).

Banks and Investment Trusts	25.8%
Coalmining	19.8%
Steelworks	17.3%
Insurance	4.3%
Shipping	3.2%
Real Estate Financials	2.9%
Flax Mills	2.5%
Printing	2.5%
Glassworks	2.5%
Sugar Refineries	2.3%
Machinery	1.9%
Other	15.0%
TOTAL	*100.0%*

Table 4. Breakdown per bank affiliation of the total number of incorporations, amount of capital raised, and average capital per company (in million francs), 1831–1839. Source: Author, from Briavoinne (1839, pp. 223–224).

	Number of Companies Founded	Amount of Capital Raised	Average Capital per Company
SG-Affiliated Firms	31	102.0	3.3
BdB-Affiliated Firms	25	74.0	3.0
Non-Affiliated Firms	95	113.0	1.2
TOTAL	*151*	*289.0*	*1.9*

throughout the period (always more than 80% of the total listed equities concerned bank-affiliated firms). That a large number of incorporated firms did not have their stock traded at the Brussels bourse, however, is not imputable to the existence of entry barriers to outsiders (Chlepner, 1926). This suggests that the shares of non-affiliated companies, which tended to be less capital-intensive (see Table 5), only circulated in restricted local circles (where information asymmetries could be lowered by personal connections: Lamoreaux, 1996), and lacked access to the official bourse. Thus, universal banks acted as gatekeepers of the general capital market. The non-existence of a market for corporate bonds corroborates this conclusion, as banks never underwrote such securities. This appears to confirm the second hypothesis – viz., that banks dominated the process of qualitative transformation of corporate assets into exchange-traded securities.

According to the *Code de Commerce*, the names of the directors of new joint-stock companies had to be explicitly mentioned in the charter: the board typically included the promoters of the enterprise and was ratified by the shareholders' general assembly only well after the floatation (Freedeman, 1965). This arrangement allowed venture capital investors to keep their grip on the firm well beyond the incorporation process. Using information from the charters of floated companies, Table 6 shows that the directors of SG and BdB were systematically advertised as 'leading administrators' of the firms incorporated by the two banks. The governor of BdB, Charles de Brouckère, was indicated as 'leading administrator' of 13 companies underwritten by his bank, with a cumulative capital of more than 55 million francs; while the governor of SG, Ferdinand de Meeus, was either directly or indirectly (as a 'leading administrator' of the two subsidiaries Société de Commerce and Société Nationale) chairing no less than 24 companies underwritten by his bank, with a cumulative capital of more than 92 million francs. In the end, the boards of all bank-affiliated companies were constantly occupied by the directors of the two underwriters (Kurgan-Van Hentenryk, 1996;

Table 5. Breakdown per asset class of the total number of securities traded at the Brussels stock exchange (end of year), 1834–1839. Source: Author, from *L'Indépendance Belge* (1834–1839).

	Domestic Sovereign and Subsovereign Bonds	Foreign Sovereign and Subsovereign Bonds	Corporate Bonds	Stocks of SG-Affiliated Firms	Stocks of BdB-Affiliated Firms	Stocks of Non-Affiliated Firms	TOTAL
1834	4	13	0	1	0	0	*18*
1835	3	12	0	4	2	0	*21*
1836	4	10	0	19	9	4	*46*
1837	4	10	0	21	14	9	*58*
1838	5	9	0	21	17	8	*60*
1839	5	9	0	21	17	8	*60*

Table 6. Belgium, 1833–1838: Names of people mentioned as 'leading administrator' of a joint-stock company in Briavoinne's treatise on Belgian industrialisation, number of companies of which the person is a 'leading administrator', and cumulative capital of the companies of which the person is a 'leading administrator'. Source: Briavoinne (1839, pp. 562–566); Laureyssens (1975).

Names of People Mentioned as 'Leading Administrator' of a Belgian Joint-Stock Company in Briavoinne (1839)	Number of Companies	Cumulative Capital of Companies (million francs)
Charles de Brouckère (BdB)	13	55.3
Ferdinand de Meeus (SG)	12	70.3
« Gérants de la Société de Commerce » (leading adm.: F. de Meeus, SG)	7	17.2
John Cockerill (BdB)	4	5.9
« Gérants de la Société Nationale » (leading adm.: F. de Meeus, SG)	4	4.9
9 other SG-related names (average)	1.9	4.6
10 other BdB-related names (average)	1.6	3.9
88 other names unrelated to SG or BdB (average)	1.1	1.0

Laureyssens, 1975). Exacerbated by extensive crossholding of affiliates through other affiliates, the phenomenon of board interlocks proved a persistent feature in Belgium (Van Overfelt, Annaert, De Ceuster, & Deloof, 2009). The fact that banks' corporate control on affiliated firms remained strongest is consistent with the idea of a lockup effect on underwritten companies. Banks' persistent involvement in the management of floated companies acted as a sort of moral guarantee in the eyes of investors, as it suggested that underwritten firms would be closely monitored and granted constant liquidity assistance by banks. On the whole, this seems to confirm the third hypothesis – viz., that banks boosted the attractiveness of floated securities by providing them with some form of credit enhancement.

5. From markets to banks

5.1. Banks as market makers: conceptual framework

According to the finance literature, markets provide two crucial functions: 'price discovery' and 'liquidity'. The two are inextricably linked, although they do not actually coincide. On the one hand, price discovery is the mechanism allowing for the incorporation of all available information into asset prices: its efficiency is hindered by the presence of information asymmetries, as uninformed traders bear a non-diversifiable risk of losses when they trade against informed ones. On the other hand, liquidity is the mechanism allowing for the matching of buyers and sellers of assets: its efficiency is hindered by the presence of transaction costs (O'Hara, 2003).

Price discovery is a particularly delicate process at the time of the first introduction of an asset into the market. In theory, even if the amount of information available to all market participants is superior to the one available to the underwriter alone, the latter's pricing errors should be randomly distributed – meaning that the difference between the issue price and the market price of the floated asset should be zero on average. In real-world markets, however, underpricing is almost constantly observed – meaning that the market price almost always exceeds the issue price. Price run-ups have been generally interpreted as unbiased indicators of information asymmetries – i.e. as the 'lemons premium' that issuers are obliged to pay in order for uninformed investors to be attracted (Rock, 1986). However, some contributions have pointed to the existence of widespread aftermarket intervention by underwriters – be it direct (such as price support) or indirect (such as sentiment creation) – which exacerbates price run-ups (Derrien, 2005; Ellis, Michaely, & O'Hara, 2000; Ritter, 2011; Welch, 1992).

Two (not mutually exclusive) explanations for aftermarket intervention have been advanced. The first (more pessimistic) one originates from the observation that securitisation is, by far, the main source of profit for venture capitalists (Lerner, 1994). If the same intermediary is both venture capitalist and underwriter of the floated firm, conflicts of interests will naturally arise in view of the obvious incentive to maximise price run-ups, and this may be conducive to cronyism (Drucker & Puri, 2007; Ritter, 2011). The second (more optimistic) explanation is linked to the sunk-cost nature of reputation. Success in the underwriting business critically depends on the underwriter's reputation as a certifier (Ljungqvist, 2007). In the case of an IPO lockup, the underwriters' need to enhance the performance of the floated securities will not only apply in the short run, but also in the long run. In order to prevent bad signals from being conveyed to the market, underwriting banks will be ready to provide subsidised lending to an underperforming affiliated firm (Kanodia, Bushman, & Dickhaut, 1989). Therefore, in order to maintain its reputation as an underwriter, a bank may find itself unable to eliminate credit risk through securitisation – meaning that the qualitative asset transformation process is incomplete. Credit risk inherent to the originated securities might actually return to the bank under the form of informal off-balance-sheet commitments – as it spectacularly did to issuers of asset-backed securities in 2007 (Acharya, Schnabl, & Suarez, 2013).

The second fundamental function of markets consists of enhancing liquidity. Exchange-traded securities naturally tend to be more liquid than other assets in view of their standardised nature and of their access to a larger pool of potential buyers. Liquidity is one of the fundamental determinants of the attractiveness of securities (Amihud, Mendelson, & Pedersen, 2005). However, liquidity can quickly evaporate in securities markets in the event of crises. As a result, the attractiveness of a financial asset is strongly increased by the presence of a lender of last resort (LLR) operating on the market for that specific asset. Through its commitment to lend on the asset at any moment at some price, the LLR provides a ceiling to transaction costs; in other words, the presence of a LLR acts as a guarantee against future liquidity shocks. Thus, assets covered by such a guarantee have a clear competitive advantage with respect to assets exposed to illiquidity risks, as they can be pledged to obtain credit at any moment. Central banks started enacting LLR policies in the mid-nineteenth century, but for many decades they limited their action to a rather narrow range of securities – mainly high-quality bills of exchange and a limited number of sovereign and quasi-sovereign bonds (Bignon, Flandreau, & Ugolini, 2012). This forced underwriters of corporate securities to step in: nineteenth-century banks saw as a positive duty the commitment to lend on the securities they had themselves issued (Flandreau & Sicsic, 2001).

From what precedes, two insights can be drawn that are relevant for understanding corporate securities markets in the very early stages of industrialisation. First, there are good reasons for underwriters to influence the price discovery mechanism – because profits can be made from price run-ups in the short run, and/or because reputation needs to be preserved in the long run. Thus, underwriting banks can be expected to actively implement market interventions in order to sustain the price and dividend performance of the underwritten companies, both in the short and in the long run. Secondly, there are good reasons for underwriters to sustain the liquidity of underwritten securities – because liquidity is an essential determinant of asset prices. Thus, underwriting banks can be expected to provide market participants with lending-of-last-resort facilities on the underwritten securities. On the whole, this means that underwriters can be expected to behave as market-makers for the securities they issue. These hypotheses will now be tested in the context of Belgium's industrial take-off.

4.2. Banks as market makers: evidence from 1830s Belgium

The most popular measure of underpricing is the IPO discount – i.e. the difference between the issue price and the market price of the stock at the end of the first day of flotation. As data on IPO discounts are only available for four stocks (see Table 1), I compute an alternative measure of underpricing, which I call the 'mid-term price run-up': this is defined as the difference between the issue price and the mid-term equilibrium price of the stock (computed as the average price over the first six months in which the stock appears on bulletins). Table 7 compares mid-term price run-ups with actual IPO discounts for the only four stocks for which the latter are available. As expected, the two measures of underpricing differ, but they are of the same order of magnitude – except for one very special case.[3] The computed mid-term price run-ups are shown in Figure 2. Three general patterns can be observed: on average, SG-affiliated stocks displayed the higher run-ups; BdB-affiliated stocks displayed lower run-ups; and non-affiliated stocks generally saw their price fall. For all classes, run-ups decline in the years following 1835.[4]

Were run-ups due to *ex-ante* underpricing (as in Rock, 1986) or to *ex-post* intervention (as in Ritter, 2011)? Direct historical evidence does not allow establishing if and to what extent underwriters intervened in the aftermarket in order to support the price of the securities they issued. One indirect way to answer this question consists of determining whether stocks were overpriced in the mid run by comparing prices and actual returns. Data on dividends are only available for ten stocks (see Table 1),[5] which are highly likely to suffer from the survivor bias – meaning that they supposedly cover only the high-quality end of the market. Past returns and prices for all assets on which information is available are

Table 7. Brussels bourse, 1835–1838: IPO discounts and mid-term price run-ups of four selected stocks. Source: Chlepner (1926, p. 92); Brion and Moreau (1998, p. 62); author's database.

		IPO Discount		Mid-Term Performance	
Company	Affiliation	Date	Price Run-Up	Period	Price Run-Up
Société de Commerce	SG	Mar. 21, 1835	24%	Jan.–Jul.1836	31.15%
Sars-Longchamps	SG	Nov. 4, 1835	14%	Jul.1836–Jan.1837	11.56%
Raffinerie Nationale	SG	Jun. 19, 1836	12%	Jan.–Jul. 1837	18.04%
Asphaltes Seyssel	None	Feb. 10, 1838	10%	Mar.–May 1838*	39.92%*

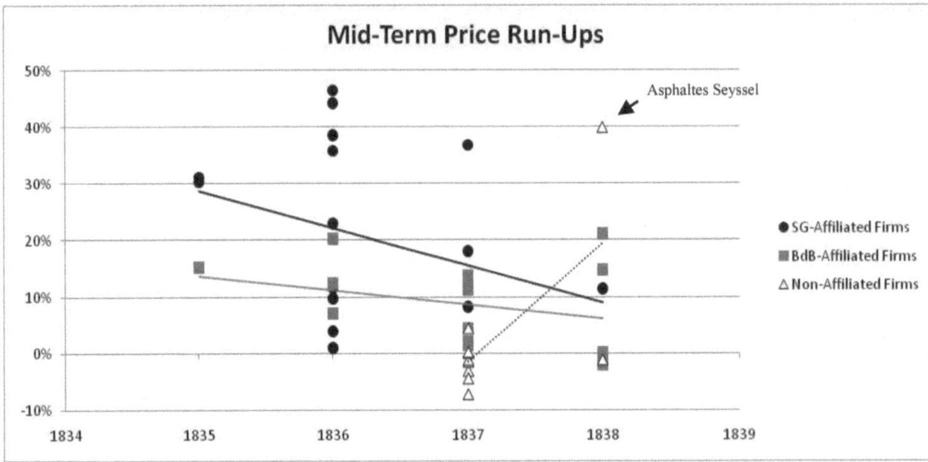

Figure 2. Mid-term price run-ups (defined as the difference between issue price and the average market price during the first six months of presence on the bulletins), 1834–1839. Source: author's database.

displayed in Figure 3. Market prices appear to reflect the returns of the assets: the stocks whose price was higher actually paid higher dividends, and vice-versa; interestingly, the yield of corporate assets was more or less in line with the yield of Belgian government bonds. On the whole, no patently aberrant pricing of stocks can be found. This might be interpreted as pointing to the absence of a stock market bubble, and as suggesting that run-ups were due to *ex-ante* underpricing rather than to *ex-post* intervention by underwriters.

Henceforth, the interpretation of underpricing as a 'lemons premium' necessary to attract outsiders to the securitisation process does not seem to be disproved by *prima facie* evidence. However, the way the underwriting process was organised suggests that there was more to the story. Initial subscribers were asked to pay only a small fraction of the nominal capital, and instalment payments were then spread across a long time span. Price run-ups thus provided a source of immediate gains for subscribers, who earned the difference between the issue price and the market price without having to put much capital on the table. In fact, the mechanism of allocation of new issues was very opaque. In the case of universal banks, bearers of affiliated securities were granted the right to subscribe new shares underwritten by the bank – which amounted to a sort of embedded call-option on future IPOs. But criteria for allocation were unclear, and insiders (typically, bank directors) managed to secure the lion's share in the business (Chlepner, 1926, pp. 87–91). Thus, directors had a clear incentive to multiply new IPOs: this may perhaps explain why the number of incorporations skyrocketed in the space of a few months. This sort of rent was extracted by subscribers at the expense of the underwriter: for newly-issued shares held on its own account, the bank was thus paid less than the aftermarket price. In modern parlance, the underwriter was 'spinning' its own managers (Ritter, 2011). However, as directors had a clear incentive in maintaining the long-term viability of the mechanism and thus in not behaving as 'wildcat bankers', the rent was more akin to a tax than to a fully-fledged exploitation of the business by insiders.

The impression that bank directors did not behave as 'wildcats' is corroborated once we look at the long-run performance of the issued securities. At the time of industrialisation, stocks were spurious securities: as firms' growth perspectives were highly uncertain, shares

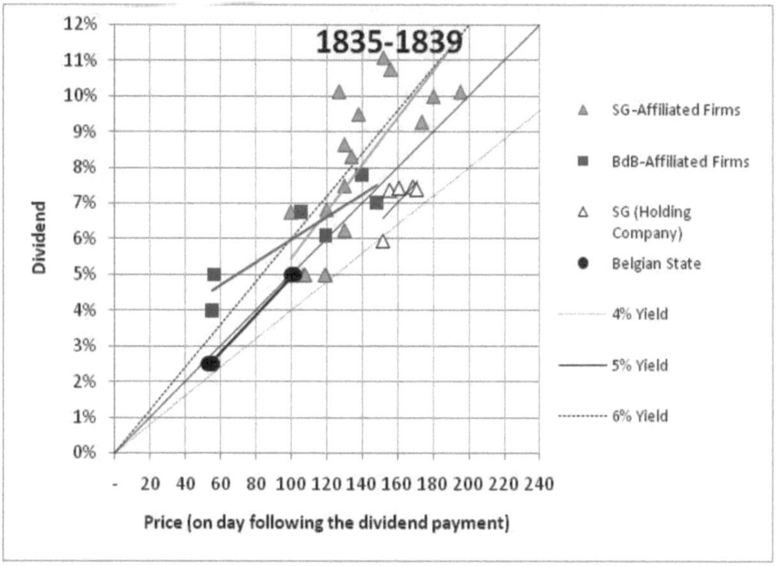

Figure 3. Total dividend yields of a number of securities by affiliation, 1835–1839. Source: author's database; SCOB database.

were often provided some enhancements, such as seniority over other liabilities or – more typically – a minimum dividend target (Baskin & Miranti, 1997). This is to be understood in the nineteenth-century context, in which dividends played as a substitute for income statement transparency and thus had a paramount signalling role (Van Overfelt, Deloof, & Vanstraelen, 2010). In 1830s Belgium, equities were generally attached a yearly minimum dividend target equal to 5% of the issue price. As missing this target was considered somewhat like a default, underwriters that were keen on defending their reputation had an interest in avoiding the dividend underperformance of affiliated firms.

Table 8 reports available data on the dividend performance of bank-affiliated firms until 1848. Before the 1839 crisis, all companies largely beat the dividend target, thus conveying bullish signals to the stock market. During the economic depression of the 1840s, dividends declined for all firms – but according to different paths. On the one hand, all BdB-affiliated companies in the sample repeatedly missed the targets; on the other hand, only two out of the eight SG-affiliated companies in the sample actually underperformed. Such different paths might have been tied to the different strategies implemented by the two banks in the aftermath of the crisis. Following its bailout, in 1841 BdB was recapitalised by a group of new investors, who vowed to transform BdB into a pure commercial bank by liquidating its investment banking activities (Chlepner, 1926). As a result, the bank lost all incentives for defending its reputation as an originator of corporate securities, and consequently stopped performing subsidised lending to affiliated companies. Conversely, SG did not consider the opportunity of changing its business model, and therefore kept a strong interest in maintaining its reputational capital. The two SG-affiliated companies which repeatedly missed their targets in the 1840s (i.e. the Sclessin and Couillet ironworks) were among those more widely held by the bank itself (50.6% and 78.0%, respectively), so that few investors were hit by the dividend cuts. Moreover, in order for the other SG-affiliated firms to avoid

Table 8. Dividend performance of bank-affiliated companies, 1835–1848. Source: Author, from SCOB database.

	SG			BdB		
	Excess Dividends with respect to the Target (% of the Stock's Issue Price): Average	Number of Companies in the Sample	Of Which Missing the Target	Excess Dividends with respect to the Target (% of the Stock's Issue Price): Average	Number of Companies in the Sample	Of Which Missing the Target
1835	0.95%	1	0	–	0	0
1836	1.52%	4	0	1.10%	1	0
1837	1.69%	7	0	2.80%	1	0
1838	3.50%	8	0	2.39%	2	0
1839	2.18%	8	0	0.00%	2	0
1840	1.35%	8	1	0.00%	2	0
1841	0.90%	8	1	0.00%	2	0
1842	−0.10%	8	2	−1.75%	2	2
1843	−0.20%	8	2	−1.43%	2	2
1844	−0.36%	8	2	−1.63%	2	2
1845	−0.04%	8	2	−2.08%	2	2
1846	1.84%	8	1	−0.80%	2	2
1847	1.26%	8	2	0.95%	2	0
1848	1.30%	8	1	−0.50%	2	1

underperformance, the bank engaged in extensive subsidised lending and sponsored efficiency-enhancing company restructurings (Brion & Moreau, 1998). As long as they were willing not to quit the business, universal banks were thus ready to 'make sacrifices' in order for the present worth of their reputation not to drop – and this, even in a period of stock market activity as limited as the 1840s (Ugolini, 2011). To summarise, while historical sources do not allow to find direct evidence of intervention by Belgian universal banks to sustain the price and dividend performance of floated companies, many pieces of indirect evidence strongly suggest that (consistent with the first hypothesis) active intervention did actually occur in the short as in the long run – at least, as long as banks attached a positive value to their reputation as securitisers.

I now turn to the question of liquidity provision. Different measures of liquidity have been proposed (Goyenko, Holden, & Trzcinka, 2009). In the simplest form, liquidity is estimated by looking at bid-ask spreads (a proxy for transaction costs): the higher the transaction costs, the lower the liquidity of the asset. In the case of emerging markets, however, even reconstructing bid-ask spreads is often an impossible task (Bekaert, Harvey, & Lundblad, 2007). This is also the case for 1830s Belgium. In order to overcome this problem, a viable alternative consists of focussing on 'non-zero returns to equity' (Lesmond, Ogden, & Trzcinka, 1999). The idea is straightforward: lack of price movements over time is interpreted as evidence of illiquidity. Figure 4 shows the number of securities listed on the Brussels stock exchange displaying non-zero week-on-week returns. It is possible to observe increasing liquidity up to the first months of 1838, and then a collapse in the summer of the same year. One element emerges from the picture: securities issued by universal banks were relatively liquid, while non-affiliated ones were utterly illiquid.

Was this due to the intervention of universal banks themselves? For both banks, available information on securities accepted as collateral covers one single date only – viz. the day they were obliged to disclose their books to inspectors in the event of their bailout: December 13, 1838 for BdB, and March 1, 1848 for SG (Tables 9.1 and 9.2).[6] It shows that universal banks almost exclusively lent on the securities they had underwritten themselves, while they only exceptionally took other securities (sovereign bonds included) as collateral. As confirmed by qualitative sources (Malou, 1863, p. 45), banks used to grant their affiliated securities eligibility for unlimited loans – i.e. they took the engagement of acting as LLR for them. Figure 5 gives the total sums lent on securities by SG and BdB during the boom-and-bust cycle. They clearly show that as time passed, banks became more and more involved in meeting the demand for such loans. In the case of SG (for which yearly averages are available), lending on securities peaked in 1839; while in the case of BdB (for which only end-of-year figures exist), lending on securities was declining at the end of 1838 – when the bank had already fallen victim to the run. As the speculative wave was losing momentum, more and more shareholders were bringing their securities to the banks in order to obtain cash. This means that borrowing conditions on the market were worse than those offered by banks. As a result, from being the lenders of last resort, banks ended up being the 'market-makers of last resort' for affiliated securities, as the market simply ceased to exist outside the banks. This explains

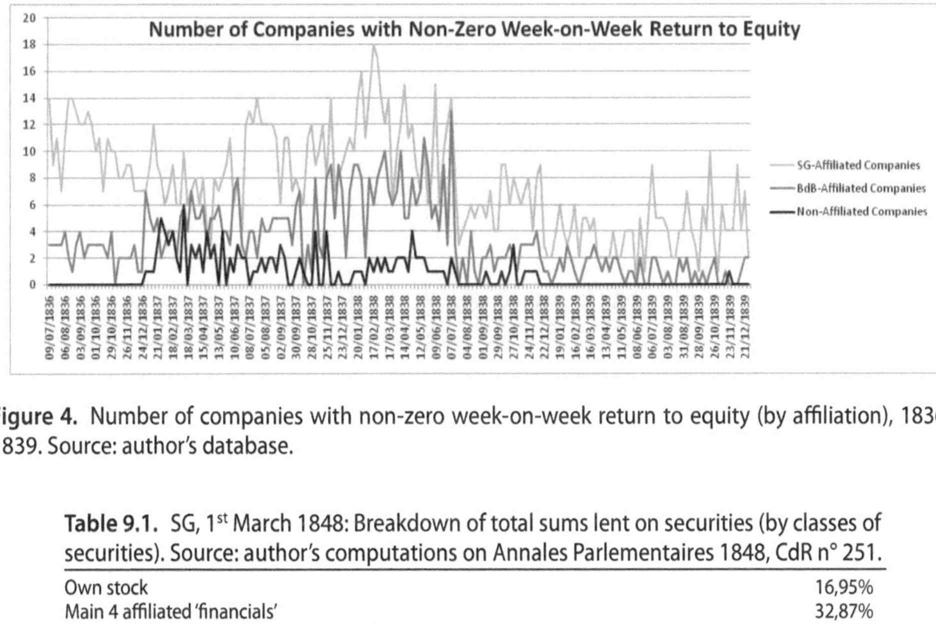

Figure 4. Number of companies with non-zero week-on-week return to equity (by affiliation), 1836–1839. Source: author's database.

Table 9.1. SG, 1st March 1848: Breakdown of total sums lent on securities (by classes of securities). Source: author's computations on Annales Parlementaires 1848, CdR n° 251.

Own stock	16,95%
Main 4 affiliated 'financials'	32,87%
Main 3 affiliated 'collieries and ironworks'	11,27%
Main 3 affiliated 'other sectors'	13,41%
Undetermined	25,51%

Table 9.2. BdB, 13th December 1838: Breakdown of total sums lent on securities (by classes of securities). Source: author's computations on AGR Brussels, Fonds Min. Finances, 307/1/15, A.

Own stock	2,12%
Listed affiliated 'financials'	24,68%
Listed affiliated 'collieries and ironworks'	34,22%
Listed affiliated 'other sectors'	9,74%
Générale group stock	1,54%
Listed non-affiliated stock	9,36%
Unlisted stock	2,14%
Sovereign bonds	16,19%

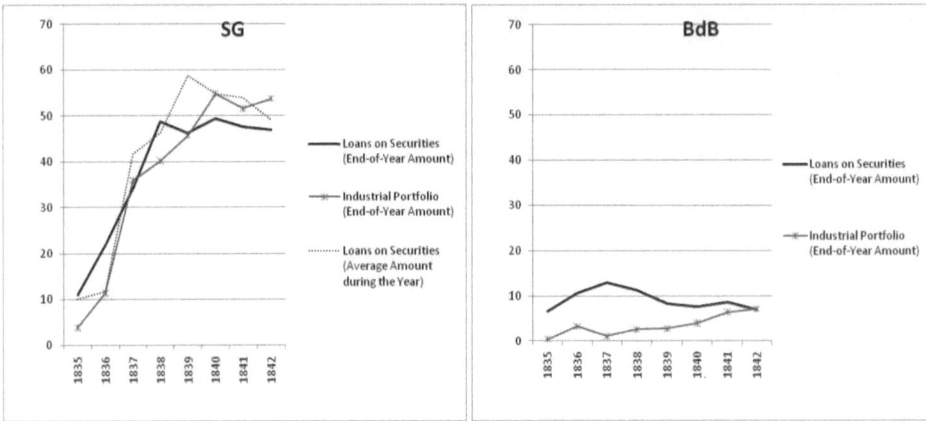

Figure 5. Loans on securities and industrial portfolio by Belgian banks (end-of-year amount, in million francs), 1835–1842. Source: Malou (1863, pp. I–IV); Chlepner (1926, pp. 78–79). SG, 1835–1842: Average amount lent on securities during the year (in million francs). Source: author's computations on Malou (1863, p. XX) and Annales Parlementaires 1848, CdR n° 251.

why, on the one hand, the observed liquidity of BdB-affiliated securities evaporated once the run prevented BdB from continuing to perform its lending policies; and why, on the other hand, the observed liquidity of SG-affiliated securities was not completely impaired by the crisis, as SG continued to lend up to the point of 'absorbing' the whole market.[7] All this confirms the second hypothesis – viz.,that banks offered lending facilities to market participants in order to sustain the performance of affiliated securities. On the whole, historical evidence confirms that banks played a primary role in the functioning of emerging markets by acting as market-makers for the securities they had themselves originated.

6. Conclusions

Building on a substantial amount of primary and secondary qualitative and quantitative evidence, this article has provided detailed microeconomic evidence on the interaction between banks and markets in the early stages of the industrialisation of a 'moderately backward' country. On the one hand, it has shown that Belgian banks played a substantial role in the creation of a stock market in Brussels in the 1830s. Before 1835, firms were rationed by the capital market and could only obtain funding from intermediaries or the state. Banks acted as venture capitalists and arranged the conditions for the transformation of high-tech 'start-ups' into exchange-listed public corporations. However, banks did not discharge all their stakes in floated companies and continued to monitor and control them. As a result, the stock market emerged not as a competitor to banks, but – quite to the contrary – as an instrument for banks to facilitate and expand their corporate finance business. On the other hand, the article has shown that Belgian banks played a considerable role not only in creating, but also in managing the Brussels stock market. First, banks created the conditions for price run-ups to happen – not only as a strategy for attracting outsiders to the stock market, but also as a way for securing profits to insiders. Second, banks continued to provide subsidisation to affiliated firms after their floatation, so that the assets that they had taken out of their balance sheet through securitisation actually reappeared on their balance sheet during the crisis. Third, banks maintained the liquidity of issued securities by acting as lenders of last resort on them, and continued to provide liquidity to their holders during and after the stock market crisis of 1839 – thus ending up 're-absorbing' *de facto* most of the securitised assets. After having partially 'externalised' their corporate finance functions to the market in the 1830s, Belgian banks were therefore forced to 're-internalise' most of them during the 1839 crisis. This was due to the fact that despite initial success, in the long term banks failed to attract enough outsiders to the new trading floor. However, the fact that the securitisation wave of the 1830s was brutally stopped and put to a stand-by in the 1840s does not mean that the methods followed by banks were necessarily fundamentally unhealthy. In fact, the very same methods were applied anew by Belgian universal banks since the 1850s, and then met a considerable success in expanding the corporate securities market and thus establishing Brussels as one of the most important financial centres in Europe (Ugolini, 2011; Van Overfelt et al., 2009).

These findings suggest that, in stark contrast to the traditional idea that markets are competitors to banks in the corporate finance sector, banks fostered the emergence of markets in order to facilitate and expand their own business. Markets and banks not only coexisted, but also coevolved: corporate assets were pushed out of intermediaries' balance sheets through securitisation, but they also jumped back to their balance sheets by means of their aftermarket interventions. All this is consistent with the conclusions of the theoretical literature on the coevolution of banks and markets (esp. Song & Thakor, 2010), but also qualifies them under one important respect. Following the traditional approach, the literature continues to consider changes in financial architecture as the result of modifications in structural (long-term) conditions. Although in an increasingly cautious way, also economic historians have continued to focus more on the structural economic, political, or legal factors impacting institutional design rather than on the contingent factors impacting the industrial organisation of finance (Fohlin, 2012, 2016). In this case study, intermediaries were found to alternatively 'externalise' and 'internalise' their corporate finance activities according to modifications not in structural, but in cyclical (short-term) conditions. Anecdotal evidence on the 'formative' phases of other national financial systems (1850s Germany, 1870s Austria, 1890s Italy) appears to be consistent with these findings on 1830s Belgium. Therefore, one might speculate that, for all its importance, the role of path dependence in shaping financial systems might perhaps have been overemphasised by economists and historians alike. Only a more systematic comparative analysis of the early emergence of financial architecture across countries will be able to tell us to what extent this may actually have been the case.

Notes

1. For a discussion on the pros and cons of "institutional" and "functional" approaches, see Ugolini (2017).
2. Ugolini (2011) discusses the choice of this proxy and the reasons for preferring the lists provided by the press (which covered the securities actually traded on the market) to the lists provided by official bulletins (which covered all securities listed regardless of their actual liquidity). He also takes into account the other relevant Belgian capital market (i.e. the Antwerp bourse), to conclude that the flotation of industrial equity was a purely Brussels-based phenomenon.
3. The price of Asphaltes Seyssel stock experienced a spectacular rise during some weeks, rapidly lost momentum, and then disappeared completely from listings: this gives a very high average price that cannot be considered as an equilibrium price.

4. The conclusion does not seem to be valid for non-affiliated companies in 1838, but the result is entirely driven by the Asphaltes Seyssel stock (see footnote 3).
5. Available data cover eight SG-affiliated companies, two BdB-affiliated companies, and no non-affiliated company. SG-affiliated companies include: SG Holding Company (financials), HF Couillet (ironworks), Hornu et Wasmes (coalmining), Levant du Flénu (coalmining), Produits au Flénu (coalmining), Sars-Longchamps (coalmining), Sclessin (ironworks), Manufacture de Glaces (glassworks). BdB-affiliated companies include: BdB Holding Company (financials), Actions Réunies (financials).
6. Although data for SG concern a much later date than the events analysed here, we know that most loans had been contracted back in 1839 and systematically rolled-over thereafter (Annales Parlementaires 1848, n° 251). We can thus expect these figures to be representative of SG's policy during the 1830s.
7. The effect of this 'absorption' of the market by the bank was the complete immobilisation of the assets side of its balance sheet: although SG managed to avoid suspending payments in 1839, its structure became extremely fragile and could not survive the following liquidity crisis in 1848 (Annales Parlementaires 1848, n° 251).

Acknowledgements

I am grateful to Michelangelo Vasta and two anonymous referees for their great help in improving this article. I thank Olivier Accominotti, Vincent Bignon, Youssef Cassis, Abe de Jong, Marc Flandreau, Juan H. Flores, Timothy Guinnane, Lars Norden, Mary O'Sullivan, and Herman Van der Wee for discussing some of the issues raised here. I am also indebted to Frans Buelens for providing access to some data series from the SCOB database. An early version of this article was circulated under the title: "Universal Banking and the Development of Secondary Corporate Debt Markets: Lessons from 1830s Belgium". The usual disclaimers apply.

Disclosure statement

No potential conflict of interest was reported by the author.

References

Acharya, V. V., Schnabl, P., & Suarez, G. (2013). Securitization without risk transfer. *Journal of Financial Economics, 107*(3), 515–536. doi:10.1016/j.jfineco.2012.09.004

Allen, F., & Gale, D. (2000). *Comparing financial systems*. Cambridge, MA: MIT Press.

Amihud, Y., Mendelson, H., & Pedersen, L. H. (2005). Liquidity and asset prices. *Foundations and Trends in Finance, 1*(4), 269–302. doi:10.1561/0500000003

Baliga, S., & Polak, B. (2004). The emergence and persistence of the Anglo-Saxon and German financial systems. *Review of Financial Studies, 17*(1), 129–163. doi:10.1093/rfs/hhg020

Baskin, J. B., & Miranti, P. J. (1997). *A history of corporate finance*. Cambridge: Cambridge University Press. doi:10.1017/CBO9780511665219

Bekaert, G., Harvey, C. R., & Lundblad, C. (2007). Liquidity and expected returns: Lessons from emerging markets. *Review of Financial Studies, 20*(4), 1–49. doi:10.1093/rfs/hhm030

Bignon, V., Flandreau, M., & Ugolini, S. (2012). Bagehot for beginners: The making of lending-of-last-resort operations in the mid-nineteenth century. *The Economic History Review, 65*(2), 580–608. doi:10.1111/j.1468-0289.2011.00606.x

Boot, A. W. A. (2000). Relationship banking: What do we know?. *Journal of Financial Intermediation, 9*(1), 7–25. doi:10.1006/jfin.2000.0282

Boot, A. W. A., & Thakor, A. V. (1997). Financial system architecture. *Review of Financial Studies, 10*(3), 693–733. doi:10.1093/rfs/10.3.693

Boot, A. W. A., & Thakor, A. V. (2010). The accelerating integration of banks and markets and its implications for regulation. In A. N. Berger, P. Molyneux, & J. O. S. Wilson (Eds.), *The Oxford handbook of banking* (pp. 58–89). Oxford: Oxford University Press. doi:10.1093/oxfordhb/9780199640935.013.0003

Boyd, J. H., & Smith, B. D. (1998). The evolution of debt and equity markets in economic development. *Economic Theory, 12*(3), 519–560. doi:10.1007/s001990050234

Brambilla, C. (2010). Assessing convergence in European investment banking patterns until 1914. In P. Baubeau & A. Ögren (Eds.), *Convergence and divergence of national financial systems: Evidence from the gold standards, 1871–1971* (pp. 89–108). London: Pickering & Chatto.

Brav, A., & Gompers, P. A. (2003). The role of lockups in initial public offerings. *Review of Financial Studies, 16*(1), 1–29. doi:10.1093/rfs/16.1.1

Briavoinne, N. (1839). *De l'industrie en Belgique, sa situation actuelle, causes de décadence et de prospérité* (Vol. 2). Brussels: Dubois.

Brion, R., & Moreau, J.-L. (1998). *The Société générale de Belgique, 1822–1997*. Antwerp: Fonds Mercator.

Cameron, R. (1967). *Banking in the early stages of industrialization: A study in comparative economic history*. New York, NY: Oxford University Press.

Chakraborty, S., & Ray, T. (2007). The development and structure of financial systems. *Journal of Economic Dynamics and Control, 31*(9), 2920–2956. doi:10.1016/j.jedc.2006.01.010

Chemmanur, T. J., & Fulghieri, P. (1994). Reputation, renegotiation, and the choice between bank loans and publicly traded debt. *Review of Financial Studies, 7*(3), 475–506. doi:10.1093/rfs/7.3.475

Chlepner, B.-S. (1926). *La Banque en Belgique: Étude historique et économique* (Vol. 1). Brussels: Lamertin.

Chlepner, B.-S. (1943). *Belgian banking and banking theory*. Washington, DC: Brookings Institution.

Confalonieri, A. (1974-6). *Banca e industria in Italia, 1894–1906*. Milan: Banca Commerciale Italiana.

Da Rin, M. (1997). Finance and technology in early industrial economies: The role of economic integration. *Research in Economics, 51*(3), 171–200. doi:10.1006/reec.1997.0047

De Troyer, M. (1974). *Financiële intermediatiepolitiek van de Société générale, 1822–1850* (Unpublished dissertation). Katholieke Universiteit te Leuven, Leuven.

Deidda, L., & Fattouh, B. (2008). Banks, financial markets and growth. *Journal of Financial Intermediation, 17*(1), 6–36. doi:10.1016/j.jfi.2006.04.003

Demoulin, R. (1938). *Guillaume Ier et la transformation économique des provinces belges 1815–1830*. Liège-Paris: Université de Liège-Droz.

Derrien, F. (2005). IPO pricing in 'hot' market conditions: Who leaves money on the table? *The Journal of Finance, 60*(1), 487–521. doi:10.1111/j.1540-6261.2005.00736.x

Drucker, S. & Puri, M. (2007). Banks in Capital Markets. In B. E. Eckbo (Ed.) *Handbook of corporate finance: Empirical corporate finance* (Vol. 1, pp. 189–232). Amsterdam: Elsevier. doi:10.1016/B978-0-444-53265-7.50019-6

Ellis, K., Michaely, R., & O'Hara, M. (2000). When the underwriter is the market maker: An examination of trading in the IPO aftermarket. *Journal of Finance, 55*(3), 1039–1074. doi:10.1111/0022-1082.00240

Federico, G., & Toniolo, G. (1991). Italy. In R. Sylla & G. Toniolo (Eds.), *Patterns of European industrialization: The nineteenth century* (pp. 197–217). London: Routledge.

Flandreau, M., & Sicsic, P. (2001). Crédit à la spéculation et marché monétaire: Le marché des reports en France de 1875 à 1914. In O. Feiertag & M. Margairaz (Eds.), *Politiques et pratiques des banques d'émission en Europe XVIIe-XXe siècle* (pp. 197–222). Paris: Albin Michel.

Fohlin, C. (2007). *Finance Capitalism and Germany's Rise to Industrial Power*. Cambridge: Cambridge University Press. doi:10.1017/CBO9780511510908

Fohlin, C. (2012). *Mobilizing money: How the world's richest nations financed industrial growth*. New York, NY: Cambridge University Press. doi:10.1017/CBO9781139045827

Fohlin, C. (2016). Financial systems. In C. Diebolt & M. Haupert (Eds.), *Handbook of cliometrics* (pp. 393–430). Berlin: Springer. doi:10.1007/978-3-642-40406-1_7

Freedeman, C. E. (1965). Joint-stock business organization in France, 1807–1867. *Business History Review, 39*(02), 184–204. doi:10.2307/3112696

Gerschenkron, A. (1962). *Economic backwardness in historical perspective: A book of essays*. Cambridge, MA: Harvard University Press.

Gerschenkron, A. (1977). *An economic spurt that failed*. Princeton, NJ: Princeton University Press.

Ghent, A., & Valkanov, R. (2016). Comparing securitized and balance sheet loans: Size matters. *Management Science, 62*(10), 2784–2803. doi:10.1287/mnsc.2015.2260

Goldsmith, R. W. (1969). *Financial structure and development*. New Haven, CT: Yale University Press.

Good, D. F. (1991). Austria-Hungary. In R. Sylla & G. Toniolo (Eds.), *Patterns of European industrialization: The nineteenth century* (pp. 218–247). London: Routledge.

Goodfriend, M. S. (1991). Money, credit, banking, and payments system policy. *Federal Reserve Bank of Richmond Economic Review, 77*, 7–23.

Goyenko, R. Y., Holden, C. W., & Trzcinka, C. A. (2009). Do liquidity measures measure liquidity? *Journal of Financial Economics, 92*(2), 153–181. doi:10.1016/j.jfineco.2008.06.002

Greenwood, J., & Smith, B. D. (1997). Financial markets in development, and the development of financial markets. *Journal of Economic Dynamics and Control, 21*(1), 145–181. doi:10.1016/0165-1889(95)00928-0

Gurley, J. G., & Shaw, E. S. (1955). Financial aspects of economic development. *American Economic Review, 45*(4), 515–538.

Hellmann, T., Lindsey, L., & Puri, M. (2008). Building relationships early: Banks in venture capital. *Review of Financial Studies, 21*(2), 513–541. doi:10.1093/rfs/hhm080

Houtman-De Smedt, H. (1997). La Société générale de 1822 à 1848: Évolution de la « banque foncière » à la « banque mixte ». In H. Van der Wee (Ed.), *La Générale de banque, 1822-1997* (pp. 13–62). Brussels: Racine.

James, C. (1995). When do banks take equity in debt restructuring? *Review of Financial Studies, 8*(4), 1209–1234. doi:10.1093/rfs/8.4.1209

Kanodia, C., Bushman, R., & Dickhaut, J. (1989). Escalation errors and the sunk cost effect: An explanation based on reputation and information asymmetries. *Journal of Accounting Research, 27*(1), 59–77. doi:10.2307/2491207

Kurgan-Van Hentenryk, G. (1996). *Gouverner la Générale de Belgique: Essai de biographie collective*. Louvain-la-Neuve: De Boeck.

Lamoreaux, N. R. (1996). *Insider lending: Banks, personal connections, and economic development in industrial New England*. Cambridge: Cambridge University Press. doi:10.1017/CBO9780511582523

Laureyssens, J. M. (1975). *Industriële naamloze vennootschappen in België 1819–1857*. Leuven: Nauwelaerts.

Lerner, J. (1994). Venture capitalists and the decision to go public. *Journal of Financial Economics, 35*(3), 293–316. doi:10.1016/0304-405X(94)90035-3

Lesmond, D. A., Ogden, J. P., & Trzcinka, C. A. (1999). A new estimate of transaction costs. *Review of Financial Studies, 12*(5), 1113–1141. doi:10.1093/rfs/12.5.1113

Levine, R. (2005). Finance and growth: Theory and evidence. In P. Aghion & S. N. Durlauf (Eds.), *Handbook of economic growth* (Vol. 1A, pp. 865–934). Amsterdam: North Holland. doi:10.1016/S1574-0684(05)01012-9.

Lévy-Leboyer, M. (1964). *Les banques européennes et l'industrialisation internationale dans la première moitié du XIXe siècle*. Paris: Presses Universitaires de France.

Ljungqvist, A. (2007). IPO underpricing. In B. E. Eckbo (Ed.), *Handbook of corporate finance: Empirical corporate finance* (Vol. 1, pp. 375–422). Amsterdam: Elsevier. doi:10.1016/B978-0-444-53265-7.50021-4

Loutskina, E. (2011). The role of securitization in bank liquidity and funding management. *Journal of Financial Economics, 100*(3), 663–684. doi:10.1016/j.jfineco.2011.02.005

Malou, J. (1863). *Notice historique sur la Société générale pour favoriser l'industrie nationale établie à Bruxelles 1823-1862*. Brussels: Decq.

Mattana, E., & Panetti, E. (2014). Bank liquidity, stock market participation, and economic growth. *Journal of Banking and Finance, 48*, 292–306. doi:10.1016/j.jbankfin.2014.01.016

Mokyr, J. (1976). *Industrialization in the Low Countries 1795-1850*. New Haven, CT: Yale University Press.

O'Hara, M. (2003). Liquidity and price discovery. *Journal of Finance, 58*(4), 1335–1354. doi:10.1111/1540-6261.00569

Petersen, M. A., & Rajan, R. G. (1995). The effect of credit market competition on lending relationships. *Quarterly Journal of Economics, 110*(2), 407–443. doi:10.2307/2118445

Puri, M. (1999). Commercial banks as underwriters: Implications for the going public process. *Journal of Financial Economics, 54*(2), 133–163. doi:10.1016/S0304-405X(99)00034-3

Rieder, K. (2017). A historic(al) run on repo: Causes of bank distress during the Austro-Hungarian Gründerkrach of 1873 (Working paper). University of Oxford, Oxford.

Riesser, J. (1911). *The German great banks and their concentration*. Washington DC: National Monetary Commission.

Ritter, J. R. (2011). Equilibrium in the initial public offerings market. *Annual Review of Financial Economics, 3*(1), 347–374. doi:10.1146/annurev-financial-102710-144845

Rock, K. (1986). Why new issues are underpriced. *Journal of Financial Economics, 15*(1-2), 187–212. doi:10.1016/0304-405X(86)90054-1

Song, F., & Thakor, A. V. (2010). Financial system architecture and the co-evolution of banks and capital markets. *The Economic Journal, 120*(547), 1021–1055. doi:10.1111/j.1468-0297.2009.02345.x

Sylla, R. (1991). The role of banks. In R. Sylla & G. Toniolo (Eds.), *Patterns of European industrialization: The nineteenth century* (pp. 45–63). London: Routledge.

Tilly, R. (1966). *Financial institutions and industrialization in the Rhineland 1815-1870*. Madison, WI: University of Wisconsin Press.

Ugolini, S. (2011). An "atypical" case? The first emergence of Brussels as an international financial centre, 1830-1860. In L. Quennouëlle-Corre & Y. Cassis (Eds.), *Financial centres and international capital flows in the nineteenth and twentieth centuries* (pp. 47–70). Oxford: Oxford University Press. doi:10.1093/acprof:oso/9780199603503.003.0003

Ugolini, S. (2016). L'invention d'un système monétaire national: Banques d'émission, supervision bancaire et développement financier en Belgique (1822–1872). In O. Feiertag & M. Margairaz (Eds.), *Les banques centrales et l'État-nation* (pp. 137–158). Paris: Presses de Sciences Po.

Ugolini, S. (2017). *The evolution of central banking: Theory and history*. London: Palgrave Macmillan. doi:10.1057/978-1-137-48525-0

Van Overfelt, W., Annaert, J., De Ceuster, M., & Deloof, M. (2009). Do universal banks create value? Universal bank affiliation and company performance in Belgium, 1905–1909. *Explorations in Economic History, 46*(2), 253–265. doi:10.1016/j.eeh.2008.07.001

Van Overfelt, W., Deloof, M., & Vanstraelen, A. (2010). Determinants of corporate financial disclosure in an unregulated environment: Evidence from the early 20th century. *European Accounting Review, 19*(1), 7–34. doi:10.1080/09638180902731539

Vargas-Martínez, M. (2010). Bank loan securitization: An alternative for banks to find liquidity (Working paper). University of Toulouse, Toulouse.

Welch, I. (1992). Sequential sales, learning, and cascades. *Journal of Finance, 47*(2), 695–732. doi:10.2307/2329120

Did French stock markets support firms of the Second Industrial Revolution?

Emilie Bonhoure and David Le Bris

ABSTRACT
Investing in the Second-Industrial-Revolution (2IR) firms at the beginning of the 20th century exposed investors to strong information asymmetries due to the novelty of these industries and the lack of legal rules on transparency and public accounting. We analysed the firms listed in Paris at the start of the 2IR. Despite the strong informational asymmetries, the Paris financial markets did provide high valuation to firms involved in emerging activities as revealed by higher Tobin's Q. This result holds when controlling for risk, liquidity, governance and nationality. Results on the dividend yield, nevertheless, do not confirm the support.

1. Introduction

The role finance plays in supporting economic growth is still an open question. While there is little doubt about the correlation between economic growth (under different definitions) and financial development (through banks or financial markets), the direction of causality remains unclear (Manning, 2003; Pasali, 2013).

From as early as Schumpeter (1912), a number of authors have viewed the financial system as a driver of economic growth. Several potential mechanisms that are more or less closely related (reduced cost of capital, better risk sharing and diversification, more efficient capital allocation, reduced agency costs, and increased role as a liquidity provider) have been pointed out (King & Levine, 1993; Levine, 1997; Manning, 2003). There is empirical evidence supporting a causal effect from finance to growth (Atje & Jovanovic, 1993; Beck & Levine, 2004). However, such relationships, at the aggregated level, could mask the phenomenon at play. Levine (2003) stresses that 'more microeconomic-based studies that explore the possible channels through which finance influences growth will foster a keener understanding of the finance-growth nexus'.

A number of studies have challenged the idea of finance as driver of economic growth. First, there are strong theoretical arguments to support the hypothesis that financial development is only a consequence of growth: growth generates new savings that mechanically result in greater financial development (Lucas, 1988; Robinson, 1952). From this perspective, causal directionality would thus be from growth to finance. A second line of thinking claims that the observed correlation may be driven by another variable, omitted or not sufficiently captured in the tests (Manning, 2003; Rajan & Zingales, 1998). Other research mitigates the observed correlation, showing that the association between finance and growth holds only under certain conditions (Law & Singh, 2014; Rousseau & Wachtel, 2011). This scepticism about the influence of the stock market is not recent. For Jean-Baptiste Say (1837), 'all these [stock market] games are the cause of so many disasters and never benefit industry and production [...]'.[1]

In the finance-growth debate, an important aspect is that finance (under different definitions) may fund firm innovations, which in turn fosters growth in the Schumpeterian sense. But here again, evidence is mixed. On the one hand, the access to external equity is found to be a determinant of innovation on both primary and secondary markets (Brown, Fazzari, & Petersen, 2009; Brown, Martinsson, & Petersen, 2012; Lian & Wang, 2019). On the other hand, the 'limited investor attention' hypothesis[2] implies that investors do not take into account the higher future profits of innovative firms and do not incorporate them into stock prices, leading to a mispricing of innovative companies' stocks (Gu, 2005; Hirshleifer, Hsu, & Li, 2013, 2018).

The relationship between finance and growth is even more confusing when going back in time. The financial market did not play a crucial role at the start of the First Industrial Revolution; for instance, very few firms were listed at the beginning of the 19th century in the US, the UK, France or Belgium (see Annaert et al., 2011, for Belgium, or Arbulu, 2007, for France). However, by the middle of the century, it had become a key player when massive investments in railways were made. For the Second Industrial Revolution, O'Sullivan (2000) pointed out that the stock market did not serve as a major source of funds for long-term business investment. The US stock exchange for industrial securities only came into existence at the turn of the 20th century, due to decisions to 'go public' made by a number of owner-controlled companies that had grown to commanding positions within their respective industries since the 1860s (Chandler, 1977; Lazonick & O'Sullivan, 1997). This weak support to 2nd IR US firms by the stock market is confirmed at a more microeconomic level focusing on Detroit (Klepper, 2007) and Cleveland (Lamoreaux, Levenstein, & Sokoloff, 2007), two leading cities for 2IR firms.

There is good reason to question the ability of the financial market to finance innovative firms in the past because of the lack of many tools, currently stressed as crucial, to reduce information asymmetry. The market efficiency hypothesis states that the expected higher future profits implied by innovative companies[3] should be valued in their stock prices, thus leading to relatively higher prices (and as a consequence higher Tobin's Q and lower dividend yield). However, the asymmetry at that time implied by the new technologies ('technological asymmetry') of these businesses and the 'institutional asymmetry' related to the lack of legal constraints on information (especially accounting) provided to investors could have prevented the financial market from giving a valuation premium to these firms.[4]

We want to test whether the French financial markets of the beginning of the 20th century helped firms involved in what is called the Second Industrial Revolution (hereafter 2nd IR) to develop despite the strong information asymmetries of the time. We focus on 1907 as a suitable time to invest in these innovative firms. The 2nd IR was clearly well under way, meaning that companies were investing strongly, requiring financial support. Additionally, we observed that two decades later, in 1929, 2nd IR firms accounted for a significant portion of the Paris stock exchanges, reflecting the achievements of this economic revolution and the high growth opportunities promised by such firms to their shareholders, from the 1907-year perspective. We can thus expect that the stock market offered a valuation premium to firms involved in 2nd IR industries at the dawn of the 2nd IR.

To explore this hypothesis, we constituted a detailed database of all the firms listed on the Paris stock exchanges in 1907. Before 1914, the French financial market was one of the most developed in the world and included an almost entirely free market segment in Paris (the *Coulisse*), adapted to promising new firms (Hautcoeur & Riva, 2012). Listing was a simple and cost-free operation at this time. However, the simple listing of 2IR firms does not provide any information on the role played by financial markets to support these firms because listing did not imply that companies had to raise equity (Ducros, 2018). Additionally, it would be possible to compute the equity raised on the financial market by these firms but such a series would require a comparison with the equity raised on the private market; unfortunately, this private funding cannot be reconstituted, preventing any comparison.[5] Overall, neither of these two measures (listing and raising equity) could directly clarify the role of the financial market in the 2nd IR.

In this article, we consider the potential role of capital markets from another perspective, assessing whether they provided the favourable financial conditions that these firms deserved, compared to other listed firms. As pointed out by Morck, Shleifer, and Vishny (1990), 'the most common view of the stock market's influence says that [it] affects investment through its influence on the cost of funds and external financing'. We assessed such potentially favourable financial conditions through the Tobin's Q and the dividend yield. Specifically, 2nd IR firms are expected to exhibit a higher Tobin's Q (as Tobin's Q captures the capitalised value of firms' future growth potential[6]), and a lower dividend yield (reflecting expectations for future high dividends[7]). For instance, we expect that a carmaker enjoyed higher Tobin's Q and lower dividend yield compared to a locomotive builder with similar characteristics. Observing these favourable financial conditions for 2IR firms in 1907 would support a causal role of the financial market in the subsequent growth of their innovative activities.

We successively modelled Tobin's Q and dividend yield with a large set of variables such as age, beta, profitability, industry, governance, etc. A dummy for 2IR firms is statistically significant and positive in explaining the Tobin's Q. However, this financial support is not confirmed when measuring it by firm dividend yield; the 2IR dummy is always non-significant. Our results are thus mixed.[8]

Finally, we ran several robustness analyses. We used standard deviation of returns as an alternative measure of risk so far captured by the beta. We used a more restrictive definition of what is a 2IR firm replacing our *2IR* dummy by a *core-2IR* one. We also again ran the above specifications on a domestic sample (namely excluding all foreign firms). Our mixed results are robust to all of these alternative specifications.

The remainder of this article is organised as follows. In Section 2, we provide a description of the 2IR firms on the French financial markets. Section 3 presents the data collection method and some descriptive statistics. We examine whether these markets provided 2IR firms with favourable financial conditions in Section 4. Section 5 offers several robustness analyses. Section 6 briefly concludes.

2. The French financial market and the Second Industrial Revolution

2.1. *The financial market at the eve of the 2IR*

Before World War I (WWI), France was already financially and economically well-developed (Herrigel, 2008). The first 40 firms in terms of market capitalisation represented about 20% of French GDP (Le Bris & Hautcoeur, 2010). This large financial market developed favourably during the first stage of the 2nd IR. According to Hautcoeur (1999), the period between 1890 and 1936 was a period of increase, for French markets, 1) in the number of listed firms, 2) in the amount of securities they listed, and 3) in the proportion of these issues in the firm's total capital.

In Paris, this massive stock market was organised into two complementary poles (Hautcoeur & Riva, 2012). Specifically, the *Parquet* was initially launched by the government at the beginning of the 19th century in order to centralise (and control) financial transactions. The government imposed a number of restrictions on this stock exchange, in particular in terms of products to be traded (derivatives like forward products or options were forbidden), and in terms of companies to be listed. It required that firms comply with certain requirements in terms of size and organisation before being listed.

In contrast, the *Coulisse* was the 'most dynamic and innovative' (Hautcoeur & Riva, 2012) but it was also the unofficial (not to say illegal) part of the Paris financial market, even though it was tolerated for most of the century. It was therefore far less, perhaps not at all, subject to regulation and government control. As a consequence, all products (especially forward ones) and firms that did not comply with *Parquet* rules were able to be listed on this parallel stock exchange; in particular, smaller, more recent or foreign companies were listed on the *Coulisse* (Hautcoeur & Riva, 2012). While the *Coulisse* allowed early listing for new firms without any requirement, these firms were able, in case of success, to migrate to the official exchange likely to offer them more liquidity and more visibility among less professional investors.

At the turn of the 20th century, listing on the *Parquet* was made upon request from the company and after acceptance of the stock exchange. The candidate firm had to submit a series of documents (statutes, general assembly reports, etc.); they were examined by the *Chambre syndicale* (the *Parquet* governing body) to accept or reject the request.[9] To list new shares, the *Parquet* was subject to the Trade Code, meaning that it had to verify the compliance of corporate statutes with the trade law (Gallais-Hamonno, 2007; Hautcoeur, 2007). It also, for its part, imposed some conditions for candidate firms: at some point they were not able to list their bonds unless they had also listed their equity (Gallais-Hamonno, 2007); they were required to have a minimum capital of two million francs (Ducros, 2018; Gallais-Hamonno, 2007). These rules also applied to foreign firms willing to be listed on the Paris market.[10] This contrasts strongly with the lack of any specific rule for listing on the unofficial *Coulisse*. To be listed on the *Coulisse* only shows that a market existed for these securities in Paris and that it was active enough to have a regularly published price. Moreover, listing on either the *Parquet* or on the *Coulisse* was completely free of charge (in terms of admission fees) for issuer companies.[11]

We retained the year 1907 because the 2nd IR was clearly underway at that time. The French economy enjoyed strong growth at this time after a long period of stagnation. While GDP in 1897 was about the same as in 1882 (Levy-Leboyer & Bourguignon, 1985), the French economy subsequently enjoyed a strong period of growth. GDP increased by about 67% between 1897 and 1914 (3.07% per year). At the middle of this *Belle Epoque*, about half of this growth was achieved in 1907. In addition, 1907 was far enough from the rise of the perils that would lead to WWI.[12]

Despite this economic growth, the stock prices of French blue chips remained very flat with declining volatility for a long period of time after the crisis of 1882 and the long economic recession that started at this point. In 1907, the level of the historical CAC40 was still around what was observed about 20 years before (Le Bris and Hautcoeur, 2010). This stable level was only broken by a small increase at the end of the century. From this peak, the market had decreased by about 10% by 1907. The stock market remained around this level until the beginning of WWI, without any marked effect of the US financial crisis of 1907. The same stable situation was observed on the debt market with the *Rente 3%* steady between 3% and 3.2% between 1906 and 1908.

Moreover, we know that many new firms were recently listed at this date. It is difficult to find sources allowing us to reconstitute public equity issues. One exception is the result of a scandal involving the bankruptcy of the banker Rochette after initial public offerings (IPOs) accompanied by false data. Following this, a Parliamentary commission led by Jean Jaurès studied all the IPOs during the previous ten years. Ducros (2018) has analysed the archives of this commission: 742 French firms have been listed across the country between 1898 and 1909, representing a total market value of 2.2 billion gold francs or 5% of 1909 French GDP.[13] Half of the value of new listings was made on the *Parquet*, a quarter on the *Coulisse* and about 13% on the *Parquet* of Lyon (other provincial market values were anecdotal).

We focus on the Paris stock exchanges due to the lack of sources for other markets and because we can assume that the most dynamic firms originally listed on other French markets were also rapidly listed on the *Coulisse*. However, in terms of number of introduced firms, about one-third (smaller in terms of size) were introduced on the Lyon stock exchange (Ducros, 2018). There is no reason why behaviours in Lyon and other provincial capital markets should differ in terms of valuation of 2IR firms compared with those in Paris; the main driver of listing on a provincial market being geographic proximity according to Ducros (2018).

2.2. *A period of poor legal protection and high information asymmetry*

The eve of the 20th century was a period of poor legal protection of investors, all over Europe,[14] but most notably in France (Hautcoeur, 1999; Herrigel, 2008). In particular, specific voting rights could be provided through preferred shares, without any legal restriction, allowing the formation of large and controlling (but not majority) block holders. At this time, little transparency and information disclosure were legally required, thus increasing information asymmetry between insider and outsider shareholders. The 1867 law for corporations (*sociétés anonymes*) had only made it mandatory to release a balance sheet and an inventory of corporate assets at each yearly shareholder general assembly, and, later, a second law required the publication of a balance sheet before the IPO (Hautcoeur, 1999). Despite the fact that no such accounting disclosure (nor any template in the balance sheet) was mandatory at the time (Nikitin, 1992), firms often provided on their own enough information to allow market yearbooks to contain simplified balance sheets.

These few accounting materials were generated without any control on the accounting methods used. However, firms did this following relatively similar templates because, from the end of the 19th century, accounting practices had been standardised through textbooks, schools and professional associations and reviews (Labardin, 2008). Even though falsifications cannot be ruled out (Lemarchand & Praquin, 2005), they were probably orthogonal to our investigations. Moreover, an advantage of using the accounting data of the time is that the stability implied by gold francs avoided any bias resulting from monetary inflation over time; this allows us for instance to be confident concerning the use of the nominal capital of firms founded at different periods.

This poor legal protection paved the way for strong agency issues, in particular between controlling (often founders) and minority (Hautcoeur, 1999) shareholders.[15] These agency problems could be extensively expressed because firms were looking for outside capital at this time of movement from family-business type capitalism to a more dispersed model (Cheffins, 2008). An increasing number of minority shareholders thus had to be considered, but despite the progressive inclusion of external investors, separation of ownership and control was not achieved fully by 1914 (Cheffins, 2008), leaving the control of the firm to few large owners. This resulted in still concentrated ownership particularly in France, both at that time (Herrigel, 2008) and even later (Goyer, 2008), reinforcing these strong agency problems.

2.3. 2IR firms at maturity

The 2IR did allow companies to generate considerable profits at maturity as revealed by a bird's eye view of the 1929 stock market. At that time, 2IR firms were massively present on the French markets, representing more than 27% of the total market capitalisation. Focusing on the ten largest 1929 2IR firms in terms of market capitalisation (see Appendix 3 for a detailed list), the most represented sectors of the 2IR were chemical products and electricity. This provides strong support for the importance of these sectors in terms of expected future profits for 1907 investors.

Importantly, the fact that 2IR firms did not clearly access favourable financial conditions in 1907 may not be inconsistent with high valuation in 1929 markets because these firms could have funded their expansion without stock markets using retained earnings or private funds. For instance, the three largest market capitalisations in 1929 (*Saint-Gobain*, *Produits chimiques et électro-métallurgiques Alais, Froges et Camargue*, and *Etablissements Kuhlmann*) experienced long and gradual development after their formal foundation, innovating and ultimately specialising in sectors of the 2nd IR (chemical products and aluminium). However, for most of their growth, it seems that they developed without a critical support from Paris stock markets.

Another case is *Air Liquide*'s initial financing which has been studied in depth (Petit-Konczyk, 2003). The firm initially relied on several engineers involved in the project and later on two banks to finance rapid expansion: it was established in Belgium and Italy by 1906, and in Japan by 1907 before its listing on the *Coulisse* in 1908, and expanded to Canada and Asia before being listed on the official market. Even after this listing, the initial investors continued subscribing to the new issues for several years.

3. Data collection and descriptive statistics

3.1. Sources and variables

Our hand-collected database details a large set of characteristics for the firms listed on the *Parquet* or on the *Coulisse* in 1907 (in total almost 1000 firms). Most data are provided by the yearbooks published for each stock exchange: *Annuaire des valeurs admises à la cote officielle* (1908 edition for data in 1907) for the *Parquet*, and *Annuaire Desfossés* (1909 edition for data in 1907) for the *Coulisse*. We used additional sources for stock prices. The *Bulletin de la Cote, de la Compagnie des Agents de Change de Paris* provided us with stock prices for the firms listed on the *Parquet*, while the *Cote Desfossés* and the *Cote du Marché des Banquiers* contain stock prices for firms listed on the *Coulisse*. Finally, besides providing us with several of the above sources, the DFIH Equipex (Data for Financial History Equipment of Excellence) has recently set up a website that we used to collect additional data especially on profit amounts.[16]

Half of the firms in our sample display their balance sheets, with their assets and liabilities and how they are broken down. This allowed us to directly extract their book value (given by the amount of their assets), which we used to calculate the Tobin's Q. Another item we had access to is firms' statutes: for most (if not all) of them, the corporate purpose is detailed (under the 'Objet' field). This allowed us to precisely determine what type of activities firms were involved in, in which factories, where, etc. In these yearbooks, firms are classified in a given industry. The *Parquet* and *Coulisse* yearbooks do not use exactly the same typology with regard to sectors, but they are quite similar.[17] We could then divide our entire sample of firms between nine large industries: *bank and insurance, railways, other carriages, coal, gold mines, other mines, the metal industry, utilities* (water, gas and electricity), and *other industries.*[18]

Our variable of interest is a dummy for firms that operate in sectors of the 2nd IR namely: the electricity industry (in both production and distribution), telephone and telegraph, cinema, photography, petroleum, the car industry, tramway construction and exploitation, chemistry (including fertilisers, phosphates, explosives, etc.), aluminium and bauxite extraction, rubber production, and other new materials production (such as cement and linoleum). This classification is built on Gordon's (2000) definition of the 2nd IR.[19]

It is worth noting that investors of the time were aware of these new industries. For instance, electricity was glorified in a Palace of Electricity during the Paris *Exposition Universelle* in 1900. Non-reported Google Ngrams of the key words (in French) of the 2IR such as 'moteur', 'électricité', 'aluminium', 'pétrole' show that these activities were on a growing trend and already discussed in the publications of that time, demonstrating clear public interest. Additionally, the use of a dummy variable to identify these firms is not more simplistic than the classifications used today to compose new-tech stock indices. Such an approach is as relevant for investors of the time as it is for current ones.

We must note that each firm is classified, on the one hand, in one of the nine large industries and, on the other, as a 2IR firm or not. For instance, a carmaker is characterised by a 1 in the *metal industry* category, and also a 1 in the 2IR series, whereas a steel producer receives a 1 for the *metal industry* category, and a 0 in the 2IR dummy.

Overall, among the 1000 companies listed on the Paris markets in 1907, the 231 firms we have identified as 2IR firms represented about 23% (8.73% of total market capitalisation).

These figures can be compared with what is currently observed on the French market. Only 489 firms are listed today in France.[20] Among these 489 firms in modern-day France, about 72 can be classified as innovative firms, thus less than 15%.[21]

The previously mentioned sources also allowed us to compute the usual financial variables such as profitability and beta (see details in Appendix 1). We additionally controlled for detailed governance features relevant for the time (board size, board member financial implication, number of stocks for one vote, number of stocks to be part of general assemblies, maximum votes per shareholder) along with agency costs proxied by the distance between Paris and successively firms' headquarters and main activities location (Bonhoure, Germain, & Le Bris, 2017). More explanation about these variables is given in Appendix 1.

3.2. Descriptive statistics

Here, we describe Tobin's Q and dividend yield characteristics by industry cluster (Table 1). Tobin's Q is rather low especially for banks and utilities (data are not available for most railways). Mining and other industries are the only activities exhibiting a ratio above 1; mining of the time was an activity enjoying strong productivity gains, and the 'other industries' group includes many 2IR activities such as cinema or chemical products. Regarding the dividend yield, the highest averages are for railways and mines. Sectors that encompass most of the 2IR firms (utilities, metal industry, other industries) display moderate levels of dividend yield compared with the 2% level of other carriages and with the 9% level of other mines.

A first approach to our question is shown in Table 2, providing descriptive statistics of Tobin's Q and dividend yield distinguishing 2IR firms from the others. 2IR firms enjoy an average higher Tobin's Q (significant at a 5% level) and a lower (non-significant) dividend yield, which might indicate financial support to these firms, as expected by the proponents of a causal effect of finance on growth. The next section investigates these relationships more deeply; the analysis confirms this first view.

Table 1. Tobin's Q and dividend yield per sector.

	Mean	Median	Maximum	Minimum	Standard Deviation	Number of observations
Tobin's Q						
Bank and insurance	0.38	0.35	5.82	0.03	0.25	71
Railways	0.15	0.13	0.28	0.05	0.12	3
Other carriages	0.70	0.68	1.52	0.12	0.42	18
Coal	0.80	0.60	1.89	0.04	0.52	25
Gold mines	1.09	0.93	3.86	0.12	0.76	57
Other mines	1.41	1.29	5.82	0.08	1.01	72
Metal industry	0.85	0.84	2.12	0.08	0.48	47
Utilities	0.42	0.39	1.43	0.04	0.35	16
Other industries	1.02	0.75	4.61	0.01	0.77	86
Dividend yield (in %)						
Bank and insurance	4.28	4.48	9.36	0.00	1.94	26
Railways	5.00	2.11	21.43	0.00	8.32	6
Other carriages	2.04	1.72	5.63	0.00	2.21	12
Coal	3.05	3.94	9.17	0.00	2.92	23
Gold mines	5.99	0.00	71.43	0.00	11.25	54
Other mines	9.15	3.50	252.66	0.00	36.46	49
Metal industry	3.77	4.24	7.07	0.00	2.22	47
Utilities	4.16	4.74	6.54	0.00	2.00	20
Other industries	4.56	5.24	11.25	0.00	2.73	79

Table 2. Tobin's Q and dividend yield across 2IR/non-2IR firms.

	Mean	Median	Maximum	Minimum	Standard Deviation	Number of observations
Tobin's Q						
2IR	1.04	0.80	4.61	0.04	0.86	74
Other firms	0.88	0.66	5.82	0.01	0.74	321
Diff. in means	0.164**					
Dividend yield (in %)						
2IR	3.68	4.71	8.72	0.00	2.55	60
Other firms	5.50	4.16	252.66	0.00	16.89	256
Diff. in means	−1.81					

Note: ***Significant at the 1 percent level, **Significant at the 5 percent level and *Significant at the 10 percent level.

4. Was a valuation premium provided to 2nd-IR firms?

We focus on two measures of valuation (both being a function of firm stock price), Tobin's Q and dividend yield, to test whether 2IR firms enjoyed a valuation premium. First, we studied firm Tobin's Q because a high Tobin's Q is expected, *ceteris paribus*, for 2IR firms that are likely to have higher growth opportunities.[22] We also studied the dividend yield, as the yield required today by investors should be lower for firms that are expected to generate future high growth of paid dividends.

Formally, we ran the following type of regression:

$$Valuation\,indicator = \alpha + \beta * 2IR + \gamma * controls \tag{1}$$

with the *Valuation indicator* variable being successively Tobin's Q and dividend yield, and the *controls* part a set of control variables including financial variables (including asset value, beta, profitability, and a measure of liquidity), governance rules, and industry fixed effects (Table 3). Our variable of interest is 2IR, a dummy taking value 1 for 2nd IR firms.

The 2IR dummy has a positive impact on Tobin's Q (column 1); this effect is significant at the 1% level. Consistent with the view of finance supporting innovative firms, financial markets provided financial support for 2IR firms. Additionally, we ran a regression excluding variables for which we have a limited number of observations (accounting variables) to provide a specification with more observations (column 2). The positive and significant effect was confirmed. However, this significance does not hold when looking at the impact of the 2IR dummy on the dividend yield. Furthermore, the R^2 is equal or close to 0.[23]

These observations are made using an exhaustive database but the lack of data leads to a lower number of observations; 258 and 206 observations for the Tobin's Q and dividend yield, respectively. We need both stock price and book value to be able to compute the Tobin's Q and both stock price and dividend to compute the dividend yield; we do not consider the lack of information on dividend as a null one because several firms explicitly display a dividend equal to 0. Additionally, accounting variables are even more infrequent leading to the exclusion of more firms, and thus to a number of observations even smaller in columns 1 and 3 when we need these variables.

These results are obtained using extensive controls for corporate governance rules. One could expect that 2IR firms used internal governance mechanisms aimed at reinforcing board monitoring and small shareholder voting power as a solution to reduce information asymmetries and thus to obtain better valuations. We first expect that *Board size* would be correlated with better valuation as the larger the board, the more able it is to monitor firm

Table 3. Did 2nd IR firms benefit from a premium?

	Dependent variable			
	Tobin's Q		Dividend yield	
	(1)	(2)	(3)	(4)
2IR	0.4279***	0.3941***	−0.0086	−0.0043
	(0.1603)	(0.1323)	(0.0589)	(0.0409)
Age	0.0029	0.0035	0.0008	0.0011
	(0.0036)	(0.0032)	(0.0014)	(0.0009)
Assets			0.0001	
			(0.0003)	
Beta	−0.0096	−0.0208	0.0002	−0.0009
	(0.0160)	(0.0135)	(0.0055)	(0.0042)
Change in profits	0.0015		−0.0007	
	(0.0051)		(0.0017)	
Coulisse	0.3222	0.2169	−0.0199	0.0059
	(0.2657)	(0.2436)	(0.1384)	(0.0337)
$Dist_{act}$	−0.0163	−0.0186	0.0239***	0.0189***
	(0.0241)	(0.0196)	(0.0089)	(0.0067)
$Dist_{HO}$	0.0338	0.0576**	−0.0219	−0.0269**
	(0.0333)	(0.0280)	(0.0158)	(0.0110)
Foreign	−0.0569	−0.1304	0.0321	0.0478
	(0.1361)	(0.1187)	(0.0549)	(0.0389)
Liquidity	−0.3003	−0.2496	−0.0516	−0.0666
	(0.1903)	(0.1589)	(0.0820)	(0.0558)
Nominal capital	−0.0010	−0.0007		
	(0.0015)	(0.0015)		
Profitability	0.2168***		0.0473	
	(0.0561)		(0.0457)	
Board size	0.0240	0.0033	−0.0079	−0.0055
	0.0162	(0.0150)	(0.0069)	(0.0045)
Board implication	13.570	9.7860	−0.9797	−0.7033
	(18.550)	(14.120)	(7.1630)	(5.5510)
Max votes	−0.0869	−0.0268	0.0715	0.0436
	0.1194	(0.1033)	(0.0499)	(0.0327)
Stocks for one vote	362.20	−357.90	−50.410	28.700
	(1634.0)	(338.70)	(571.50)	(179.40)
Stocks for GM	−383.00	330.30	48.900	−26.020
	(1634.0)	(339.20)	(571.40)	(179.10)
Industry FE	Yes	Yes	Yes	Yes
Observations	198	258	142	206
R^2	0.2984	0.2211	0.0000	0.0084

Note: Heteroscedasticity-robust standard errors are reported in parentheses. ***Significant at the 1 percent level, **Significant at the 5 percent level and *Significant at the 10 percent level.

insiders. Secondly, the more shares board members are required to hold (*Board implication*), the more aligned their interests will be with other shareholders, and the more protected these other shareholders will then be. Regarding voting rules, a low level of *Maximum votes* for one shareholder (ie lower cap of voting rights) may reassure minority shareholders that the largest shareholders will not gain control of the firm and impose their own views at their expense (Cheffins, 2008). These minority investors may be able to more efficiently exert their 'right to say' with a lower minimum ownership threshold (namely a lower number of *Stock for one vote*), while a lower minimum number of shares required to vote at general assemblies (*Stock for GM)* would enable them to be more part of the decision-making process (Enriques & Volpin, 2007). Despite descriptive statistics consistent with the usual financial hypotheses (see in Appendix 1), these governance characteristics do not seem to influence valuation premium. Indeed, none of them is significant in explaining the Tobin's Q and the dividend yield.[24]

Regarding other control variables, very few of them significantly impact the dependent variables. Profitability is positively associated with the Tobin's Q, suggesting that a higher current level of profits may also be related to future growth opportunities. Considering dividend yield, the distance between Paris and firm activities has the most prevalent effect on it, which is consistent with Bonhoure et al. (2017).

5. Robustness analyses

5.1. *An alternative measure of risk*

Risk is a crucial factor for innovative firms but the beta used in the previous tests may not be the appropriate measure of risk. To use beta as the correct risk measure implies accepting the idea that investors hold a market portfolio and look for any stock allowing them to diversify their main investment and to avoid too strong a correlation with the market risk. In a single asset world, risk is better captured by the standard deviation of firm stock returns.

To take this last point into account, we switch our risk measure from the beta to the standard deviation of returns. Again, the results are in line with what has already been provided through our main specifications (Table 4: we have only reproduced detailed results for our variable of interest): while being a 2IR firm did yield at the time a significantly higher Tobin's Q, this meant nothing in terms of dividend yield. A last point to note is that, similarly to the beta, the new risk measure is non-significant.

5.2. *A more restrictive definition of the 2IR firms*

We then tested the robustness of our results to an alternative sample built according to a more restrictive definition of what a 2IR firm is. Importantly, some firms combined businesses of both the 2nd IR and prior industries; typical examples include 'electrical' firms that also operated in the gas sector, or tramway companies involved in the railway business (which rather come from the 1st IR). We included them in the 2IR measure. However, for this reason, our classification of 2IR firms could be viewed as too broad. Another reason for this is that

Table 4. Did 2nd-IR firms benefit from a premium? (Alternative measure of risk).

	Dependent variable			
	Tobin's Q		Dividend yield	
	(1)	(2)	(5)	(6)
2IR	0.4265***	0.3910***	−0.0086	−0.0044
	(0.1601)	(0.1330)	(0.0589)	(0.0409)
Standard deviation of returns	−0.1879	−0.0418	0.0113	−0.0066
	(0.2017)	(0.1553)	(0.0700)	(0.0548)
Financial and other characteristics (excl. accounting)	Yes	Yes	Yes	Yes
Accounting characteristics	Yes	No	Yes	No
Governance characteristics	Yes	Yes	Yes	Yes
Industry FE	Yes	Yes	Yes	Yes
Observations	198	258	142	206
R^2	0.3004	0.2135	0.0000	0.0082

Note: Heteroscedasticity-robust standard errors are reported in parentheses. ***Significant at the 1 percent level, **Significant at the 5 percent level and *Significant at the 10 percent level.

tramway companies may also be regarded as too similar to the railway business (as the distinction between tramways and electrical trains was unclear at the time) to be accounted for as pure 2IR firms. Similarly, for firms distributing electricity (without producing it), their assimilation with other 2IR firms, while they are not involved in any manufacturing activity, might be considered spurious.

Consequently, we propose an alternative dummy variable, core-2IR, including a more restrictive set of firms involved in the 2nd IR: firms that 1) operate only in the 2nd IR sectors, and 2) are involved in a production process (thus excluding firms that only sell goods and services but do not produce them). One must note that the high precision of our sources (both yearbooks) allowed us to determine whether firms were involved in production and distribution or only in distribution (notably for the electricity and gas sectors). Appendix 2 shows the list of firms classified in our 2IR and core-2IR dummy variables. These core-2IR firms represented 3.60% of the total market capitalisation (versus 8.73% for the previous 2IR dummy).

Using this more restrictive dummy, we ran our main specifications. Results (Table 5) are again similar to what we provide in the main tests. The coefficients when explaining Tobin's Q decrease slightly, suggesting that this core-2IR sample does not allow us to capture firms enjoying higher Tobin's Q.

5.3. Domestic sample

As another robustness check, we ran the same tests as above but on the domestic sample only, namely on firms whose head office was located in France and its colonial empire. As a consequence, we rely on a reduced number of observations. National regulations (La Porta, Lopez-de-Silanes, Shleifer, & Vishny, 2000) or domestic bias (Coval & Moskowitz, 1999) could affect the valorisations we observe, and even the relationship with investors.

Results (Table 6) confirm our previous findings. The 2IR dummy still has a positive and significant impact on the Tobin's Q, while it does not on the dividend yield despite a rise of the R^2.

Table 5. Did 2nd-IR firms benefit from a premium? (more restrictive 2IR set).

	Dependent variable			
	Tobin's Q		Dividend yield	
	(1)	(2)	(3)	(4)
Core 2IR	0.4000**	0.3751***	0.0002	0.0075
	(0.1647)	(0.1399)	(0.0594)	(0.0427)
Financial and other characteristics (excl. accounting)	Yes	Yes	Yes	Yes
Accounting characteristics	Yes	No	Yes	No
Governance characteristics	Yes	Yes	Yes	Yes
Industry FE	Yes	Yes	Yes	Yes
Observations	198	258	142	206
R^2	0.2935	0.2157	0.0000	0.0085

Note: Heteroscedasticity-robust standard errors are reported in parentheses. ***Significant at the 1 percent level, **Significant at the 5 percent level and *Significant at the 10 percent level.

Table 6. Did 2nd-IR firms benefit from a premium? (domestic sample).

	Dependent variable			
	Tobin's Q		Dividend yield	
	(1)	(2)	(3)	(4)
2IR	0.4175**	0.3969***	−0.0093	−0.0117
	(0.1642)	(0.1371)	(0.0080)	(0.0071)
Financial and other characteristics (excl. accounting)	Yes	Yes	Yes	Yes
Accounting characteristics	Yes	No	Yes	No
Governance characteristics	Yes	Yes	Yes	Yes
Industry FE	Yes	Yes	Yes	Yes
Observations	129	171	94	142
R^2	0.3410	0.2702	0.3548	0.0732

Note: Heterosedasticity-robust standard errors are reported in parentheses. ***Significant at the 1 percent level, **Significant at the 5 percent level and *Significant at the 10 percent level.

6. Conclusion

Focusing on the 2nd IR in France and on the Paris stock exchanges in 1907, we add further insights to the long-standing debate over the relationship between finance and growth. We have provided mixed support for the view that finance (stock markets in our setting) did cause growth by providing 2IR firms with favourable financial conditions when they needed funds. More specifically, we show that firms that operated in the sectors of the 2nd IR did benefit from a valuation premium on the Paris markets, as modelled by the Tobin's Q. However, our results are not confirmed on the dividend yield.

These results are obtained on an exhaustive database of the firms listed on the Paris markets at the beginning of the 20th century and controlling for a large set of variables. In particular, we control for the specific governance rules these innovative companies could have adopted to reduce information asymmetries.

Notes

1. 'Tous ces jeux qui entraînent beaucoup de malheurs et dont l'industrie et la production ne profitent jamais [...]' (Say, 1837).
2. Investors do not value (and thus do not incorporate into stock prices) information that is difficult for them to know about and understand. Information about innovation expenses, new technologies, etc. are typical examples of what investors may have difficulty processing.
3. Innovative enterprises are indeed shown to have, on average, higher future profits (Toms, 2013), that do turn into actual higher earnings and cash flows in the future (Brown et al., 2012; Gu, 2005; Hirshleifer, Hsu, & Li, 2013, 2018; Lian & Wang, 2019; Matolcsy & Wyatt, 2008).
4. We use the term 'valuation premium' to refer to the additional amount that a buyer was willing to pay for a given company's stock (in our case, 2IR firms), compared with its peers, broadly said to be a lower cost of capital for the firm. This concept should not be confused with the 'value premium' (the difference in returns between 'value' and 'growth' stocks) or with the 'equity premium' (the difference in returns between stocks and risk-free rates).
5. There is no exhaustive homogeneous source for private funding. Only few cases could be observed through surviving private corporate archives when they have recorded details about their shareholders.

6. The Tobin's Q is often used as a measure of the investment opportunities of a firm. In that sense, younger firms and those with more investment opportunities are shown to have a higher Tobin's Q (eg Braggion & Moore, 2011; Fama & French, 2001; Rauh, 2006).
7. Consistently, younger companies and those with more investment opportunities are shown to pay out a lower dividend yield (eg Fama & French, 2001; Toms, 2013).
8. One could consider that the control firms (ie non-2IR firms) may have enjoyed high profits at the time thanks to monopoly rents. However, such a rent is not accompanied by a potential growth in future profits that is captured by a high Tobin's Q and a low dividend yield. Controlling for benefits, industries and nominal capital, we are confident that we capture more the potential growth in profits than the current level of profits.
9. In terms of requirements, the promotion of a new equity issue was regulated by a 1907 law making mandatory the publication of an informative notice in the *Bulletin des annonces légales et obligatoires* (Ducros, 2018). However, the firms we studied were listed before the implementation of this law.
10. Foreign companies nonetheless remained subject to the national regulations of their head office country. However 1) cross listings were frequent for such firms as the listing on the French capital market was mostly to target local (French) investors, and 2) most of the non-French firms in our sample were listed on the *Coulisse* thus without any pre-listing requirements.
11. Firms may bear the burden of indirect costs linked to the publication of notices and information before an equity issue. However, there was no such legal obligation at the time except for the mandatory notice publication from 1907 (see footnote 9).
12. This macroeconomic situation is reflected in the interest rates. From a maximum of about 4%, the rate on the main French state bond, the *Rente 3%*, declined gradually to 2.90%, reached at the end of the stagnation period in 1897. An upward trend started with the growth period, with this trend accelerating after 1910.
13. As a matter comparison, Burhop, Chambers, and Cheffins (2014) found about the same 5% for the 728 IPOs made in London between 1900 and 1911 but more recently, as reported by Ducros (2018), the firms introduced on all the US markets between 2005 and 2016 represented only 1.8% of US GDP.
14. For instance, in the UK (Braggion & Moore, 2011; Campbell & Turner, 2011; Cheffins, 2008) or in Belgium (Moortgat, Annaert, & Deloof, 2017).
15 We here consider the agency relationship between controlling and minority shareholders. In such a relationship, controlling shareholders (the agent) can take advantage of their position to extract some private benefits at the expense of minority investors (the principal).
16. Profits amounts have been collected in later yearbooks that provided historical accounts.
17. The *Parquet* yearbook gathers firms according to 15 different industries: insurance, banks, canals, railways and tramways, docks and water, electricity, spinning, gas, forges and foundries, collieries, metal mines, chemical products (phosphate, fertilisers, and others), ports, carriages, and other firms. The *Coulisse* yearbook distinguishes 11 industries, namely insurance, banks and credit institutions, railways, tramways and carriages, car and related industries, utilities (gas, electricity, and water), collieries, the metal industry, gold mines, other mines, and other firms. For greater convenience and higher visibility (15 industries is too large a number especially when some of them include only a few companies), we aggregated them into the nine different sectors.
18. The 'Other industries' group gathers many different types of firms, which are too few to constitute a single industry on their own: newspapers, restaurants, cinema, rubber plantations, stores, museums, cement, spinning, etc.
19. Robert Gordon (2000) broadly distinguishes the 'group of four' major innovations in the pre-WWI period: 1) electricity, 2) internal combustion engine, 3) petroleum and all chemical processes (plastics, pharmaceuticals and other chemical products), and 4) entertainment and communication innovations (telephone and telegraph, cinema, etc.).
20. This fall in the number of listed firms over the 20th century has already been observed on other markets (Annaert et al., 2011).

21. Specifically, 489 are present on the CAC All Shares index displayed by Euronext (see https://www.euronext.com/products/indices/QS0010989141-XPAR/market-information). Among these 489 companies, we considered those included in the 'Technology' and 'Telecom' sectors as innovative.
22. Formally, Tobin's Q (which is the ratio of firm market value to its asset value) stands for corporate investment or growth opportunities: firms with Tobin's Q lower than 1 usually have fewer investment opportunities, while those whose Tobin's Q is higher than 1 have more growth opportunities.
23. This very low R^2, not rare in financial studies, may be due to the fact that the dividend yield captures other issues in addition to investment aspects (see the literature that studies possible explanations of why firms pay dividends). Moreover, it appears that foreign firms were sensitive to different factors because the R^2 strongly rises when focusing on domestic sample (see Table 6).
24. In a non-reported investigation, we actually did not observe that 2IR firms exhibited statistically different governance from other firms.
25. Another mechanism consisted of granting a number of votes to shareholders depending on their stake (graduated voting rights).

Disclosure statement

No potential conflict of interest was reported by the authors.

References

Annaert, J., Buelens, L., Cuyvers, F., de Ceuster, M., Deloof, M., & de Schepper, A. (2011). Are blue chip stock market indices good proxies for all-shares market indices? The case of the Brussels Stock Exchange 1833–2005. *Financial History Review, 18*(3), 277–308. doi:10.1017/S0968565011000187

(1909). *Annuaire Desfossés – Valeurs Cotées en Banque à la Bourse de Paris*. Paris: E. Desfossés and Fabre Frères.

Arbulu, P. (2007). Le Marché Parisien des Actions au XIXème Siècle. In G. Gallais-Hamonno (Ed.) *Le marché financier français au XIXème siècle* (vol. 2). Paris: Publications de la Sorbonne.

Atje, R., & Jovanovic, B. (1993). Stock markets and development. *European Economic Review, 37*(2–3), 632–640. doi:10.1016/0014-2921(93)90053-D

Beck, T., & Levine, R. (2004). Stock markets, banks, and growth: Panel evidence. *Journal of Banking & Finance, 28*(3), 423–442. doi:10.1016/S0378-4266(02)00408-9

Bonhoure, E., Germain, L., & Le Bris, D. (2017). Active versus speculative monitoring: Evidence from pre-WWI Paris-Listed firms. Working paper.

Braggion, F., & Moore, L. (2011). Dividend policies in an unregulated market: The London Stock Exchange, 1895-1905. *Review of Financial Studies, 24*(9), 2935–2973. doi:10.1093/rfs/hhr026

Brown, J., Fazzari, S., & Petersen, B. (2009). Financing innovation and growth: Cash flow, external equity, and the 1990s R&D boom. *The Journal of Finance, 64*(1), 151–185. doi:10.1111/j.1540-6261.2008.01431.x

Brown, J., Martinsson, G., & Petersen, B. (2012). Do financing constraints matter for R&D? *European Economic Review, 56*(8), 1512–1529. doi:10.1016/j.euroecorev.2012.07.007

Burhop, C., Chambers, D., & Cheffins, B. (2014). Regulating IPOs: Evidence from going public in London, 1900–1913. *Explorations in Economic History, 51*, 60–76. doi:10.1016/j.eeh.2013.07.003

Campbell, G., & Turner, J. (2011). Substitutes for legal protection: Corporate governance and dividends in Victorian Britain. *The Economic History Review, 64*(2), 571–597. doi:10.1111/j.1468-0289.2010.00545.x

Chandler, A. D. Jr. (1977). *The visible hand: The managerial revolution in American business*. Cambridge, Mass: Harvard University Press.

Cheffins, B. (2008). *Corporate ownership and control: British business transformed*. Oxford: Oxford University Press.
Compagnie des Agents de Change près la Bourse de Paris. (1908). *Annuaire des Valeurs Admises à la Cote Officielle*. Paris: Chambre Syndicale. Kept at the CAEF (Centre Des Archives Economiques et Financières [Centre for Economic and Financial Archives]) and Scanned by the DFIH (Data for Financial History) Equipex (Equipment of Excellence).
Compagnie des Agents de Change près la Bourse de Paris. (1908). *Bulletin de la Cote, de la Compagnie des Agents de Change de Paris*. Paris: Chambre Syndicale.
Coval, J., & Moskowitz, T. (1999). Home bias at home: Local equity preference in domestic portfolios. *The Journal of Finance, 54*(6), 2045–2073. doi:10.1111/0022-1082.00181
Desfossés, (1907). Cours de la Banque et de la Bourse. *Journal Quotidien de la Bourse*. Paris: Cote Desfossés.
Ducros, J. (2018). *Role of regional financial markets and competition among exchanges: The rise and fall of the Lyon Stock Exchange, 1800-1945*. (Unpublished doctoral dissertation). EHESS, Paris.
Enriques, L., & Volpin, P. (2007). Corporate governance reforms in continental Europe. *Journal of Economic Perspectives, 21*(1), 117–140. doi:10.1257/jep.21.1.117
Fama, E., & French, K. (2001). Disappearing dividends: Changing firm characteristics or lower propensity to pay? *Journal of Financial Economics, 60*(1), 3–43. doi:10.1016/S0304-405X(01)00038-1
Gallais-Hamonno, G. (2007). *Le Marché Financier Français au XIXème Siècle, Volume 2. Aspects Quantitatifs des Acteurs et des Instruments à la Bourse de Paris*. Paris: Editions de la Sorbonne.
Gordon, R. (2000). Interpreting the 'One Big Wave' in U.S. long-term productivity growth. In B. van Ark, S. Kuipers, & G. Kuper (Ed.), *Productivity, technology, and economic growth*. Boston: Kluwer.
Goyer, M. (2008). The transformation of corporate governance in France. In Culpepper, P., Hall, P., & Palier, B. (Ed.), *Changing France: The politics that markets make*. London: Palgrave Macmillan.
Gu, F. (2005). Innovation, future earnings, and market efficiency. *Journal of Accounting, Auditing and Finance, 20*(4), 385–418. doi:10.1177/0148558X0502000405
Hautcoeur, P.-C. (1999). Asymétries d'Information, Coûts de Mandat et Financement des Entreprises Françaises (1890-1936). *Revue Économique, 50*(5), 1053–1087. doi:10.3406/reco.1999.410131
Hautcoeur, P.-C. (2007). *Le Marché Financier Français au XIXème Siècle, Volume 1. Récit*. Paris: Editions de la Sorbonne.
Hautcoeur, P.-C., & Riva, A. (2012). The Paris financial market in the 19th Century: Complementarities and competition in microstructures. *The Economic History Review, 65*(4), 1326–1353. doi:10.1111/j.1468-0289.2011.00632.x
Herrigel, G. (2008). Corporate governance. In G. Jones, & J. Zeitlin (Ed.), *The Oxford Handbook of business history*. Oxford: Oxford University Press.
Hirshleifer, D., Hsu, P.-H., & Li, D. (2013). Innovative efficiency and stock returns. *Journal of Financial Economics, 107*(3), 632–654. doi:10.1016/j.jfineco.2012.09.011
Hirshleifer, D., Hsu, P.-H., & Li, D. (2018). Innovative originality, profitability, and stock returns. *Review of Financial Studies, 31*(7), 2553–2605. doi:10.1093/rfs/hhx101
John, K., Knyazeva, A., & Knyazeva, D. (2011). Does geography matter? Firm location and corporate payout policy. *Journal of Financial Economics, 101*(3), 533–555. doi:10.1016/j.jfineco.2011.03.014
King, R., & Levine, R. (1993). Finance, entrepreneurship, and growth: Theory and evidence. *Journal of Monetary Economics, 32*(3), 513–542. doi:10.1016/0304-3932(93)90028-E
Klepper, S. (2007). Disagreements, spinoffs, and the evolution of Detroit as the capital of the U.S. automobile industry. *Management Science, 53*(4), 616–631. doi:10.1287/mnsc.1060.0683
Labardin, P. (2008). *L'Emergence de la Fonction Comptable en France* (Doctoral dissertation). Université d'Orléans, Orléans.
Lamoreaux, N., Levenstein, M., & Sokoloff, K. (2007). Financing Invention during the second industrial revolution: Cleveland, Ohio, 1870-1920. In Lamoreaux, N., & Sokoloff, K. (Ed.) *Financing innovation in the United States, 1871 to the Present*. Cambridge, Mass.: MIT Press.
La Porta, R., Lopez-de-Silanes, F., Shleifer, A., & Vishny, R. (2000). Investor protection and corporate governance. *Journal of Financial Economics, 58*(1-2), 3–27. doi:10.1016/S0304-405X(00)00065-9

Law, S. H., & Singh, N. (2014). Does too much finance harm economic growth? *Journal of Banking & Finance, 41*, 36–44. doi:10.1016/j.jbankfin.2013.12.020

Lazonick, W., & O'Sullivan, M. (1997). Finance and industrial development: The United States and the United Kingdom. *Financial History Review, 4*(1), 7–29. doi:10.1017/S0968565000000810

Le Bris, D., & Hautcoeur, P.-C. (2010). A challenge to triumphant optimists? A blue chips index for the Paris Stock-Exchange (1854-2007). *Financial History Review, 17*(2), 141–183. doi:10.1017/S096856501000003X

Lemarchand, Y., & Praquin, N. (2005). Falsifications et Manipulations Comptables. La Mesure du Profit comme Enjeu Social, 1856-1918. *Comptabilité-Contrôle-Audit, 11*(3), 15–33. doi:10.3917/cca.113.0015

Levine, R. (1997). Financial development and economic growth: Views and agenda. *Journal of Economic Literature, 35*(2), 688–726.

Levine, R. (2003). More on finance and growth: More finance, more growth? *Review, 85*(4), 31–46. doi:10.20955/r.85.31-46

Levy-Leboyer, M., & Bourguignon, F. (1985). *L'Economie Française au XIXème Siècle*. Paris: Economica.

Lian, Q., & Wang, Q. (2019). How does the primary market value innovations of newly public firms? *Journal of Accounting, Auditing and Finance, 34*(1), 3–29.

Lucas, R. (1988). On the mechanics of economic development. *Journal of Monetary Economics, 22*(1), 3–42. doi:10.1016/0304-3932(88)90168-7

Manning, M. J. (2003). Finance causes growth: Can we be so sure? *The B.E. Journal of Macroeconomics, 3*(1), 1–24.

Matolcsy, Z., & Wyatt, A. (2008). The association between technological conditions and the market value of equity. *The Accounting Review, 83*(2), 479–518. doi:10.2308/accr.2008.83.2.479

Moortgat, L., Annaert, J., & Deloof, M. (2017). Investor protection, taxation and dividend policy: Long-run evidence, 1838–2012. *Journal of Banking & Finance, 85*, 113–131. doi:10.1016/j.jbankfin.2017.08.013

Morck, R., Shleifer, A., & Vishny, R. (1990). The stock market and investment: Is the market a sideshow? *Brookings Papers on Economic Activity, 2*, 157–215. doi:10.2307/2534506

Nikitin, M. (1992). *La Naissance de la Comptabilité Industrielle en France* (Doctoral dissertation). Université Paris Dauphine – Paris IX, Paris.

O'Sullivan, M. (2000). The innovative enterprise and corporate governance. *Cambridge Journal of Economics, 24*(4), 393–416. doi:10.1093/cje/24.4.393

Pasali, S. S. (2013). Where is the cheese? Synthesizing a giant literature on causes and consequences of financial sector development. *Policy Research Working Paper Series* n°6655. Washington DC: World Bank.

Petit-Konczyk, M. (2003). Le Financement d'une Start-Up: L'Air Liquide, 1898 - 1913. *Revue Finance Contrôle Stratégie, 6*(4), 25–58.

Rajan, R., & Zingales, L. (1998). Financial dependence and growth. *American Economic Review, 88*(3), 559–586.

Rauh, J. (2006). Investment and financing constraints: Evidence from the funding of corporate pension plans. *The Journal of Finance, 61*(1), 33–71. doi:10.1111/j.1540-6261.2006.00829.x

Robinson, J. (1952). The generalisation of the general theory. In J. Robinson (Ed.), *The rate of interest and other essays*. London: MacMillan.

Rousseau, P., & Wachtel, P. (2011). What is happening to the impact of financial deepening? *Economic Inquiry, 49*(1), 276–288. doi:10.1111/j.1465-7295.2009.00197.x

Say, J.-B. (1837). *Cours Complet d'Economie Politique Pratique* (3rd ed.). Brussels: H. Dumont.

Schumpeter, J. (1912). *Theorie der Wirt-schaftlichen Entwicklung [The Theory of Economic Development]*. Leipzig: Dunker & Humblot.

Syndicat des Banquiers en Valeurs au Comptant près la Bourse de Paris. (1907). *Cote du Marché des Banquiers en Valeurs au Comptant près la Bourse de Paris*. Paris: Imprimerie Bienvenu, Dubois et Bauer. Scanned by the DFIH (Data for Financial History) Equipex (Equipment of Excellence).

Toms, S. (2013). The life cycle of corporate governance. In Wright, D., Siegel, D., Keasey, K., & Filatotchev, I. (Ed.), *The oxford handbook of corporate governance*. Oxford: Oxford University Press.

Appendix 1

Variables considered in this article – list, specifications, descriptive statistics

List of the variables:

Tobin's Q_i	Tobin's Q	Calculated as the ratio of the market capitalisation of the firm *i* over the book value of the assets of firm *i*
Div yield$_i$	Dividend yield	Calculated as the ratio of the dividends paid by firm *i* in 1907 over the last available price of 1906
$2IR_i$	Dummy for firms operating in sectors of the 2nd IR	Dummy variable which is equal to 1 if the firm main activities are in sectors of the 2nd IR, and 0 otherwise
core-$2IR_i$	Dummy for firms operating (only) in the 2nd IR, excluding distribution	Dummy variable which is equal to 1 if the firm activities are only in sectors of the 2nd IR and if the firm not only distributes but also produces what it sells, and 0 otherwise
Age_i	Age	Calculated as the year 1907 minus the date of creation of the firm *i*
$Assets_i$	Firm assets	Value of assets of firm *i* as given by its balance sheet. Expressed in million francs
$Beta_i$	Beta	Calculated as the ratio of the covariance of 12 monthly returns of the stock *i* with 12 market returns over the variance of market returns
Change in profits$_i$	Change in profits from 1906 to 1907	Calculated as the percentage of change in profits of firm *i* in 1907 compared with the profits of firm *i* in 1906
$Coulisse_i$	Dummy for firms listed on the *Coulisse*	Dummy variable which is equal to 1 if the firm is listed on the *Coulisse*, 0 otherwise (i.e. if it is listed on the *Parquet*)
$Dist_{i,act}$	Distance between Paris and activities location	Distance in km between Paris and the place where most activities of the firm *i* take place
$Dist_{i,HO}$	Distance between Paris and the head office	Distance in km between Paris and the city of firm *i*'s head office
$Foreign_i$	Dummy for foreign firms	Dummy variable which is equal to 1 if the firm head office is not in France (and broadly not in the French colonial empire), and 0 otherwise
$Liquidity_i$	Proportion of zero returns	Calculated as the ratio of the number of monthly stock returns equal to 0 over the number of available monthly returns, for firm *i*
Nominal capital$_i$	Nominal capital	Calculated as the total number of shares of firm *i* time the nominal value of each share. Expressed in million francs
$Profitability_i$	Ratio of profits over nominal capital	Calculated as the ratio of profits of firm *i* over the nominal capital of firm *i*
SD of returns$_i$	Standard deviation of stock returns	Calculated as the standard deviation of the 12 monthly returns of stock *i*
Board size$_i$	Number of board members	Number of board members of firm *i* in 1907
Board implication$_i$	Board involvement into the firm capital	Calculated as the ratio of the minimum number of shares of firm *i* that board members have to hold over the total number of shares of firm *i*
Max votes$_i$	Maximum votes a shareholder can have	Calculated as the ratio of the maximum votes (expressed as the corresponding number of shares) a shareholder of firm *i* can have over the total number of shares of firm *i*
Stocks for one vote$_i$	Number of stocks necessary to get one vote	Calculated as the ratio of the number of shares of firm *i* necessary for one vote over the total number of shares of firm *i*
Stocks for GM$_i$	Number of stocks to participate in the firm GMs	Calculated as the ratio of the minimum number of shares necessary to participate in firm *i*'s General Assemblies (GMs) over the total number of shares of firm *i*
$Industry_i$	Industry fixed-effects	Dummy variables for nine industries: bank and insurance, railways (and tramways), other carriages, coal, gold mines, other mines, metal industry, utilities (water gas and electricity), other industries

Financial characteristics

We provide here the descriptive statistics for some important control variables we use (namely firm risk, measured by its beta, and liquidity) as well as for alternative measures we implement in the robustness section (Table 7). These statistics are also provided for 2IR and non-2IR firms separately (Table 8).

Table 7. Beta, standard deviation of returns, and liquidity.

	Mean	Median	Maximum	Minimum	Standard Deviation	Number of observations
Beta	0.83	0.49	44.18	−23.69	2.24	671
SD of returns	7.53%	4.62%	356.63%	0.00%	18.44%	662
Liquidity	25.69%	16.67%	100.00%	0.00%	29.25%	662

Table 8. Beta, standard deviation of returns, and liquidity across 2IR/non-2IR firms.

	Mean	Median	Maximum	Minimum	Standard Deviation	Number of observations
Beta						
2IR	0.89	0.42	6.70	−2.88	1.50	154
Other firms	0.82	0.52	44.18	−23.69	2.42	517
SD of returns						
2IR	6.59%	4.17%	40.80%	0.00%	6.48%	153
Other firms	7.81%	4.71%	356.63%	0.00%	20.72%	509
Liquidity						
2IR	24.34%	10.00%	100.00%	0.00%	28.85%	153
Other firms	26.10%	16.67%	100.00%	0.00%	29.39%	509

Among these financial characteristics, liquidity was more difficult to measure. The traditional way (using traded volumes) was not suitable because data have never been reported for the French markets; neither was the bid-ask spread, sometimes used as a proxy for volumes. As a rough proxy for liquidity, we used the 'zero-return' observation which is the proportion of the monthly returns equal to 0, meaning no change in the stock price compared with the last month, and thus, most of the time, the absence of transactions.

Distance variables

We control for agency costs, proxied by the distance between investors and companies (in particular their managers). It has been suggested in the literature that asymmetry of information, and thus agency issues, increase with the distance between the principal and the agent of a firm (Bonhoure et al., 2017; John, Knyazeva, & Knyazeva, 2011); the point is that a similar firm far from its shareholders would be costlier to monitor. Since this increase in agency issues is detrimental to shareholders, it should negatively affect stock prices (and Tobin's Q and dividend yield, accordingly).

Specifically, we control for the impact of two types of distances as defined in Bonhoure et al. (2017). First, $dist_{act}$ measures the distance between Paris (where most shareholders are considered to be) and the firm's main activities, and thus how severe asymmetry of information between shareholders and (operational) managers is. Secondly, $dist_{HO}$ measures the distance between Paris and the firm's head office, in other words asymmetry of information between shareholders and (decisional) managers.

Governance characteristics

The governance variables we use are specific to the context and thus require further explanation:

- *Board implication:* computes the fact that most statutes in our dataset require board members to hold a minimum number of firm's shares to be part of the board. We measure their implication (assuming that financial incentive matters) by the ratio of this minimum number of required stocks over the total number of firm shares.
- *Stocks for one vote:* deviations from the current one-share-one-vote rule were very common through several mechanisms, in particular granting one vote for a given number of shares (captured by our *Stocks for one vote* variable)[25].
- *Max votes:* it was also common practice to cap the number of votes a single shareholder may have. For instance, the total number of votes for one single investor might be limited to a fifth of the capital (in other words to one fifth of total firm votes). The *Max votes* variable is a measure of this maximum number of votes granted to a single shareholder.
- *Stocks for GM:* shareholders were required to hold a minimum number of stocks to be able to participate in general assemblies, measured by the *Stocks for GM* variable.

To help the understanding of these controls we detail here some descriptive statistics. We first distinguish firms according to their industry (Table 9). One striking observation is that banks and insurance companies have, by far, the largest *Board size* consistent with the view that these activities are difficult to monitor.

We can distinguish three groups in terms of board implication. First, sectors with low dispersion (in other words, all firms across these sectors require a more or less similar minimum number of shares to be held), and with a relatively low median number, include mature ones with potential entry barriers (bank and insurance, coal). Gold mines exhibit remarkably low board implication. Secondly, a more diverse group (other mines, railways, utilities, and other industries) is characterised by medium to high dispersion, which is difficult to explain given the diversity of sectors (both mature and young ones, with both high and low entry barriers, etc.). Thirdly, metal and other carriage industries are characterised by an even higher variation of required board implications, without necessarily presenting a higher median.

Most industries impose relatively low levels of *Maximum votes*, which may deter the formation of large and controlling block holders. There is one exception to this: gold mines, which, despite the fewer observations display the highest mean and a 100%-median of levels of maximum votes, meaning that at least 50% of gold mines allowed their shareholders to have complete control over them. Here again, the governance of gold mines appears very specific. The *Stocks for one vote* and *Stocks for GM* variables, on their hand, display rather similar characteristics.

Now, we turn to the distribution of our corporate governance features according to age quintiles (Table 10). The size of the board increases with the age of the firm, which is not surprising because size and complexity should also increase along with corporate lifetime. The other governance features seem, broadly, not to be impacted by the age of the firm, providing two insights: the type of governance rules did not evolve over time (one could have suspected different practices in governance rules according to the date of firm creation) and firms did not change their governance rules when becoming older. The only remarkable rule is that the oldest firms seem to favour small investors through a low maximum vote and low numbers of stocks required to be part of the general meeting and to have one vote at the meeting.

Finally, we provide the same distribution but following size quintiles (Table 11). Specifically, we measured size by the nominal capital to take into account the 'regular' size of each firm. It is consistently observed that the size of the board increases with the size of the firm. It also clearly appears that the involvement of board members strongly decreases with the size of the firm. Less in favour of

Table 9. Governance characteristics per sector.

	Mean	Median	Maximum	Minimum	Standard Deviation	Number of observations
Board size						
Bank and insurance	10.13	9.00	30	3	4.00	135
Railways	8.98	7.00	26	3	5.64	101
Other carriages	7.98	7.00	32	1	5.24	47
Coal	7.56	7.00	18	3	2.95	55
Gold mines	6.36	6.00	12	3	1.97	67
Other mines	6.66	6.00	16	3	2.47	118
Metal industry	7.67	7.00	20	2	3.29	96
Utilities	7.65	7.00	16	3	2.89	94
Other industries	6.57	6.00	20	3	3.01	227
Board implication (in %)						
Bank and insurance	0.24	0.23	1.25	0.003	0.23	132
Railways	0.30	0.17	2.50	0.01	0.41	97
Other carriages	0.44	0.25	3.13	0.004	0.58	45
Coal	0.25	0.17	0.78	0.002	0.19	47
Gold mines	0.11	0.05	0.63	0.001	0.14	53
Other mines	0.31	0.23	2.00	0.0001	0.29	103
Metal industry	0.45	0.27	7.50	0.01	0.86	87
Utilities	0.39	0.21	2.17	0.01	0.42	85
Other industries	0.50	0.35	2.50	0.004	0.47	209
Max votes (in %)						
Bank and insurance	35.86	2.50	100.00	0.05	46.33	118
Railways	44.24	20.00	100.00	0.05	46.09	91
Other carriages	25.00	10.00	100.00	0.06	35.26	42
Coal	34.52	7.50	100.00	0.31	44.02	50
Gold mines	74.68	100.00	100.00	0.33	43.57	19
Other mines	41.86	16.67	100.00	0.02	44.70	88
Metal industry	36.71	10.00	100.00	0.45	43.48	86
Utilities	39.81	11.24	100.00	0.13	44.90	86
Other industries	35.86	10.00	100.00	0.06	43.07	210
Stocks for one vote (in %)						
Bank and insurance	0.07	0.04	0.83	0.0003	0.10	115
Railways	0.09	0.05	0.56	0.0004	0.11	90
Other carriages	0.09	0.05	0.63	0.0001	0.14	42
Coal	0.07	0.05	0.25	0.0002	0.06	49
Gold mines	0.03	0.02	0.13	0.0002	0.04	19
Other mines	0.07	0.05	0.40	0.0001	0.08	87
Metal industry	0.10	0.07	0.67	0.0003	0.11	86
Utilities	0.13	0.06	1.00	0.001	0.19	86
Other industries	0.15	0.10	1.43	0.0002	0.19	208
Stocks for GM (in %)						
Bank and insurance	0.07	0.04	0.83	0.0003	0.10	132
Railways	0.08	0.05	0.56	0.0002	0.10	95
Other carriages	0.09	0.05	0.63	0.0001	0.14	42
Coal	0.07	0.04	0.25	0.0002	0.07	49
Gold mines	0.03	0.02	0.13	0.0002	0.04	19
Other mines	0.07	0.04	0.40	0.0001	0.08	88
Metal industry	0.09	0.06	0.67	0.0003	0.11	89
Utilities	0.12	0.06	1.00	0.001	0.18	89
Other industries	0.15	0.10	1.43	0.0002	0.19	210

Table 10. Governance characteristics per age quintile.

	Mean	Median	Maximum	Minimum	Standard Deviation	Number of observations
Board size						
0 to 2 years	6.17	6.00	26.00	2.00	2.80	191
2 to 9 years	7.39	7.00	17.00	3.00	2.99	189
9 to 18 years	7.43	7.00	30.00	3.00	3.44	192
18 to 30 years	7.70	7.00	20.00	1.00	3.41	184
30 to 107 years	9.80	9.00	32.00	3.00	4.97	184
Board implication (in %)						
0 to 2 years	0.48	0.32	7.50	0.0001	0.71	174
2 to 9 years	0.38	0.25	2.17	0.001	0.39	171
9 to 18 years	0.34	0.17	2.22	0.002	0.42	176
18 to 30 years	0.31	0.21	3.13	0.01	0.38	168
30 to 107 years	0.27	0.20	1.25	0.003	0.24	169
Max votes (in %)						
0 to 2 years	54.06	40.00	100.00	0.40	45.70	149
2 to 9 years	38.48	16.00	100.00	0.20	41.80	159
9 to 18 years	44.21	20.00	100.00	0.33	44.29	156
18 to 30 years	37.31	6.25	100.00	0.06	45.71	163
30 to 107 years	18.98	1.04	100.00	0.02	37.25	163
Stocks for one vote (in %)						
0 to 2 years	0.11	0.07	0.83	0.0001	0.13	147
2 to 9 years	0.11	0.07	1.00	0.0002	0.15	158
9 to 18 years	0.12	0.05	1.43	0.0002	0.18	153
18 to 30 years	0.09	0.05	1.00	0.0002	0.13	163
30 to 107 years	0.08	0.05	0.83	0.0003	0.10	161
Stocks for GM (in %)						
0 to 2 years	0.11	0.07	0.83	0.0001	0.13	152
2 to 9 years	0.11	0.07	1.00	0.0002	0.15	161
9 to 18 years	0.13	0.05	1.43	0.0002	0.20	155
18 to 30 years	0.09	0.05	1.00	0.0001	0.13	170
30 to 107 years	0.08	0.05	0.83	0.0002	0.10	175

small investors, the number of shares to vote and to be part of the general assemblies clearly decreases with size, meaning that small firms offer lower powers to small investors. This is more consistent with the view of founders or existing shareholders being reluctant to give too much power to external ones.

Table 11. Governance characteristics per size quintile.

	Mean	Median	Maximum	Minimum	Standard Deviation	Number of observations
Board size						
0 to 2	5.42	5.00	13.00	1.00	1.99	213
2 to 4	6.46	6.00	14.00	3.00	2.13	168
4 to 8	7.36	7.00	18.00	3.00	2.79	190
8 to 18.85	8.29	8.00	21.00	3.00	2.88	184
18.85 to 69,444.44	11.26	10.00	32.00	3.00	5.30	180
Board implication (in %)						
0 to 2	0.71	0.50	7.50	0.01	0.74	190
2 to 4	0.46	0.34	2.17	0.004	0.40	162
4 to 8	0.28	0.21	2.00	0.0001	0.23	176
8 to 18.85	0.19	0.17	0.63	0.001	0.13	166
18.85 to 69,444.44	0.08	0.07	0.50	0.001	0.07	160
Max votes (in %)						
0 to 2	39.96	13.89	100.00	0.36	43.78	185
2 to 4	31.79	10.00	100.00	0.31	40.19	145
4 to 8	34.98	8.33	100.00	0.10	43.33	157
8 to 18.85	39.65	10.00	100.00	0.02	45.71	153
18.85 to 69,444.44	45.11	10.00	100.00	0.05	48.18	146
Stocks for one vote (in %)						
0 to 2	0.20	0.13	1.43	0.0003	0.23	185
2 to 4	0.13	0.13	0.45	0.001	0.10	145
4 to 8	0.08	0.05	0.40	0.0001	0.07	154
8 to 18.85	0.05	0.05	0.25	0.0002	0.05	152
18.85 to 69,444.44	0.02	0.01	0.20	0.0001	0.03	142
Stocks for GM (in %)						
0 to 2	0.20	0.13	1.43	0.0003	0.23	190
2 to 4	0.14	0.13	0.93	0.001	0.12	147
4 to 8	0.08	0.05	0.40	0.0001	0.07	163
8 to 18.85	0.05	0.04	0.25	0.0002	0.05	158
18.85 to 69,444.44	0.02	0.01	0.15	0.0001	0.02	151

Note: The size quintiles are expressed in million francs. Specifically, the first quintile is at 2,000,000 francs, the second one at 4,000,000 francs, the third at 8,000,000, the fourth at 18,848,580, and the fifth at 69,444,444,444 francs.

Appendix 2

List of the firms classified as 2nd-IR

All the firms classified as 2IR are reported in the table below, which contains their name, their industry, the stock exchange they are listed on, and whether they are part of the core-2IR subsample.

Firms	Ind.*	SE**	Core 2IR
Chemins de Fer sur Routes d'Algérie	R	P	No
Paris à Arpajon (Compagnie du chemin de fer sur route de)	R	P	No
Chemin de Fer Métropolitain de Paris	R	P	No
Nord-Sud de Paris (Chemin de fer électrique souterrain)	R	P	No
Tramways Algériens	R	P	No
Tramways d'Amiens	R	P	No
Tramways Electriques d'Angers	R	P	No
Tramways Electriques et Omnibus de Bordeaux (Compagnie française de)	R	P	No
Compagnie Générale Française de Tramways	R	P	No
Compagnie Française de Tramways (Indo-Chine)	R	P	No
Tramways de Nice et du Littoral	R	P	No
Tramways Electriques d'Oran	R	P	No
Compagnie Générale Parisienne de Tramways	R	P	No
Tramways de l'Est Parisien	R	P	No
Tramways Electriques Nord Parisiens	R	P	No
Tramways de l'Ouest Parisien	R	P	No
Tramways de la Rive Gauche de Paris	R	P	No
Tramways de Roubaix et de Tourcoing	R	P	No
Tramways de Rouen	R	P	No
Tramway de Paris à Saint-Germain	R	P	No
Tramways de Paris et du Département de la Seine (Compagnie des)	R	P	No
Tramways des Deux-Sèvres	R	P	No
Tramways du Var et du Gard	R	P	No
Société Versaillaise de Tramways Electriques et de Distribution d'Energie	R	P	No
Compagnie Générale des Eaux	WGE	P	No
Eaux de la Banlieue de Paris	WGE	P	No
Eaux Minérales de la Bourboule	WGE	P	No

Firms	Ind.*	SE**	Core 2IR
Société Générale des Compteurs de Voitures (Taxamètres)	OI	P	No
Naphte de Bakou	OI	P	Yes
Sucreries et Raffinerie d'Egypte	OI	P	No
Compagnie des Automobiles "l'Auto-Parisienne"	OC	C	No
Compagnie Française des Automobiles de Place	OC	C	No
Compagnie Générale des Automobiles-Taximètres	OC	C	No
L'Electrique Lille-Roubaix-Tourcoing	OC	C	No
The F.I.A.T. Motor Cab Company Limited	OC	C	No
The General Motor Cab Company Limited	OC	C	No
The Rio-de-Janeiro Tramway, Light and Power Company, Limited	OC	C	No
Société des Taxi-Autos de Dion-Bouton	OC	C	No
Compagnie des Tramways Electriques de Brest	OC	C	No
Tramways Electriques de Douai	OC	C	No
Compagnie des Tramways Electriques de Limoges	OC	C	No
Société Anonyme des Tramways de Tiflis	OC	C	No
Tramways de Tunis	OC	C	No
Compagnie Française du Tramway à vapeur de Versailles à Maule et à Meulan	OC	C	No
Tramways et Eclairage Electriques de Vladicaucase	OC	C	No
Union des Tramways	OC	C	No
Compagnie Générale des Voitures Automobiles	OC	C	No
Société des Automobiles Brasier (anciennement Société des Anciens Etablissements Georges Richard Société de Construction d'Automobiles Le Trèfle à Quatre Feuilles)	MI	C	Yes
Usines d'Automobiles G. Brouhot	MI	C	Yes
Société Parisienne de Carrosserie Automobile	MI	C	Yes
La Charrue Automobile	MI	C	Yes
Société des Anciens Etablissements Chenard et Walcker	MI	C	Yes
Delahaye and C°, Limited	MI	C	Yes
Société des Anciens Etablissements Falconnet-Pérodeaud	MI	C	Yes

Eaux pour l'Etranger (Compagnie générale des)	WGE	P	No	Compagnie Commerciale des Fiacres Automobiles à Taximètre	MI	C	Yes
Société Lyonnaise des Eaux et de l'Eclairage	WGE	P	No	Société des Garages Kriéger et Brasier	MI	C	Yes
Compagnie Générale d'Eaux Minérales et de Bains de Mer	WGE	P	No	Anciens Etablissements Mestre et Blatgé et Hénon et Mestre	MI	C	Yes
Eaux Minérales de Vals	WGE	P	No	Société d'Electricité Nilmelior	MI	C	Yes
Etablissement Thermal de Vichy (Compagnie fermière de l')	WGE	P	No	Le Palladium	MI	C	Yes
Eaux et Electricité de l'Indo-Chine	WGE	P	No	A. Védrine and C° Ltd	MI	C	Yes
Gaz et Eaux de Tunis	WGE	P	No	Société Anonyme du Bec Auer pour l'Europe du Nord	WGE	C	No
L'Eclairage Electrique	WGE	P	No	The Universal Gas Methane and "Buisson Hella" Company, Limited	WGE	C	No
Compagnie Continentale Edison	WGE	P	Yes	La Canalisation Electrique (Anciens Etablissements G. et Henri B. De La Mathe)	WGE	C	Yes
Compagnie Générale d'Electricité	WGE	P	Yes	Société Départementale d'Usines à Gaz	WGE	C	No
"Est-Lumière" (Compagnie d'Electricité de l'Est-Parisien)	WGE	P	No	Société française d'Eclairage et de Chauffage	WGE	C	No
Compagnie d'Electricité de l'Ouest Parisien (Ouest-Lumière)	WGE	P	No	Société Française des Manchons Farkas	WGE	C	No
Secteur de la Place Clichy (Société d'éclairage électrique du)	WGE	P	Yes	Société française des Manchons "Hella"	WGE	C	No
Secteur de la Rive Gauche de Paris (Compagnie électrique du)	WGE	P	No	Compagnie centrale d'Eclairage et de Force par l'Electricité (Electricité de Limoges)	WGE	C	No
Société d'Eclairage et de Force par l'Electricité à Paris	WGE	P	No	Compagnie Electrique de la Loire	WGE	C	Yes
Société d'Electricité de Paris	WGE	P	Yes	Compagnie Centrale d'Electricité	WGE	C	Yes
Cie Générale de Distribution d'Energie Electrique	WGE	P	Yes	Est-Lumière	WGE	C	No
Energie Electrique du Littoral Méditerranéen	WGE	P	Yes	Etablissement thermal de Bagnoles-de-l'Orne	WGE	C	No
Société Générale Electrique et Industrielle	WGE	P	No	Compagnie des Eaux minérales de la Bourboule	WGE	C	No
Société Havraise d'Energie Electrique	WGE	P	Yes	Société générale des Eaux de Calais	WGE	C	No
Société Indo-Chinoise d'Electricité	WGE	P	Yes	Société des Eaux Minérales de Chatel-Guyon	WGE	C	No
Société Industrielle d'Energie Electrique	WGE	P	Yes	Société nouvelle des Eaux de Martigny-les-Bains (Vosges)	WGE	C	No
Electricité de Varsovie	WGE	P	No	Compagnie des Eaux minérales de Pougues et autres	WGE	C	No
Forces Motrices du Rhône (Société Lyonnaise des)	WGE	P	No	Compagnie Générale des Eaux Minérales de Royat	WGE	C	No
Accumulateurs Electriques "Union" (Compagnie Française des)	WGE	P	Yes	Société des Eaux Minérales de Thonon-les-Bains	WGE	C	No
Société d'Applications Industrielles (Compagnie d'entreprises électriques)	WGE	P	Yes	Société Générale de Forces Motrices et d'Eclairage de la Ville de Grenoble	WGE	C	Yes
Maison Breguet	WGE	P	Yes	Société des Forces Motrices de la Haute-Durance	WGE	C	Yes
Société Gramme	WGE	P	Yes	La Française Electrique	WGE	C	Yes

Travaux d'Eclairage et de Force (Compagnie générale de)	WGE	P	Yes	Société Anonyme Ottomane du Gaz de Beyrouth	WGE	C	No
Le Triphasé	WGE	P	Yes	Gaz Franco-Belge, R. Lesage et Cie	WGE	C	No
L'Union Electrique	WGE	P	No	Compagnies réunies Gaz et Electricité	WGE	C	No
Procédés Thomson-Houston (Compagnie française pour l'Exploitation des)	WGE	P	Yes	Société du Gaz de Maubeuge et extensions	WGE	C	No
Cables Télégraphiques (Compagnie française des)	WGE	P	No	Compagnie hellénique d'électricité, système Thomson-Houston	WGE	C	No
Société Industrielle des Téléphones	WGE	P	Yes	Hudson River Electric Power Company	WGE	C	Yes
Compagnie Générale Madrilène d'Electricité	WGE	P	Yes	Compagnie Electrique du Secteur de la Rive Gauche de Paris	WGE	C	No
Thomson-Houston de la Méditerranée (Compagnie d'Electricité)	WGE	P	Yes	Société Anonyme du Gaz de Villerupt	WGE	C	No
Télégraphes du Nord	WGE	P	No	Amiantes de Poschiavo	OM	C	No
Eclairage, Chauffage et Force Motrice (Société d')	WGE	P	No	The Canadian General Mining Cy Ltd	OM	C	Yes
Gaz de Beauvais	WGE	P	No	The Canadian Metal Company Limited	OM	C	Yes
Eclairage de Bordeaux (Compagnie générale d')	WGE	P	No	Colombia	OM	C	Yes
Compagnie Centrale d'Eclairage par le Gaz Lebon et Cie	WGE	P	No	The General Phosphate Company Limited	OM	C	Yes
Société Gaz et Eaux	WGE	P	No	Pétroles de Grosnyi	OM	C	Yes
Gaz pour la France et l'Etranger (Compagnie général du)	WGE	P	No	Compagnie Française de Pétroles	OM	C	Yes
Compagnie Française d'Eclairage et de Chauffage par le Gaz	WGE	P	No	Phosphates Tunisiens	OM	C	Yes
Compagnie Générale Française et Continentale d'Eclairage	WGE	P	No	Société Française d'Etudes et d'Exploitation des Phosphates en Tunisie	OM	C	Yes
Fusion des Gaz	WGE	P	No	The Spies Petroleum Company Limited	OM	C	Yes
Eclairage par le Gaz d'Huile (Société internationale d')	WGE	P	No	"Steaua Romana" Etoile Roumaine	OM	C	Yes
Gaz et Electricité de Marseille	WGE	P	No	L'Air Liquide	OI	C	Yes
Gaz et Electricité de Melun	WGE	P	No	La Bellignite	OI	C	Yes
Gaz de Mulhouse	WGE	P	No	Compagnie d'Electro-Chimie de Bozel	OI	C	Yes
Gaz du Nord et de l'Est (Société des usines à)	WGE	P	No	British South African Explosives Company	OI	C	Yes
Gaz de Paris	WGE	P	No	Le Camphre	OI	C	Yes
Union des Gaz	WGE	P	No	Fabrique Rouennaise de Cellulose	OI	C	No
Eclairage des Villes et Fabrication des Compteurs et Appareils Divers	WGE	P	No	Société des Ciments de Domme	OI	C	Yes
Compagnie Générale (Belge) pour l'Eclairage et le Chauffage par le Gaz	WGE	P	No	Cinéma-Exploitation	OI	C	Yes
Compagnie Madrilène d'Eclairage et de Chauffage par le Gaz	WGE	P	No	Société Générale des Cinématographes "Eclipse"	OI	C	Yes

Société Italienne pour le Gaz (Gaz de Turin)	WGE	P	No
Phosphates du Dyr	OI	P	Yes
Phosphates et Chemins de Fer de Gafsa	OI	P	Yes
Société Centrale de Dynamite	OI	P	Yes
Société Générale de Dynamite et de Produits Chimiques	OI	P	Yes
Etablissements Malétra (Société anonyme de produits chimiques)	OI	P	Yes
Glaces et Produits Chimiques de Saint-Gobain - Chauny et Cirey (Manufactures des)	OI	P	Yes
Matières Colorantes et Produits Chimiques de St-Denis (Etablissements A. Poirrier et G. Dalsace)	OI	P	Yes
Matières Plastiques (Société générale pour la fabrication des)	OI	P	Yes
L'Oyonnithe	OI	P	Yes
Produits Chimiques et d'Explosifs (Société franco-russe de)	OI	P	Yes
Produits Chimiques de Saint-Denis (Société anonyme de)	OI	P	Yes
Ancienne Compagnie Richer - Entreprise générale d'engrais, de vidanges et produits chimiques, Fresne & Cie	OI	P	Yes
Anciennes Maisons Ternois et Guinon (Vidanges, Engrais et Equarrissage)	OI	P	Yes
Société Chimique des Usines du Rhône	OI	P	Yes
Dynamite Nobel	OI	P	Yes
The Lagunas Nitrate Company, Limited	OI	P	Yes
The Lautaro Nitrate Company, Limited	OI	P	Yes
Union Espagnole des Explosifs	OI	P	Yes
Auto-Transports	OC	P	No
Compagnie Générale de Traction	OC	P	No
Voitures pour le Service des Chemins de Fer (Compagnie générale des)	OC	P	No
Automobiles Mors	MI	P	Yes
Compagnie des Cinéma-Halls	OI	C	Yes
Société Anonyme Omnia (Cinéma Montmartre et Extensions)	OI	C	Yes
Compagnie des Cinématographes Théophile Pathé	OI	C	Yes
The Colombian India Rubber Exploration Cy Ltd	OI	C	Yes
Société générale pour la Fabrication de la Dynamite (Dynamite Française)	OI	C	Yes
Société Générale des Engrais organiques	OI	C	Yes
Etablissements Bognier et Burnet	OI	C	Yes
Etablissements Gaumont	OI	C	Yes
Etablissements Hutchinson (Compagnie Nationale du Caoutchouc Simple)	OI	C	Yes
Société des Etablissements Keller-Leleux pour les Alliages électro-thermiques	OI	C	Yes
Société des Etablissements Porcher	OI	C	Yes
Le Film d'Art	OI	C	Yes
Société Générale des Freins Lipkowski	OI	C	Yes
Société du Caoutchouc par le Latex (Procédés du docteur Lucien Morisse)	OI	C	Yes
Compagnie Française du Lithophone (Société anonyme pour l'exploitation des produits barytiques)	OI	C	Yes
De Mello Brazilian Rubber Company Ltd	OI	C	Yes
Société Petitcollin	OI	C	Yes
Compagnie Générale de Phonographes Cinématographes et Appareils de Précision	OI	C	Yes
Société des Phonographes et Cinématographes "Lux"	OI	C	Yes
Société Industrielle de Photographie	OI	C	Yes
Société anonyme des Plaques, Pellicules et Papiers photographiques J. Jougla	OI	C	Yes
Société des Plaques et Papiers Photographiques A. Lumière et ses Fils	OI	C	Yes
Société des Produits Chimiques de Marseille-L'Estaque	OI	C	Yes

Société des Ciments Français et des Portland de Boulogne-sur-Mer	OI	P	Yes	Société Anonyme des Produits chimiques et Huileries d'Odessa	OI	C	Yes
Ciments de Laitier de Donjeux	OI	P	Yes	Société de Produits Electro-Chimiques et Métallurgiques des Pyrénées	OI	C	Yes
Ciments Portland du Boulonnais	OI	P	Yes	Société des Fabriques Russes-Françaises pour la production des articles de Caoutchouc, de Gutta-percha et de Télégraphie, sous la raison "Prowodnik"	OI	C	Yes
Ciments Portland Artificiels de l'Indo-Chine	OI	P	Yes	Raffinerie François	OI	C	No
Compteurs et Matériel d'Usines à Gaz (Compagnie pour la fabrication des)	OI	P	No	Compagnie des Sucreries de Porto-Rico	OI	C	No
Société des Glacières de Paris	OI	P	No	Société Générale des Sucreries et Raffineries en Roumanie	OI	C	No
Société Française d'Incandescence par le Gaz (Système Auer)	OI	P	No	Société Sud-Russe pour la Fabrication et la Vente de la Soude et d'autres Produits Chimiques	OI	C	Yes
Compagnie Industrielle des Pétroles	OI	P	Yes	Société des Plantations de Caoutchouc de Tapanoelie	OI	C	Yes
Procédés Raoul Pictet	OI	P	No	Unione Italiana fra consumatori e fabbricanti di concimi e Prodotti chimici	OI	C	Yes
Raffinerie et Sucrerie Say	OI	P	No				

Classification

Ind* stands for the industry the firm is part of:

BI	Bank and insurance
R	Railways (and tramways)
OC	Other carriages
C	Coal
GM	Gold mines
OM	Other mines
MI	Metal industry
WGE	Water, gas, and electricity (namely utilities)
OI	Other industries

SE** stands for the stock exchange the firm is listed on:

P	*Parquet*
C	*Coulisse*

Appendix 3

The 2nd-IR blue chips in 1929 and market history

2IR blue chips in 1929 (ten largest 2IR firms in terms of market capitalisation), and their market capitalisation in francs:

1	*Manufacture des glaces et produits chimiques de Saint-Gobain*	3,345,600,000
2	*Compagnie des produits chimiques et électro-métallurgiques Alais, Forges et Camargue*	1,668,000,000
3	*Etablissements Kuhlmann (Compagnie nationale des matières colorantes et manufactures de produits chimiques du Nord réunis)*	1,004,400,000
4	*Compagnie parisienne de distribution d'électricité*	847,500,000
5	*Société lyonnaise des eaux et d'éclairage*	813,600,000
6	*Compagnie générale de distribution de l'énergie électrique (1907), Union d'électricité (1929)*	806,400,000
7	*L'Air liquide (Société pour l'étude et l'exploitation des procédés Georges Claude)*	801,000,000
8	*Société anonyme André Citroën*	704,000,000
9	*Est-Lumière (Compagnie d'électricité de l'Est-Parisien)*	692,550,000
10	*Compagnie de l'Ouest parisien (Ouest-Lumière)*	688,800,000

Core-2IR blue chips in 1929 (the ten largest core-2IR firms in terms of market capitalisation), and their market capitalisation in francs:

1	*Manufacture des glaces et produits chimiques de Saint-Gobain*	3,345,600,000
2	*Compagnie des produits chimiques et électro-métallurgiques Alais, Forges et Camargue*	1,668,000,000
3	*Etablissements Kuhlmann (Compagnie nationale des matières colorantes et manufactures de produits chimiques du Nord réunis)*	1,004,400,000
4	*L'Air liquide (Société pour l'étude et l'exploitation des procédés Georges Claude)*	801,000,000
5	*Société anonyme André Citroën*	704,000,000
6	*Compagnie française pour l'exploitation des procédés Thomson-Houston*	558,000,000
7	*Compagnie générale d'électricité*	492,000,000
8	*Energie électrique du Nord de la France*	470,000,000
9	*Electricité et gaz du Nord*	462,000,000
10	*Energie électrique du littoral méditerranéen*	420,000,000

2IR blue chips in 1929 and brief history

Name	Rank 2IR mkt cap	Rank core-2IR mkt cap	Date of foundation	Nominal capital at the foundation	Date of listing	Nominal capital at listing	Increase in nominal capital at listing	Nominal capital in 1907 (if relevant)	Nominal capital in 1929
Manufacture des glaces et produits chimiques de Saint-Gobain, Chauny et Cirey	1	1	"1858"	NA (4,600 shares without mention of face value)	1892	NA (4,600 shares without mention of face value)	NA	60 000 000	225 000 000
Compagnie des produits chimiques et électro-métallurgiques Alais, Forges et Camargue	2	2	1855	600 000	1914	15 750 000	15 150 000	NA	208 000 000
Etablissements Kuhlman (Compagnie nationale des matières colorantes et manufactures de produits chimiques du Nord réunis)	3	3	1854	6 000 000	1919	60 000 000	54 000 000	NA	250 000 000
Compagnie parisienne de distribution d'électricité	4	NA	1907	50 000 000	1908	50 000 000	–	NA	100 000 000
Société lyonnaise des eaux et d'éclairage	5	NA	1880	50 000 000	1880	50 000 000	–	18 000 000	115 000 000
Compagnie générale de distribution de l'énergie électrique (1907), Union d'électricité (1929)	6	NA	1904	1 000 000	1907	12 000 000	11 000 000	12 000 000	275 000 000
L'Air liquide (Société pour l'étude et l'exploitation des procédés Georges Claude)	7	4	1902	100 000	1908	1 500 000	1 400 000	NA	66 000 000
Société anonyme André Citroën	8	5	1919, 1924 (*société anonyme*)	300 000 000	1927	300 000 000	–	NA	400 000 000
Est-Lumière (Compagnie d'électricité de l'Est-Parisien)	9	NA	1900	2 000 000	1907	6 000 000	4 000 000	6 000 000	67 500 000
Compagnie de l'Ouest parisien (Ouest-Lumière)	10	NA	1900	6 000 000	1905	8 000 000	2 000 000	12 000 000	110 000 000
Compagnie française pour l'exploitation des procédés Thomson-Houston	13	7	1893	1 000 000	1896	15 000 000	14 000 000	40 000 000	330 000 000
Compagnie générale d'électricité	15	8	1898	10 000 000	1898	10 000 000	–	15 000 000	100 000 000
Energie électrique du Nord de la France	17	9	1907	1 500 000	1910	7 000 000	5 500 000	NA	118 750 000
Electricité et gaz du Nord	18	10	1910	25 000 000	1911	25 000 000	–	NA	100 000 000
Energie électrique du littoral méditerranéen	20	12	1900	4 000 000	1904	32 000 000	28 000 000	32 000 000	330 000 000

Debating banking in Britain: The Colwyn committee, 1918

Mark Billings, Simon Mollan and Philip Garnett

ABSTRACT

By 1918 the British banking system had reached a degree of maturity and concentration, with a small number of large banks dominating the sector. Political concerns about the rise of financial power led to the appointment of the Colwyn Committee to investigate the amalgamations process, and consider the issue of concentration with reference to the role of banking in the economy. In this article we explore this critical inflection point in British banking history and argue that the Committee's proceedings reveal that many current concerns about banking correspond to those of a century ago. We also argue that–contrary to some historical interpretation–the Committee did not unequivocally favour financial interests, but rather sought to stabilise organisational change in the sector, and introduce new restrictions on the freedom of banks in respect of amalgamation, as well as supervision and regulation.

Introduction

The link between financial development and economic growth has been widely investigated and most evidence points to a positive causal effect.[1] Gerschenkron (1962) and Goldsmith (1969) debated the relative merits of bank-based versus market-based financial systems in financial development several decades ago. More recently Fohlin argued that 'the specific type of financial system or institutions that develop is far less important for economic growth than the development of *some* well-functioning financial system' (Fohlin, 2016, p. 426, emphasis in original).[2] Recent historical evidence similarly indicates that both banks and stock markets contribute to economic growth (for example, Carlin & Mayer, 2003; Levine & Zervos, 1998; Rajan & Zingales, 1998). Nevertheless, the variations in the structure and form of financial services provision – specifically with respect to the financing of industry – are often used to express essentialist notions of which is preferable, or better suited, to the promotion of economic growth more generally.

The financial system of the United Kingdom – like that of the United States of America – is generally characterised as stock market-oriented, in contrast to the bank-oriented financial systems of France, Germany and Japan (Allen & Gale, 2000; Newton, 2010). The particular combination of stock market capital provision and banking in the UK has been the subject of a long-running and wide-ranging debate about whether the financial sector as a whole performed poorly in its wider economic function of promotion of economic growth (Best & Humphries, 1986; Ingham, 1984; Nicholls, 1988; Peters, 1993). In turn this provokes questions about how a specific financial system developed historically, and the extent to which it emerged or was intentionally structured. Richard Grossman identified four themes that shape the historical development of banking: financial and institutional crises, bailouts, periods of amalgamation and merger, and regulation (Grossman, 2010, p. xviii). All of these elements are relevant to this article, especially the latter two.

We focus on the British banking system at an arguably critical moment in its historical development. The UK arguably had a highly competitive financial system at the outbreak of World War One and delivered at least broadly comparable outcomes in business finance to Germany (Hannah, 2017, especially pp. 91–95). Table 1 provides some measures of financial development in 1913 and reinforces the view that the financial systems of several major countries were not dissimilar in terms of outcomes and structures. However, by 1918 concerns around amalgamations in British banking led to the establishment of an influential official investigation, the Treasury Committee on Banking Amalgamations (sometimes referred to by the name of its chairman, Lord Colwyn, and hereafter 'the Committee'). The main outcome of the Committee was to check the progress of banking amalgamations, which began in the late eighteenth century, and intensified in the period after 1810, creating the structure of British domestic banking which remains recognisable today. This inflection point is widely discussed in the existing historiography mainly by reference to the Committee's findings rather than its deliberations. We place the Committee's political deliberations into the organisational context of the business/financial history of the period, and explore how that discourse contributed to shaping the subsequent development of the UK financial sector.

The central contribution of this article is to contextualise, problematise, and interpret the unpublished evidence presented to the Committee with reference to contemporary concerns relating to the nature, development and future of British banking and the wider financial system. The Committee's terms of reference required it to consider and report on the effect of bank amalgamations on 'the industrial and mercantile community' and what, if any, legislation or other safeguards should be introduced. These terms of reference raise the question of how the Committee and its witnesses interpreted the role of banks in the provision of business finance. In particular, did amalgamations impact on competition so

Table 1. Comparative financial development, 1913.

		Banking system characteristics				
Country	Lending/GDP (%)	Universal? (0–2 subjective scale)	Bank seats on company boards	Equity shareholdings by banks	Extensive branch networks (0/1)	Equity market development (0–2 subjective scale)
Canada	n/a	1	Some	Some	1	1
France	16/29	1	1	Some	1	2
Germany	28	2	1	Some	1	2
Italy	28	2	Top banks	1	1	1
UK/England	33	0	Few	Few	1	2
United States	30	1	1	1	0	2

Source: Lending/GDP: Hannah (2017), p. 85; all other data: Fohlin (2016, pp. 402–405, 415–416).

as to create a tension between banks' 'public utility role' and the stability of the financial system? If so, what solutions, if any, could the Committee offer?

The article is structured as follows. The next section outlines the development of the British banking system in the nineteenth and early twentieth centuries, and considers the amalgamation process that shaped the sector to place the Committee's deliberations in broader context. The third section outlines the background to the Committee, briefly discussing its membership, the witnesses, its proceedings and their outcome. The fourth section addresses the issues raised by witnesses and attempts to place their evidence in the context of academic scholarship on banking, concepts of banking and theories of financial development. The fifth and final section concludes.

The amalgamation movement and the development of the British banking system

In the late nineteenth and early twentieth centuries British banking was subject to general corporate law but otherwise essentially unregulated. Banks were predominantly limited liability companies, there was no deposit insurance, there were no ratio-based capital or liquidity regulations, and there were no limits on branching or mergers and acquisitions. Against the background of the gold standard with freedom of capital movement, and a largely passive Bank of England, bankers operated without intrusive regulation (Capie, 2016).

Victorian banks developed significant branch networks before 1880 but these were not national (Barnes & Newton, 2018). Sykes summarised the perceived advantages of local decision-making: 'the provinces have the benefits derived from a management working in the midst of provincial and local conditions, maintaining responsive and intimate touch with industrial changes' (Sykes, 1926, p. 189). Histories of British banking typically describe a system with lending decisions based on borrower reputation and the availability of a broad range of collateral rather than detailed analysis of prospects, loan characteristics, and client distress (Capie & Collins, 1999a, 1999b; Collins & Baker, 2003). This system evolved through amalgamations from the late eighteenth century onwards from one with hundreds of unit banks, unable to expand because of limiting legislation removed in the first half of the nineteenth century, into a highly concentrated system.[3]

The periodisation of the amalgamation movement owes much to the classic work by Sykes (1926). In identifying 1825 as the beginning of the period, Sykes was essentially correct. Although the population of British banks began to decline from its peak in 1810, the process of amalgamation began in earnest only in the 1820s (Garnett, Mollan, & Bentley, 2015; Garnett, Mollan, & Bentley, 2017).[4] Figure 1 indicates that there were in broad terms four phases of heavy amalgamation. The first began around 1825 and ended in the early 1840s. The second began around 1854, terminating in the late 1860s. The third, and most significant, began in the early 1880s and continued until the outbreak of World War One in 1914. The final, less significant phase began around the end of the war in 1918 and terminated, as Sykes suggests, around 1924.

Figure 2 shows that the population of British banks (in comparison with 1810–1924) was broadly stable between 1924 and 1987 when it again began to decline, although there is evidence of population instability from the 1960s onwards when measured as the year-on-year change in the population. What is incontrovertible, however, is that the end of the amalgamation movement as a secular trend in the population of British banks was followed

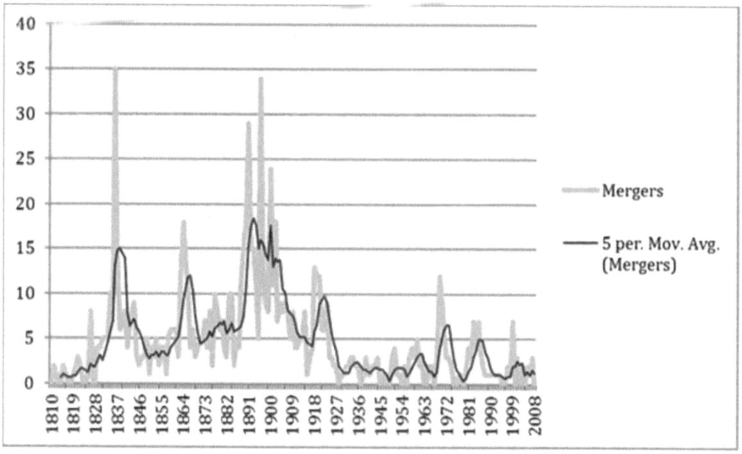

Figure 1. Mergers in the population of British banks, 1810–2008.

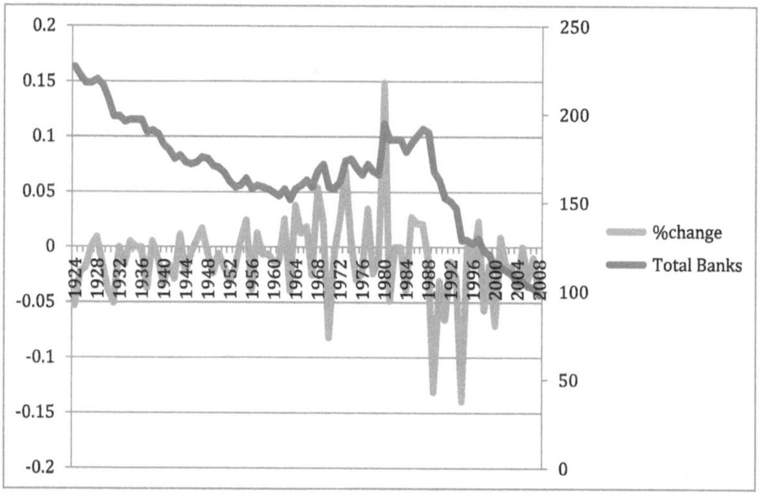

Figure 2. The population of British banks, 1924–2008 (left axis: percentage change year to year; right axis: absolute number of total banks).

by about half a century or so of relative population stability from the interwar period until at least the 1960s, and arguably until the 1980s. This highlights the importance of the policies that stem from the Committee, and brought to a close a period of profound consolidation in British banking.

Figures 3 and 4 show that the amalgamation process during the 40 years or so preceding the Committee was also a process of creation of new banks, and failure of existing banks. Between 1880 and 1918 there were 382 mergers between banks, 599 bank failures, and 251 new banks created. These individual events drove fundamental trends in the overall banking population, notably the late-nineteenth century emergence of the large retail banks and the later dominance of the Big Five, which had grown through amalgamation (Capie & Rodrik-Bali, 1982). For example, Barclays emerged through the 1896 merger of 12 private banks, and expanded its geographical footprint into the country's industrial areas through

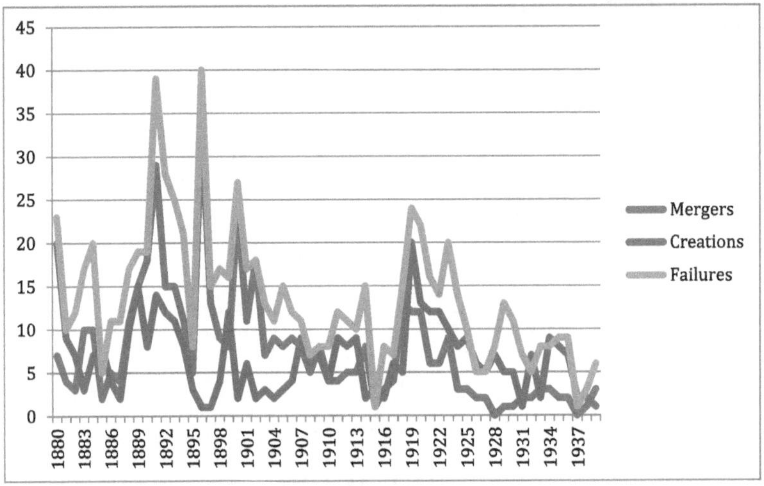

Figure 3. Mergers, creations and failures of British banks, 1880–1939 (absolute numbers).

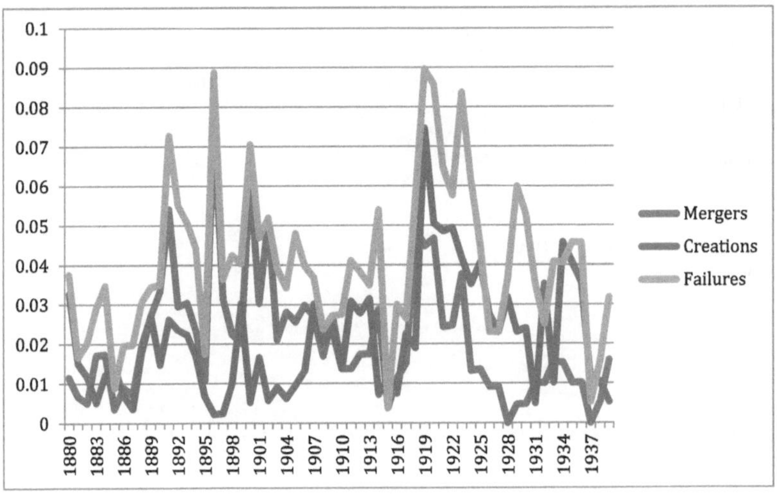

Figure 4. Mergers, creations and failures of British banks, 1880–1939 (normalised).

later amalgamations (Ackrill & Hannah, 2001, pp. 55–58, 60–61). Another of the Big Five, the Midland, illustrates the relative importance of amalgamations and organic growth through branch openings. From 1880 to 1919 the Midland added 921 branches through amalgamations against 536 through new branch openings, with only 16 branch closures in the period (Crick & Wadsworth, 1936, p. 333). Concentration in the share of bank deposits and branch numbers increased considerably between 1910 and 1921 (see Table 2), especially through several large amalgamations in 1917 and 1918 (Alhadeff, 1968, pp. 244–246; Capie & Rodrik-Bali, 1982; Turner, 2014, p. 43).

This process created banks with large branch networks and dominant market shares. These banks were well-diversified geographically and across different sectors of the economy, and their asset structures had become more liquid and conservative with a gradual shift to lower capital ratios with more (notionally short-term) overdraft lending, tougher

Table 2. UK Banking in outline, 1900–1921.

	Total number of UK		Five largest UK banks' percentage share of total bank	
Year	Joint-stock banks	Bank branches	Deposits	Branches
1900	188	5,922	24.7	21.9
1905	137	6,759	28.7	19.8
1910	112	7,564	36.7	32.5
1915	96	8,494	39.8	39.9
1921	70	9,998	79.4	78.5

Sources: total numbers of banks and branches: Capie and Webber (1985, pp. 577–578); five largest banks: Turner (2014, p. 45). Turner's data include those banks which were wholly owned by the Big Five but remained separate entities.

lending terms, higher cash balances, and greater holdings of high quality investments (Baker & Collins, 2002; Collins & Baker, 2001a, 2001b, 2003). Lending power and decision-making were generally concentrated in these banks' head offices, which had gravitated to London even if some had origins in the provinces.[5]

Historians have tended to focus on two aspects of increased concentration in British domestic banking: the potential negative impact on competition and customers, particularly small and medium-sized enterprises and innovative businesses; and the potential positive impact on stability.[6] The alleged failings, together with the failure of these banks, the Bank of England, and government to facilitate industrial restructuring, are central to some versions of the 'declinist' narrative on British economic history (Best & Humphries, 1986; Elbaum & Lazonick, 1984, 1986; Tomlinson, 2009). Others contest these claims and argue that these criticisms and the differences between British banks and those elsewhere, particularly in continental Europe, have been exaggerated, and that the banks could claim that their role in the provision of finance was expected to be limited (Ackrill & Hannah, 2001, pp. 93–95; Collins, 1998; Newton, 2003; Ross, 1990, 1996).

The latter stages of the amalgamation process aroused popular fears of a 'Money Trust' (i.e. the control of the financial system by elite interests, concentrated in an oligopoly made up of a small number of banks), partly influenced by debates on banking in the US following the 1907 financial crisis.[7] Examination of the trend in the UK banking population offers some insight into the reasonableness of this concern. Figure 5 shows two fitted lines, one fitted to the real population, and the other to a linear trend line based on the consolidation rate in the population as a whole measured from its peak in 1810 to the point of the Committee's deliberations in 1918. This fitted linear trend line indicates that the population of UK banks would have become very small by the 1950s. This crude counter-factual device does not 'predict' what would have happened without the Committee. Rather, it shows the banking sector population demographic context which the Committee faced – the trend was towards continued consolidation through amalgamation – and that concerns about a 'Money Trust' were not unreasonable when viewed from this perspective.

The committee

Public and political disquiet at the prospects of further consolidation in the sector led the government to appoint the Committee on 11 March 1918. The majority of the Committee's 12 members and 22 witnesses were elite bankers and businessmen. The chairman Lord Colwyn was a businessman and banker.[8] Other members included the Governor of the Bank

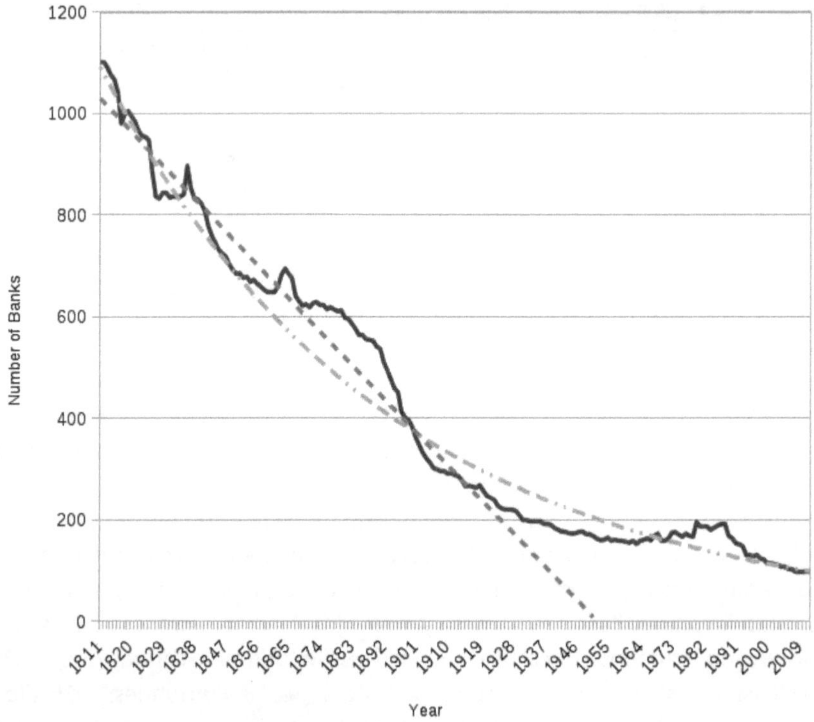

Figure 5. The population of British banks, 1810–2008.

Table 3. The Committee members.

Name	Background
Lord Colwyn (Chairman)	See note 8
Lord [Walter] Cunliffe	Governor, Bank of England, 1913–1918
Hon. Rupert Beckett	Partner, Beckett & Co., private bankers, c.1890–1921; Director, London County Westminster and Parr's [Westminster] Bank 1921–50, Deputy Chairman 1927–30, Chairman 1930–50
Hon. Herbert Gibbs	Partner, Antony Gibbs and Sons; sometime member and chairman of Public Works Loan Board
Sir Arthur Haworth Bt.	President, Manchester Liberal Federation; Liberal MP Manchester South, 1906–1912, cotton yarn agent; President, Manchester Royal Exchange
Sir Richard Vassar-Smith Bt.	Chairman, Lloyds Bank, 1909–1922
Sir John Purcell KCB	Chairman, National Bank
Captain H. [Henry] Keswick	Chairman, Hong Kong and Shanghai Banking Corporation
Mr. E. [Edward] Manville	Electrical engineer and motor manufacturer with numerous business interests; member Excess Profits Duty Board of Referees; Unionist MP 1918–23 and member of various government committees
Mr. H. [Harry] McGowan	Chairman and managing director, Explosives Trades Limited; explosives industrialist
Mr. John Rae	Treasurer, Bank of Scotland; Director, Westminster Bank 1926–1932
Mr. Douglas Vickers	Director, Vickers Limited.; armaments industrialist

Source: names as shown in Treasury Committee on Bank Amalgamations (1918).

of England, Lord Cunliffe, several bank chairmen or directors, a merchant banker, and several businessmen and industrialists (see Table 3). The witnesses were more mixed, with nine joint-stock bank directors, a variety of other representatives of the financial community, a handful of other businessmen of various types, two economists, one an academic and the other a civil servant, and, intriguingly, the Fabian socialist Sidney Webb (see Table 4). The

Table 4. The witnesses to the Committee.

Name	Background	Number of pages of written evidence
Oswald Stoll	[Theatre promoter]	15
Thomas Goodwin	Manager, Co-operative Wholesale Society's Bank	10
Sir Charles Stewart Addis	Hong Kong and Shanghai Banking Corporation, Ltd. [member, Bank of England Court from May 1918]	10
Gordon Selfridge	[Department store owner]	6
Viscount Cowdray	[Partner in S. Pearson & Son, contractors]	9
D. Drummond Fraser	Joint Managing Director, Manchester and Liverpool District Banking Co.	13
Sidney Webb	[Fabian socialist]	17
A.W. [Sir Alfred William] Flux	[Statistical Department], Board of Trade	11
Thomas Courtney Johnston	Pountney & Co. Ltd, Bristol	8
Christopher Nugent	Union Discount Company of London, Ltd.	10
Sir Herbert Hambling	Chairman, London and South-Western Bank Limited	10
John Ford Darling	General Manager, London Joint Stock Bank Limited	14
Sir Edward Holden	Chairman and Managing Director, London, City and Midland Bank	34
Professor H.S. [Herbert Somerton] Foxwell	Professor of Political Economy, University of London	21
Owen Charles Quekett	Chairman of the Stock Exchange Committee	2
Gaspard Farrer	Baring Brothers and Co. Ltd.	8
Harold Edward Snagge	Edward Boustead & Co., East India merchants	5
Henry Bell	Director and General Manager, Lloyds Bank	20
Mr. [John William] Beaumont Pease	Deputy Chairman [Chairman, 1922–1945], Lloyds Bank	23
Sir James Hope Simpson	General Manager, Bank of Liverpool Ltd.	12
Lord Inchcape	Director, National Provincial and Union Bank of England, Ltd.; [shipping magnate]	13
Walter Leaf	Chairman, London County, Westminster and Parr's Bank, Ltd.	9

Source: TNA, T1/12267/50326, file 1 of 2; the witnesses are listed in the order in which their evidence appears on file, cross-checked against the list of witnesses in Treasury Committee on Bank Amalgamations (1918), with additional background information in parentheses.

process by which witnesses were selected is unknown.[9] The mix of Committee members and witnesses appears cosy and conflicted by modern standards. Several members (Cunliffe, Beckett, Gibbs) and witnesses (Addis, Farrer, Inchcape) were simultaneously sitting together as members of the Committee on Currency and Foreign Exchanges after the War, chaired by Cunliffe.[10] The witnesses Addis, Bell and Beaumont Pease were faced by their own bank chairmen (Keswick and Vassar-Smith) as members of the Committee.[11]

On 1 May 1918, the Committee published a short report, heavily influenced by the witnesses' oral evidence. Although the report has been referred to widely in the historical literature, only a handful of scholars appear to have consulted the transcripts of evidence (Carnevali, 2005; Grossman, 1999; Kynaston, 1999; Sayers, 1976). One of these, Francesca Carnevali, characterised the Committee as follows: 'financial interests set up the committee and shaped the direction of its investigation. Bankers were asked by bankers whether bank amalgamations should be allowed to continue' (Carnevali, 2005, p. 19). Thus Carnevali effectively argues that the Colwyn process was fundamentally flawed, having been captured by banking interests which would resist meaningful change. We argue, however, that this interpretation fails to acknowledge the many insights the evidence offers on the nature and structure of contemporary banking and the British financial system more generally, as well as the outcome of the Committee.

The Committee's report noted that it was '... forced to the conclusion that the possible dangers resulting from further large amalgamations are material enough to outweigh the arguments against Government interference ... and some measure of Government control is essential' (Treasury Committee on Bank Amalgamations, 1918, p. 7). The Joint Stock Banks (Amalgamation Control) Bill was drafted in 1919 to require government approval for future changes of ownership and control in banking, but no legislation was passed.[12] However, the mechanism proposed in the draft Bill was introduced on a non-statutory basis: an Advisory Committee on Bank Amalgamations was appointed in May 1919 by the Chancellor of the Exchequer, Andrew Bonar Law. This committee had two members: Colwyn (as 'commercial representative') and Lord Inchcape, a shipping magnate, director of one of the Big Five, the National Provincial, and witness to the Committee (as 'banking representative').[13] The Committee witness Sir James Hope Simpson appears to have provided the idea for this advisory committee when he advocated 'a confidential body' to judge amalgamations on merits rather than by rules.

Despite the failure to legislate on amalgamations, official opinion was resolutely opposed to further domestic expansion by the Big Five and amalgamations between members of the London Clearing House, and official policy thwarted various transactions, although several amalgamations in progress when the Committee was appointed were allowed without intervention.[14] Nevertheless, the keenness of two of the Big Five, Barclays and Lloyds, to test the boundaries of the restrictions greatly irritated Cunliffe's successor, Montagu Norman, who was particularly concerned about the possibility of contagion from their expanding international activities.[15]

The evidence

Many of the questions on which the Committee heard evidence, such as the relationship between competition and financial stability and the merits of geographic spread, continue to attract the interest of economists.[16] Witnesses ranged beyond the Committee's terms of reference in the breadth of issues they addressed: the implications of amalgamations for customers large and small, from local to international; the size and number of banks needed to ensure effective competition; the impact of amalgamations on branch networks; their impact on capital levels in banking, and hence financial stability; the belief of some witnesses that British banks needed to amalgamate in order to compete with other large international banks; the implications of amalgamations for the state, including pressures to assume a larger role in banking, to intervene in the affairs of struggling banks, and the possible nationalisation of banks; and comparisons between the British financial system and those of other countries, notably Germany, the US and Canada. We address these issues below.

The rationale for bank amalgamations

Banking literature identifies offensive and defensive motivations in banking mergers and acquisitions. Foremost among these is that amalgamations offer the easiest way to expand geographical coverage and establish branch networks (Dymski, 2012, p. 572). This view is consistent with the suggestion that British banks found amalgamation an advantageous way to expand (Garnett et al., 2015). The literature considers amalgamations as broadly acceptable if the banking market remains contestable and stability is preserved (Dymski, 2012).

For the most part the evidence of the Committee's banking witnesses is consistent with this literature. These witnesses favoured amalgamations and saw no reason to make them more difficult. Ford Darling suggested several motives for the proposed merger of his own bank with the London, City and Midland: its lack of geographical spread, its under-representation in industrial centres, the cost of opening branches, and its lack of foreign business and infrastructure to support it. Hambling considered it easier for a bank to amalgamate with another than to establish new branches. Drummond Fraser believed that amalgamations offered the possibility of economies of scale and supported those that did not involve geographical overlaps of branches or decrease the ratio of paid-up capital to deposits. The non-banker Cowdray felt that bigger banks were able to draw on larger pools of management talent. Other justifications for amalgamations are considered below.

The Committee's report focused heavily on the changing nature of amalgamations, adopting a distinction made principally by the economist Foxwell. He identified three types: those between small unit banks within regions, which he saw as positive in terms of risk-spreading; those between larger banks (possibly created through the previous type) in different regions to achieve 'national' coverage, which he again favoured as spreading risk geographically and by industry of borrower; and finally those of already-large banks with some degree of national coverage, which he saw negatively as reducing competition.

The need for big banks

Several witnesses discussed the need for large banks, with two strands to this argument: first, the necessity of large banks to accommodate the needs of individual customers; and secondly, the need for scale in banking to support economic development. Ford Darling cited the business needs of large customers as a reason for his bank's planned amalgamation, although it had never yet struggled to accommodate these needs.[17] Several non-banking witnesses accepted the need for scale in banking. Courtney Johnston favoured amalgamations in principle, not only of banks, as 'absolutely essential' to be able to compete. Selfridge argued that US trusts '... have been of the greatest possible assistance to the States ...', and advocated what we might contemporarily describe as distinctly 'Chandlerian' views on the desirable scale and scope of banking enterprises: 'It seems to me that all our businesses should be bigger in this country ... If you are going to put out a fire you are going to the biggest reservoir for your water. You do not want a lot of little reservoirs'. Cowdray considered that a contractor such as Pearson benefited from using bank-provided project finance before floating securities in completed and proven projects. He argued that small banks were less useful for this purpose: big banks were better able to assess such projects, whereas smaller banks were more inclined to show favouritism to certain customers. He considered that British banks needed to grow to match the size of the largest US banks and agreed when Colwyn asked whether the country had lost business in, say, 'the East and South America – because our banks have not been large enough to deal with it?' Foxwell thought that the size of banks in countries such as France and Germany '... makes it necessary, I think, that we should have in this country very large and powerful banks, but how large and how powerful, of course, it is impossible to lay down *a priori*'. His argument was echoed by Holden who considered amalgamation 'is the only means of obtaining individual Banks of a size and power at all commensurate with those now being formed or developed in America and Germany'. He argued that large banks would help maintain London's importance as a financial centre, even though the UK's population was smaller than those of Germany and the US.

'Too-small-to-survive' banks

The two witnesses from Lloyds Bank, Bell and Beaumont Pease, discussed the weakness of small local banks. Bell had been at the 11-branch Liverpool Union Bank, which he claimed was sound but was forced to amalgamate with Lloyds in 1900 due to the seasonality of its business in which customer needs would exceed its deposits available to lend and individual customers could borrow in excess of the bank's capital.[18] The bank therefore faced the dilemma of turning away sound business from good customers or amalgamating with a larger bank. He claimed that all Liverpool's local banks were under similar strain 'until the big joint stock banks came into the city and brought resources from all over the country'. Purely local mergers would not have solved the problems of seasonality and narrowness of the deposit base.

Holden described his bank's amalgamations in Liverpool, Manchester and Oldham, and maintained that all had contributed positively to competition, stability and lending in these locations. The London banker Ford Darling presented a different argument: for all but 'three industrial centres' in which his bank was present, 'country branch' deposits exceeded advances, so its head office provided profitable investment outlets for surplus funds. Hambling similarly considered '... that banks should become national ... [and] operate in all areas. ... they should be able to collect their deposits where deposits can be collected and ... they should be able to lend them where commerce wants them'. The Liverpool banker Hope Simpson also favoured amalgamations of regional banks 'into' London.[19]

Bell described a small proportion of Lloyds' amalgamations as 'rescues' and Beaumont Pease went further, claiming some were with insolvent banks. Sayers (1957, pp. 256–257) offers some support for this view, identifying two 1902 acquisitions, the Bucks and Oxon Union Bank and the Cornish Bank, as financially weak. Holden appeared to support the view of Bell and Beaumont Pease. He highlighted that there had been very few bank failures in the period 1900–1913 and linked this to the willingness of the larger banks to 'immediately take up [a weak bank] and prevent disaster' through amalgamation or some other form of support. Holden offered only two specific examples where banks worked together to prevent crisis: the cases of Barings in 1890 and the Yorkshire Penny Bank.[20]

The evidence of Drummond Fraser, in his '25th year in Manchester in a managerial capacity', contrasted, and in some respects contradicted, that of the other bankers. He claimed never to have been in the position of being unable to accommodate customers' requirements for advances. He noted that customer and shareholder objections had defeated two proposed combinations between Manchester and London banks and anticipated similar objections to other such proposals.[21]

Lending practice, local banks and competition

Addis doubted that amalgamations offered customers greater access to credit and thought they created the potential for reduced competition. But the banking witnesses generally maintained that post-amalgamation practices were unchanged from earlier banking arrangements. Holden argued that each of his own bank's amalgamations had increased lending, quoted statistics on its lending to the 'small man', and maintained that 'there is no trouble whatever in the small man getting accommodation'. Bell offered to produce extensive evidence of 'uncovered' (i.e. unsecured) lending to small traders and Beaumont Pease provided an extensive commentary on lending practice in private banks versus joint-stock banks, claiming the latter lent no less, and sometimes more, liberally at local level. Ford Darling claimed that his own bank's lending to smaller customers would be unaffected by its proposed amalgamation as '... our managers have got their discretionary limits, which they use without reference to Head Office at all, for the smaller advances'. In contrast, Inchcape thought that '... I do not think the banks compete very much with each other. I will tell you what they compete in ... is mostly in civility to their customers'. A non-banking witness, Courtney Johnston, thought that 'In the old days the private banker knew the local people, and the local industries and helped them'.

Beaumont Pease claimed that where amalgamations reduced the number of banks in a town or district other banks opened new branches. Bell used the example of Liverpool to illustrate his claim that amalgamations increased competition even if there were fewer banks – small local banks tended to 'live together in the greatest amity' but larger banks were more competitive. Ford Darling thought that in places such as Newcastle there were sufficient banks to ensure competition despite the overlapping branch networks of amalgamating banks.

In Manchester Drummond Fraser felt well able to compete with London banks. His customers wanted 'the real personal, sympathetic touch ... the close personal touch ... [not] based on the inelastic stereotyped rules necessary under a London control'. He claimed to have acquired numerous sound business customers offering security for loans but unwilling to offer the personal guarantees sought by London banks. Equally, he was willing to lose business to London banks when only very fine margins were available. Webb was sceptical of the value of the 'personal touch' in banking as borrowers formed only a small proportion of customers; the 'personal touch' was irrelevant to the vast majority of depositors.

The claims of these witnesses in relation to the effects of amalgamations on competition can be related to recent literature. Hannah details intense pre-World War One local competition in financial services in the city of Oxford (Hannah, 2017, pp. 79–83). Braggion, Dwarkasing, and Moore (2017), however, find that amalgamations reduced competition: borrowers of comparable quality in counties with higher concentration in banking received smaller loans and posted more or higher quality collateral.

Concentration, competition and state control

Simpson argued that '... the public is, on the whole, better served by banks today than it was when there was a large number of small banks'. He was supported by other bankers, most robustly by Holden in a lengthy opening statement. Opinions on the number of banks necessary to secure effective competition varied: Cowdray suggested five or six; Ford Darling thought ten; Foxwell thought that 'You can have just as keen a competition between three separate interests as between 30'. He was relaxed about competition in London given the presence there of foreign banks but thought it preferable to avoid amalgamations which created banks with more than £250 million in deposits. Holden specified no number, merely stating that there should be a 'sufficient number of powerful Banks to ensure free competition'.

Goodwin's Co-operative Wholesale Society's Bank acted for the Co-operative Movement and did not compete directly for commercial banking business. It did, however, use other banks as agents and he considered further amalgamations could be detrimental to his own bank's interests. Goodwin articulated a point made by several witnesses of different persuasions: '… the very fact of the banking business of the country getting into a few hands will … make it all the more easy for a transfer to State control'. Addis thought that continuing amalgamations encouraged socialists to counter the too-big-to-fail problem: 'No Government, obviously, could afford, for National reasons, to allow one of those banks to become insolvent. From guarantee to control is only a step, and from control to Socialism is only one step more removed'.

The only socialist witness, Webb, faced sceptical but respectful questioning.[22] He viewed deposit banking as a natural monopoly or oligopoly in that the fewer banks existed, the less inclined depositors would be to 'run' on an individual bank. He thought that the banks would bring nationalisation upon themselves by pursuing amalgamations which would lead to '… too perilous a power to remain in the hands of private persons for private purposes'. The logical solution was for a single bank 'under public control'. He declined to specify any particular form of public ownership saying 'I should put it into the hands of the community', but defended the Labour Party against assertions that it advocated nationalisation without compensation. He confirmed bank shareholders should be bought out on 'quite equitable terms' with 'full and complete compensation'. In response to Keswick's question '… where is nationalisation to stop', Webb replied: 'I should be sorry to put a limit to it, because we are only at the beginning of eternity. I cannot say where it would stop'.[23] Other Committee members (Manville and Purcell) pressed Webb as to why the state should take on banking risks. In response he cited the Commonwealth Bank of Australia as an example of state involvement in banking and argued for separation of the deposit-taking and lending functions; the state should take deposits and lend or provide capital to financial corporations to undertake business lending.

Attitudes to regulation

Witnesses' attitudes to regulation varied, with some in favour and others deeply opposed. Cowdray proposed legislation to require banks to report to the Board of Trade any actual or contemplated anti-competitive arrangements. Farrer thought that amalgamations should have been deferred during wartime and had tried to persuade the Board of Trade of this. Stoll advocated safeguards against the excessive power of banks. Courtney Johnston argued for safeguards around banking to prevent local funds being used to finance 'foreign competitors'. Webb, however, thought that legislation to control amalgamations would be 'sham'.

Some witnesses stressed the importance of transparency. Drummond Fraser called for transparency of capital ratios and advocated monthly publication of uniform balance sheets. Flux discussed the nature and regulation of banking in Canada, noting transparency through publication of shareholder lists, monthly accounts, and loans to directors and businesses connected to them. He also detailed Canadian regulation of bank amalgamations, noting that the 1913 Banking Act required the authority of the Minister of Finance for an amalgamation and gave shareholders the right to appoint an auditor from a panel of 40 nominated by the general managers of all banks, although external auditors were assumed to be less effective monitors than insiders due to their lack of familiarity with a bank's affairs.

Foxwell thought legislation and government control over banking would be too rigid. Other witnesses objected more strongly. Hambling was deeply distrustful: 'I hate competent Government Authorities. I have the strongest possible objection to Government interference because from my short experience I find they do not exercise them [sic] very wisely. I think banks can do their own business better ...'.[24] Inchcape expressed similar views: 'I have a very strong objection to Government Control. I think the less Government interferes with the business of the country the better'.

Banks' capital structures

Discussions around contingent capital or extended liability have revived in recent years as part of the response to the twenty-first century financial crisis, with economists arguing for a form of capital which would 'bail in' shareholders in the event of distress, and therefore provide disincentives to excessive risk-taking (Chennells & Wingfield, 2015; Turner, 2014). In theory such a mechanism still existed in 1918 and later. Banks with limited liability typically issued at least some shares that were partly – rather than fully – paid up, with the balance callable at directors' discretion. Banks sometimes also issued shares with reserve liability, callable only in a winding-up, similar to extended liability regimes in US banks (Grossman, 2010, pp. 237–240). These arrangements supposedly protected depositors by providing resources which could be called up to boost banks' capital positions. Share classes which were not fully paid and/or carried reserve liability typically carried rights to higher dividends to compensate for the (at least notional) risk that the uncalled elements would be called up. These contingent capital arrangements appear to have reduced risk-taking by British banks before World War One, particularly among banks with higher leverage (Grossman & Imai, 2013). The Committee's report, however, noted that amalgamations had weakened capital ratios, and that uncalled capital in particular had been reduced, '... with substantial benefits to shareholders ... purchased at the expense of some of the security of depositors' (Treasury Committee on Bank Amalgamations, 1918, p. 6).[25]

Many witnesses spontaneously commented on, or were questioned about, the effect of amalgamations on bank capital. Holden actually claimed that amalgamations increased capital. Foxwell noted that paid-up capital had fallen in relative terms, with deposits and total liabilities more than doubling in the preceding decade, with no increase in capital. Addis also noted that amalgamations sometimes eliminated shareholders' uncalled liability, which he considered disadvantageous. He also claimed that, in contrast to British amalgamations, German bank amalgamations increased paid-up capital.

Ford Darling regarded uncalled capital as a disincentive to shareholders in banks in general and a constraint on his own bank's ability to amalgamate with others. His bank's proposed amalgamation with the London City and Midland Bank would reduce its uncalled liability to £38 per share from £85 per share which he considered beneficial to his shareholders. Inchcape told the Committee that in his bank every share transfer came before a board committee where '... the standing, employment, and responsibility of the transferee are considered' to ensure that calls on uncalled capital could be met. He also likened the possible impact of such calls to the 1878 collapse of the unlimited-liability City of Glasgow Bank which prompted banks to rush to limited liability status (Acheson & Turner, 2008; Button, Knott, Macmanus, & Willison, 2015). Foxwell was sceptical of the ability of banks to call up uncalled capital. He also identified the moral hazard problem in a concentrated banking sector, linking the too-big-to-fail argument to the decline in capital ratios:

> ... institutions of a certain size are 'too large to let go'. It inspires the customers with confidence when a bank reaches a certain size; they say that whatever the state of things this bank will not be allowed to fall: a crash would carry the market away. I confess I think this rather an unfortunate presumption, though it may be a sound one, because I believe it is partly responsible for the very slender reserves which our banks carry, and the very small proportionate capital.

International comparisons and 'money trust' claims

Witnesses made some comparisons to the banking systems of other countries, generally the US, Canada, France, and, most often and usually favourably, Germany. Hambling praised the German system and claimed '... it will be necessary after the war to have these big institutions [i.e. banks similar to Germany's *Grossbanken*] to be able to compete with the fierce competition we shall meet with'. Foxwell contrasted German universal banks with British banks, suggesting 'We have carried specialising, I venture to think, rather too far. Everything is specialised here', and saw value in amalgamations which would result in less specialised institutions. Stoll viewed Germany very differently, arguing that 'four great German banks ... in partnership with the German Government ... keep that [German] population in shackles more complete than was serfdom in England in the age of Feudalism' and claimed the Pujo Committee had evidenced a similar situation in the US. Committee members questioned him sceptically and appear to have largely disregarded his evidence, although the Committee Report mentions the possibility that bank amalgamations could create a 'Money Trust' in Britain.

Stoll claimed that the trend to fewer, larger banks would drive a similar trend in industry, regardless of other factors. In his view 'The hundred or so directors of five banks are more or less closely bound up with concerns in Banking, Finance, Insurance, Shipping, Railways, Mining, Electricity etc.' and would tend to favour customers with whom board links existed. The only other witness to address the question of a 'Money Trust' directly was Holden, who rubbished Stoll's argument: 'Inter-locking directors are unknown in our banking world. A director of an English Bank is not permitted to sit on the Board of another English Bank, and no individual or Corporation is allowed to acquire a controlling interest in their stock'. At the time of the Committee bank directors usually did not hold full-time management roles. The business, educational, social, political, marital and other family connections of bank directors undoubtedly created a loose elite of gentlemanly capitalists in the Victorian era (Braggion & Moore, 2013; Cain & Hopkins, 2002; Daunton, 1992). Recent research suggests that directors of leading banks were central to corporate networks, but that directors from non-bank financial institutions increased their presence on corporate boards as the twentieth century progressed (Wilson, Buchnea, & Tilba, 2018). So while Holden may have been right about inter-bank interlocks, doubt remains about finance-industry links, or how this affected industrial finance.

Carnevali (2005) argued that some witnesses misrepresented German banking, ignoring the role of German regional banks and exaggerating the need for large banks to compete.[26] Fohlin (2002, pp. 248–251) saw strong similarities between British and German banking: similar levels of concentration from around 1890, with a surge during and after World War One, suggesting that concentration was a natural tendency in banking regardless of the dominance of universal or more specialised banks. Burhop (2006, p. 57) reinforces this view, arguing that the development of large joint-stock credit banks in Germany had beneficial effects in diversifying risk across regions and industrial sectors. As Table 1 indicates, the US was an exception, where regulation constrained branch banking and diversification, resulting in a fragmented system with thousands of unit banks, contributing to instability (Calomiris & Haber, 2014).

Conclusions

The discussion and the findings of the Committee reveal that the banking sector that had emerged by 1918 had reached a level of systematic maturity, with many essential features that endure into the present. The sector was dominated by a small number of large banks formed from amalgamations. As such, the development of the system exhibited hysteresis – there could be no return to the system as it had been composed in the nineteenth century. However, the secular process that had led to that position in turn aroused policy-concerns about the desirability and efficacy of a consolidated and concentrated banking system, and it was these that the Committee sought to address.

The discourse of the Committee reveals that the British banking sector had changed. The simultaneous expression of both too-big-to-fail and too-small-to-survive arguments in relation to bank size, concerns about declines in capital ratios, alongside the implicit – and to some extent explicit – acknowledgement that the state (government and Bank of England) was the ultimate guarantor of the system were indicative of awareness of that change – and reflected some concern about its implications. This reveals an awareness of the moral-hazard concerns that persist into the present in relation to who carries the systemic risks of a banking sector dominated by a small number of systemically-important large banks.

The arguments for big banks were given as scalar benefits, greater managerial depth, enhanced services for industrial clients, enhanced competition, national rather than regional coverage and international competitiveness. These were set against the inverse for small banks: they lacked scale, managerial depth, and national coverage (but rather operated cosy regional oligopolies/cartels), could not offer services clients needed, and were not internationally competitive. For some witnesses amalgamation was necessary to rescue small banks, and was also the easiest means of expansion for larger banks. These arguments were, at one level, entirely self-serving since they represented the organisational rationale for many of the larger banks. However, they also reflected the ways in which the sector had developed. This shows the ways in which historical actors operate within a bounded episteme: this was the world as they understood it to be, but also revealed that the sector had reached a saturated level of concentration.

There is nuance in understanding what the interests of bankers and banks might be, individually and collectively. Even though further amalgamation might benefit a bank (or banks) that might become even bigger, it would potentially lead to a monopoly seen as undesirable from a free-market perspective and stimulate calls for nationalisation by a future socialist Labour government –something that the financial elites certainly wished to forestall. So the Committee did arrive at conclusions that were not unequivocally in the interests of bankers. Any further mergers in the sector were to be approved by the Treasury and the Board of Trade, thereby terminating the amalgamation movement as an organic and unregulated process. Thereafter, any amalgamations took place within a governmental and regulated context. This substantial change reflected a turn away from *laissez faire* and towards more interventionist roles for both government and also, in a supervisory context, the Bank of England. As such, the banks now accepted limits on their actions.

Acknowledgements

The authors thank the editors of this special issue and the two referees. Earlier versions of this article were presented at the 2018 conferences of the Association of Business Historians, the Business History Conference, and the Economic and Business History Society, and the authors thank participants for their many comments.

Notes

1. See, for example, the recent meta-analyses of post-World War Two studies by Arestis, Chortareas, and Magkonis (2015), and Valickova, Havranek, and Horvath (2015). See also Fohlin (2016, pp. 423–425) and Levine (1997).
2. Levine (2002) reached a broadly similar conclusion in a study based on data from 48 countries covering the period 1980–1995.
3. The banking sector was exceptional in that amalgamations proceeded earlier and more rapidly than in other sectors of the British economy. See Hannah (1983).
4. The database/dataset used to construct the figures which appear in this article is that which two of the co-authors of this article have drawn on in two previous articles in this journal which describe the sources and methodology (Garnett et al., 2015, 2017). These data were collected as part of the Tipping Points project at Durham University funded by the Leverhulme Trust, grant number F/00128/BF. The data sources are Moore (1992) and Anonymous (2009). Bond (2016) presents similar data for the period 1790–1982 rather than 1810–2008. He uses similar sources but a different methodology to determine which banks to include in his data.
5. For example, the head office of Lloyds was in Birmingham until 1902, with joint head offices in Birmingham and London from 1902 to 1912, and then London only from 1912 (Sayers, 1957, pp. 261–263, 289).
6. Carnevali (2005) and Scott and Newton (2007), for example, argue that banks were uncompetitive in their lending and deposit rates, were excessively conservative, failed to provide long-term capital to industry, demanded unreasonable security from borrowers, and generally exploited their 'cartel' to enjoy a quiet and comfortable life. But British banking enjoyed relative interwar stability when many other countries experienced severe problems: Billings and Capie (2011) and Grossman (1994).
7. O'Sullivan (2016) has recently argued that evidence of a money trust in the US was exaggerated.
8. Colwyn's business interests were mainly in rubber and cotton. He was a director of the Lancashire and Yorkshire Bank from 1912 and its chairman from June 1919. He was a member of various other official committees: the Treasury Committee on [wartime munitions] Contracts set up in 1918; chair of standing committees on contracts and stores established in response to that Committee's report; chair of the Royal Commission on Income Tax, 1919–20; chair of the Committee on National Debt and Taxation, set up in 1924 which reported in 1927; and

chair of the 1924–5 Committee on Navy, Army, and Air Force Expenditure (Chandler, 1968, pp. 574–575; Peden, 2000, p. 117; Sayers, 1976, p. 237).

9. Webb, for example, stated in his evidence that he 'did not proffer myself as a witness'.
10. The purpose of this committee was to consider issues relating to post-World War One monetary and exchange rate arrangements.
11. The typed transcripts of the witnesses' oral evidence total 280 pages and are available in the UK's National Archives. The original source of all the evidence given to the Committee is The National Archives, Kew, London (hereafter 'TNA'), file T1/12267/50326. The evidence of individual witnesses varied considerably in length: the mean page length per witness is 13 pages and the median 11. The shortest evidence, only two pages, came from the London Stock Exchange chairman, whereas that of Sir Edward Holden runs to 34 pages. Some witnesses read a prepared statement before questioning, others simply responded to Committee members' questions. Several (including Bell and Beaumont Pease) commented on having been called to testify at short notice, some even the same day. For most witnesses only one version of their evidence is on file. Occasionally a second with minor handwritten amendments can be found. There are also occasional references to unminuted confidential statements and Webb referred to having submitted a memorandum but none is on file. It is unclear why the evidence remained unpublished; the file contains correspondence with various witnesses asking them to confirm the transcripts of their evidence and whether they would object to publication. Their usual answer was that they did not.
12. TNA, T1/12313/17061 and T1/12313/17061/40169; also see discussion in Sayers (1976, pp. 237–241).
13. TNA, T1/12325/20697/18509; Grieves (2008). Gaspard Farrer of Barings, another Committee witness, served as an alternate to Lord Inchcape when the latter was in ill-health (TNA, T1/12325/20697/23401).
14. Bank of England Archive, London (hereafter 'BoE'), G1/9.
15. Ackrill & Hannah, 2001, pp. 81–85; Jones, 1993, pp. 141–142; Sayers, 1976, pp. 244–245; BoE, G1/9, and G1/10; TNA, T160/711/F6070 and T160/805/F11588.
16. See, for example, Berger, Klapper, and Turk-Ariss (2009) and Goetz, Laeven, and Levine (2016).
17. Carnevali (2005) regarded this argument as spurious on the grounds that, as noted in footnote 3, bank amalgamations preceded those in other sectors of the economy.
18. Newton (1996, p. 74) discusses a similar example and its consequences: the heavy exposure of the Sheffield Union Bank to Naylor, Vickers & Co.
19. His own bank amalgamated with a member of the London Clearing House, Martins, in 1919.
20. See Larson, Ward, and Wilson (2010) on the latter.
21. See Gregory (1936, pp. 32, 34, and 122) on the failed amalgamations of the Manchester and Liverpool District and Lloyds and the Lancashire and Yorkshire and Parr's in 1903 and 1910 respectively.
22. Webb was involved in drafting the Labour party's constitution in 1917 and wrote the party's object (Clause IV) seeking 'the common ownership of the means of production, distribution and exchange and control of each industry or service' (Davis, 2004).
23. Webb drafted the 1918 Labour manifesto which called for land nationalisation, a capital levy and 'the immediate nationalisation and democratic control of vital public services, such as mines, railways, shipping, armaments and electric power' (Craig, 1970, p. 56). The party did not commit itself to the nationalisation of banks until the 1931 manifesto: 'The Labour Party is convinced, in the light particularly of experience since 1925, that the banking and credit system of the country can no longer be left in private hands. It must be brought directly under central ownership and control' (ibid., 69–70). In 1926 a private member's bill for nationalisation of the Bank of England failed (Hennessy, 1992, p. 206).
24. Hambling was a member of the Financial Advisory Committee appointed to advise the wartime Ministry of Munitions (TNA, IR74/229).
25. Turner has recently evidenced the reduction in capital as the amalgamation movement progressed (Turner, 2014, p. 129, Table 5.10 and p. 133, Figure 5.2).
26. See also Lehmann (2014) on the relationship between universal banks and regional joint-stock banks in stock market IPOs.

Disclosure statement

No potential conflict of interest was reported by the authors.

References

Acheson, G. G., & Turner, J. D. (2008). The death blow to unlimited liability in Victorian Britain: The city of Glasgow failure. *Explorations in Economic History*, *45*(3), 235–253. doi:10.1016/j.eeh.2007.10.001

Ackrill, M., & Hannah, L. (2001). *Barclays: The business of banking 1690–1996*. Cambridge: Cambridge University Press.

Alhadeff, D. A. (1968). *Competition and controls in banking: A study of the regulation of bank competition in Italy, France and England*. Berkeley, CA: University of California Press.

Allen, F., & Gale, D. (2000). *Comparing financial systems*. Cambridge, MA: MIT Press,

Anonymous (2009). Bankers' Almanac. East Grinstead: Reed Business Information.

Arestis, P., Chortareas, G., & Magkonis, G. (2015). The financial development and growth nexus: A meta-analysis. *Journal of Economic Surveys*, *29*(3), 549–565. doi:10.1111/joes.12086

Baker, M., & Collins, M. (2002). English commercial bank stability, 1860-1914. *Journal of European Economic History*, *31*(3), 493–512.

Barnes, V., & Newton, L. (2018). How far does the apple fall from the tree? The size of English bank branch networks in the nineteenth century. *Business History*, *60*(4), 447–473. doi:10.1080/00076791.2017.1323883

Berger, A. N., Klapper, L. F., & Turk-Ariss, R. (2009). Bank competition and financial stability. *Journal of Financial Services Research*, *35*(2), 99–118. doi:10.1007/s10693-008-0050-7

Best, M. H., & Humphries, J. (1986). The city and industrial decline. In B. Elbaum & W. Lazonick (Eds.), *The decline of the British economy* (pp. 223–239). Oxford: Clarendon Press.

Billings, M., & Capie, F. H. (2011). Financial crisis, Contagion, and the British banking system between the world wars. *Business History*, *53*(2), 193–215. doi:10.1080/00076791.2011.555105

Bond, I. (2016). The British banking population: 1790-1982. In M. Hollow, F. Akinbami, & R. Michie (Eds.), *Complexity and crisis in the financial system: Critical perspectives on the evolution of American and British banking* (pp. 85–117). Cheltenham: Edward Elgar Publishing.

Braggion, F., Dwarkasing, N., & Moore, L. (2017). Nothing special about banks: Competition and bank lending in Britain, 1885 to 1925. *The Review of Financial Studies*, *30*(10), 3502–3537. doi:10.1093/rfs/hhx044

Braggion, F., & Moore, L. (2013). The economic benefits of political connections in late Victorian Britain. *The Journal of Economic History*, *73*(1), 142–176. doi:10.1017/S0022050713000053

Burhop, C. (2006). Did banks cause the German industrialisation. *Explorations in Economic History*, *43*(1), 39–63. doi:10.1016/j.eeh.2005.04.005

Button, R., Knott, S., Macmanus, C., & Willison, M. (2015). Desperate adventurers and men of straw: The failure of city of Glasgow Bank and its enduring impact on the UK banking system. *Bank of England Quarterly Bulletin*, *55*(1), 23–35.

Cain, P. J., & Hopkins, A. G. (2002). *British imperialism 1688–2000*. London: Pearson Education.

Calomiris, C. W., & Haber, S. (2014). *Fragile by design: The political origins of banking crises and scarce credit*. Princeton, NJ: Princeton University Press,

Capie, F. H. (2016). Trust, financial regulation, and growth. *Australian Economic History Review, 56*(1), 100–112. doi:10.1111/aehr.12082

Capie, F. H., & Collins, M. (1999a). Banks, industry and finance 1860–1914. *Business History, 41*(1), 37–62. doi:10.1080/00076799900000201

Capie, F. H., & Collins, M. (1999b). Organisational control and English commercial bank lending to industry in the decades before world war one. *Revista de Historia Económica/Journal of Iberian and Latin American Economic History, 1*, 187–210. doi:10.1017/S0212610900007618

Capie, F. H., & Rodrik-Bali, G. (1982). Concentration in British banking, 1870–1920. *Business History, 24*(3), 280–292. doi:10.1080/00076798200000052

Capie, F. H., & Webber, A. (1985). *A Monetary history of the United Kingdom, 1870–1982: Data, sources, methods* (Vol. 1). London: George Allen & Unwin.

Carlin, W., & Mayer, C. (2003). Finance, investment, and growth. *Journal of Financial Economics, 69*(1), 191–226. doi:10.1016/S0304-405X(03)00112-0

Carnevali, F. (2005). *Europe's advantage: Banks and small firms in Britain, France, Germany and Italy since 1918*. Oxford: Oxford University Press.

Chandler, G. (1968). *Four centuries of Banking. The northern constituent banks* (Vol. 2). London: B.T. Batsford Ltd.

Chennells, L., & Wingfield, V. (2015). Bank failure and bail-in: An introduction. *Bank of England Quarterly Bulletin, 55*(3), 228–241.

Collins, M. (1998). English bank development within a European context, 1870-1939. *The Economic History Review, 51*(1), 1–24. doi:10.1111/1468-0289.00081

Collins, M., & Baker, M. (2001a). English commercial bank liquidity, 1860-1913. *Accounting, Business and Financial History, 11*(2), 171–191. doi:10.1080/713757309

Collins, M., & Baker, M. (2001b). Sectoral differences in English bank asset structures and the impact of mergers, 1860-1913. *Business History, 43*(4), 1–28. doi:10.1080/713999245

Collins, M., & Baker, M. (2003). *Commercial banks and industrial finance in England and Wales, 1860-1913*. Oxford: Oxford University Press.

Craig, F. W. S. (1970). *British general election manifestos, 1918–1966*. Chichester: Political Reference Publications.

Crick, W. F., & Wadsworth, J. E. (1936). *A hundred years of joint stock banking*. London: Hodder and Stoughton.

Daunton, M. (1992). Financial elites and British society, 1880–1950. In Y. Cassis (Ed.), *Finance and financiers in European history, 1880–1960* (pp. 121–146). Cambridge: Cambridge University Press.

Davis, J. (2004). Webb [née Potter], (Martha) Beatrice (1858–1943) and Sidney James Webb, Baron Passfield (1859–1947). In *Oxford dictionary of national biography*. Oxford: Oxford University Press. Online edition. http://www.oxforddnb.com/view/article/36799. Accessed 3 May 2017.

Dymski, G. A. (2012). Financial mergers and acquisitions: From regulation to strategic repositioning to geo-economics. In D. Faulkner, S. Teerikangas, & R. J. Joseph (Eds.), *The Oxford handbook of mergers and acquisitions* (pp. 566–592). Oxford: Oxford University Press.

Elbaum, B., & Lazonick, W. (1984). The decline of the British economy: An institutional perspective. *The Journal of Economic History, 44*(2), 567–583. doi:10.1017/S0022050700032149

Elbaum, B., & Lazonick, W. (1986). An institutional perspective on British decline. In B. Elbaum & W. Lazonick (Eds.), *The decline of the British economy* (pp. 1–17). Oxford: Clarendon Press.

Fohlin, C. (2002). Regulation, taxation and the development of the German universal banking system, 1884–1913. *European Review of Economic History, 6*(2), 221–254. doi:10.1017/S1361491602000096

Fohlin, C. (2016). Financial systems. In C. Diebolt & M. Haupert (Eds.), *Handbook of cliometrics* (pp. 393–430). Berlin: Springer-Verlag,

Garnett, P., Mollan, S., & Bentley, R. A. (2015). Complexity in history: Modelling the organisational demography of the British banking sector. *Business History, 57*(1), 181–201.

Garnett, P., Mollan, S., & Bentley, R. A. (2017). Banks, births, and tipping points in the historical demography of British banking: A response to J.J. Bissell. *Business History, 59*(5), 814–820. doi:10.1080/00076791.2017.1301429

Gerschenkron, A. (1962). *Economic backwardness in historical perspective: A book of historical essays*. Cambridge, MA: Harvard University Press.

Goetz, J. C., Laeven, L., & Levine, R. (2016). Does the geographic expansion of banks reduce risk? *Journal of Financial Economics, 120*(2), 346–362. doi:10.1016/j.jfineco.2016.01.020

Goldsmith, R. W. (1969). *Financial structure and development*. New Haven, CT: Yale University Press.

Gregory, T. E. (1936). *The Westminster Bank: Through a century* (Vol. 2). London: Westminster Bank Limited.

Grieves, K. (2008). Mackay, James Lyle, first Lord Inchcape (1852–1932). In *Oxford dictionary of national biography*. Oxford: Oxford University Press. Online edition. http://www.oxforddnb.com/view/article/34741. Accessed 23 December 2016.

Grossman, R. S. (1994). The shoe that didn't drop: Explaining banking stability during the great depression. *The Journal of Economic History, 54*(3), 654–682. doi:10.1017/S0022050700015072

Grossman, R. S. (1999). Rearranging deck chairs on the Titanic: English banking concentration and efficiency, 1870–1914. *European Review of Economic History, 3*(3), 323–349. doi:10.1017/S1361491699000155

Grossman, R. S. (2010). *Unsettled account: The evolution of banking in the industrialized world since 1800*. Princeton, NJ: Princeton University Press.

Grossman, R. S., & Imai, M. (2013). Contingent capital and bank risk-taking among British banks before the first world war. *Economic History Review, 66*(1), 132–155. doi:10.1111/j.1468-0289.2011.00638.x

Hannah, L. (1983). *The rise of the corporate economy* (2nd ed.). London: Methuen & Co.

Hannah, L. (2017). Banks and business finance before 1914: A comparative evaluation. In P. Di Martino, A. Popp, & P. Scott (Eds.), *People, places and business cultures: Essays in honour of Francesca Carnevali* (pp. 75–97). Woodbridge: The Boydell Press.

Hennessy, E. A. (1992). *A domestic history of the bank of England 1930–1960*. Cambridge: Cambridge University Press. doi:10.1086/ahr/99.4.1319

Ingham, G. K. (1984). *Capitalism divided? The city and industry in British social development*. London: Macmillan.

Jones, G. (1993). *British multinational banking 1830-1990*. Oxford: Oxford University Press.

Kynaston, D. (1999). *The city of London: Illusions of gold 1914-1945* (Vol. 3). London: Chatto and Windus.

Larson, M. J., Ward, K., & Wilson, J. F. (2010). Banking from Leeds, not London: Regional strategy and structure at the Yorkshire Bank, 1859-1952. *Accounting, Business and Financial History, 20*(2), 117–133. doi:10.1080/09585206.2010.485744

Lehmann, S. H. (2014). Taking firms to the stock market: IPOs and the importance of large banks in imperial Germany, 1896-1913. *Economic History Review, 67*(1), 92–122. doi:10.1111/1468-0289.12016

Levine, R. (1997). Financial development and economic growth: Views and agenda. *Journal of Economic Literature, 35*(2), 688–726.

Levine, R. (2002). Bank-based or market-based financial systems: Which is better? *Journal of Financial Intermediation, 11*(4), 398–428. doi:10.1006/jfin.2002.0341

Levine, R., & Zervos, S. (1998). Stock markets, banks and economic growth. *American Economic Review, 88*(3), 537–558.

Moore, C. (1992). *The bankers' almanac register of bank name changes & liquidations: Amalgamations, absorptions, and liquidations of international banks since 1750*. London: Reed Information Services.

Newton, L. A. (1996). Regional bank-industry relations during the mid-nineteenth century: Links between bankers and manufacturing in Sheffield, c. 1850 to c.1885. *Business History, 38*(3), 64–83. doi:10.1080/00076799600000095

Newton, L. (2003). Government, the banks and industry in inter-war Britain. In T. Gourvish (Ed.), *Business and politics in Europe, 1900-1970: Essays in honour of Alice Teichová* (pp. 145–168). Cambridge: Cambridge University Press.

Newton, L. (2010). The birth of joint stock banking: England and New England compared. *Business History Review, 84*(1), 27–52. doi:10.1017/S0007680500001239

Nicholls, D. (1988). Fractions of capital: The aristocracy, the city and industry in the development of modern British capitalism. *Social History, 13*(1), 71–83. doi:10.1080/03071028808567702

O'Sullivan, M. A. (2016). *Dividends of development: Corporate America: Securities markets in the history of US capitalism, 1866–1922*. Oxford: Oxford University Press.

Peden, G. C. (2000). *The Treasury and British public policy, 1906-1959*. Oxford: Oxford University Press.

Peters, J. (1993). The British government and the city-industry divide: The case of the 1914 financial crisis. *Twentieth Century British History*, *4*(2), 126–148. doi:10.1093/tcbh/4.2.126

Rajan, R. G., & Zingales, L. (1998). Financial dependence and growth. *American Economic Review*, *88*(3), 559–586.

Ross, D. M. (1990). The clearing banks and industry—New perspectives on the inter-war years. In J. J. van Helten & Y. Cassis (Eds.), *Capitalism in a mature economy: Financial institutions, capital exports and British industry, 1870–1939* (pp. 52–70). Aldershot: Edward Elgar.

Ross, D. M. (1996). Commercial banking in a market-oriented financial system: Britain between the wars. *Economic History Review*, *44*(2), 314–335. doi:10.2307/2597918

Sayers, R. S. (1957). *Lloyds Bank in the history of English banking*. London: Oxford University Press.

Sayers, R. S. (1976). *The Bank of England 1891-1944* (Vol. 3). Cambridge: Cambridge University Press. doi:10.1086/ahr/83.2.442

Scott, P., & Newton, L. (2007). Jealous monopolists? British banks and responses to the Macmillan gap during the 1930s. *Enterprise and Society*, *8*(04), 881–919. doi:10.1093/es/khm104

Sykes, J. (1926). *The amalgamation movement in English banking, 1825–1924*. London: P.S. King and Son.

Tomlinson, J. (2009). Thrice denied: "Declinism" as a recurrent theme in British history in the long twentieth century. *Twentieth Century British History*, *20*(2), 227–251. doi:10.1093/tcbh/hwp019

Treasury Committee on Bank Amalgamations (1918). Parliamentary papers (Report Cmnd. 9052). London: His Majesty's Stationery Office.

Turner, J. D. (2014). *Banking in crisis: The rise and fall of British banking stability, 1800 to the present*. Cambridge: Cambridge University Press.

Valickova, P., Havranek, T., & Horvath, R. (2015). Financial development and economic growth: A meta-analysis. *Journal of Economic Surveys*, *29*(3), 506–526. doi:10.1111/joes.12068

Wilson, J. F., Buchnea, E., & Tilba, A. (2018). The British corporate network, 1904–1976: Revisiting the finance-industry relationship. *Business History*, *60*(6), 779–806. doi:10.1080/00076791.2017.1333106

Corporate networks in post-war Britain: Do finance–industry relationships matter for corporate borrowing?

Philipp Kern and Gerhard Schnyder

ABSTRACT

The relationship between interlocking directorates and corporate finance patterns is a widely-researched aspect of the literature on national financial systems. This literature often considers the United Kingdom to be analogous to the United States, without directly investigating the nature and impact of finance–industry relationships. Based on a hand-collected data set covering eight benchmark years between 1950 and 2010, the authors start filling this gap by combining historical narratives, social network analysis, and regression analysis. They investigate whether finance–industry relations affect corporate borrowing patterns differently across time periods. The authors find that network-embedding had an impact on corporate borrowing from the 1950s to 1970s, but not thereafter. They also find that network structure and its function do not always evolve in parallel, highlighting limitations of purely structural approaches to understanding the link between corporate networks and firm behaviour and the importance of the historical idiosyncrasies of each country case.

1. Introduction

The United Kingdom occupies a special place in the literature on national financial systems. Alexander Gerschenkron's (1962) seminal book explained the emergence of universal banking systems as a strategy of late industrialising nations to substitute banks for financial markets to catch up with early industrialisers. This elevated the UK – as the first industrialiser – to the status of a benchmark with a heavily market-based financial system, where firms rely on financing through well-capitalised stock markets or by issuing bonds, with bank lending playing a minor role.

While this early work saw the UK as a fairly unique case, more recent research in the comparative capitalism and law and finance tradition tends to describe it as a generic market-based financial system akin to that of the US, Canada, and other Anglo-Saxon economies (Bordo & Sylla, 1995; Hall & Soskice, 2001; La Porta, Lopez-de-Silanes, Shleifer, & Vishny, 1998; Whitley, 2007). A problematic consequence of treating the UK as a generic liberal system is that insights on finance–industry relationships generated elsewhere – often the US – are frequently assumed also to apply to the UK without empirical investigation.

Furthermore, the literature's common distinction between bank-based and market-based systems may obscure the more important underlying aspect of long-term versus short-term financing of corporations. Although bank loans are typically an important source of long-term finance in some countries, financial markets too can provide 'patient capital' (Deeg, Hardie, & Maxfield, 2016). Therefore, in this article we focus on long-term borrowing by corporations – as opposed to short-term financing – rather than the narrower aspect of long-term bank lending.

A central characteristic of finance–industry relationships is interlocking directorates, ie the links created between firms by directors who sit on multiple boards. Such interlocks have been shown to affect lending and corporate finance: banks lend more to firms they have board interlocks with and, conversely, firms with ties to banks borrow more (Davis & Mizruchi, 1999; Mizruchi & Stearns, 1994; Mizruchi, Stearns, & Marquis, 2006). Research has confirmed this relationship in countries as disparate as the US and Germany, suggesting that it holds true not just across Anglo-Saxon countries, but across financial systems. Yet, the historically unique development of the British financial system should cast doubt on generalisations in this regard. Indeed, recent research on the history of banking systems (Fohlin, 2012) reasserts the uniqueness of the UK's model, including the rarity of interlocking directorates between finance and industry (see also Windolf & Nollert, 2001), which starkly contrasts with continental European cases such as Germany (Fohlin, 2007) and Italy (Vasta, Drago, Ricciuti, & Rinaldi, 2017). This raises questions over the evolution of finance–industry relationships over time and whether they have the same effect on bank lending and corporate borrowing in the UK as in other countries. We therefore seek to answer the following research questions related to finance–industry ties and a more general network effect on corporate borrowing:

Do direct and indirect finance–industry ties affect levels of corporate borrowing?

Does the borrowing behaviour of network neighbours affect corporate borrowing?

Prior research on the UK company network in general and finance–industry relations in particular tends either only to provide snapshots of interlocking directorates (Scott, 1987) or simply to describe trends over time, inferring their impact on borrowing patterns, if at all, from historical accounts rather than using firm-level accounting data to conduct more formal tests (Schnyder & Wilson, 2014; Wilson, Buchnea, & Tilba, 2017; Windolf & Nollert, 2001). Braggion (2005) investigates the impact of board interlocks and proximity to banks on firm performance more directly, but only for a short period at the turn of the twentieth century. As the impact of interlocks on corporate finance behaviour may change over time (Mizruchi et al., 2006), such indirect and cross-sectional approaches are unsatisfactory. We fill this gap by providing, to our knowledge, the first systematic and longitudinal analysis for the UK of the relationship between a company's embedding in the interlocking directorate network and its use of long-term debt to finance its operations. We attempt to answer the following additional research question regarding the temporal nature of network functionality:

Does the effect of network ties change over time, in particular as financial firm strategies and non-financial companies' corporate finance strategies evolve?

Our work can therefore be situated as part of a 'second generation' of research on interlocking directorates (Cronin, 2011), which seeks to empirically investigate network effects on firm behaviour in order to address more fully the 'so what?' question (Mizruchi, 1996).[1]

We apply a mixed methods approach that combines exploratory social network analysis with regression analysis to understand both the structure and the function of finance–industry ties in Britain between 1950 and 2010. Our data set consists of the 50 largest financial firms and 200 largest non-financial firms in eight census years across the period.

We make three contributions to research in this area. First, we provide what is to our knowledge the most in-depth account of post-war finance–industry relationships in the UK to date. Second, we go beyond mapping and describing the network patterns by empirically testing whether corporate borrowing is related to interlocking directorates. Our results suggest that British corporate finance patterns are related to board interlocks only in historically exceptional circumstances, suggesting a less relationship-based system than that of the US. The UK should therefore not be seen as a generic market-based financial system. Third, our results hint at the importance of going beyond a purely structural analysis of corporate networks by investigating their effect. We find evidence of changes in the impact of network ties on corporate finance patterns over time that are not paralleled by changes in the network's structural features. We also find phases where the network structure changes, but the effect of network ties on borrowing remains the same. Beyond our country case, this highlights the need to understand corporate networks as well as national financial systems in historical and geographical context.

2. Theory: the role of interlocking directorates in corporate finance

The role of board-level links between finance and industry has been debated since the beginning of the twentieth century. American politicians and commentators at the time were concerned with the outsized influence of bankers, who were seen to create a 'money monopoly' or 'money trust' to tightly control access to capital via interlocking directorates. Although such fears have abated, the centrality of financial institutions in corporate networks has been confirmed for most developed countries (Davis & Mizruchi, 1999; Vasta & Baccini, 1997; Windolf, 2009; Windolf & Nollert, 2001) as well as some developing countries (eg Musacchio & Read, 2007). Research has focused on the effects of bank centrality, in particular lending patterns and corporate finance behaviours (Mintz & Schwartz, 1985a), and whether having bankers on the board has a positive or negative effect on the firm. This section provides an overview of these debates.

The literature differentiates two views of the purpose of finance–industry interlocks. The resource dependence approach (Selznick, 1949) sees organisations as co-opting financiers on to their boards in order to establish personal relationships and secure access to key resources. A related view holds that companies co-opt bankers on to their boards to acquire financial expertise – particularly before the professionalisation of the in-house finance function since the 1970s (Mizruchi et al., 2006).

A second approach sees interlocks not as co-optation, but as a mechanism to monitor or control an organisation (Mizruchi, 1996). In this view, bankers sit on the board of companies they lend to in order to monitor their credit lines – which is of particular importance in capital-intensive industries (Windolf, 2009). There are several flavours of this approach. A more extreme version is the 'bank control thesis', suggesting that banks use board seats to extract rents through asset stripping and similar strategies (Fitch & Oppenheimer, 1970; Kotz, 1978). The more moderate variant, the 'bank hegemony' model (Mintz & Schwartz, 1985b), acknowledges banks' power but sees them exercising it through guidance and boundary setting for managerial action rather than overt control. Here, board interlocks are primarily understood as a communication mechanism (Mizruchi, 1996). Whichever view one subscribes to, the implication of finance–industry interlocks is that they influence non-financial companies' finance patterns by facilitating access to debt and providing financial expertise.

Several studies have empirically investigated these claims. They found that corporate finance patterns are shaped by the kind of bankers companies have on their boards: investment bankers are associated with bond issues and commercial bankers with short-term debt (Mizruchi & Stearns, 1994; Stearns & Mizruchi, 1993). Some research suggests that industrial companies actively seek to appoint bankers to their boards when they are in financial difficulties (Davis & Mizruchi, 1999; Mizruchi & Stearns, 1988), thereby increasing the availability of short-term funding (Richardson, 1987; Stearns, 1986). Similarly, Ratcliff (1980) has shown that banks with more network ties tend to lend more to industry, while those with fewer ties tend to specialise in the mortgage market, suggesting that bank–industry ties increase non-financial firms' access to finance.

Recent contributions have sought to understand when finance–industry links are best understood from a resource dependence, bank hegemony, or bank control perspective. Evidence suggests that access to finance via board interlocks can substitute for well-developed financial markets, making personal relationships an important resource in emerging economies to access finance at all (Musacchio, 2009), or on preferential conditions (Kroszner & Strahan, 2001; Laeven, 2001; Rajan & Zingales, 1998). Rubio-Mondéjar and Garrués-Irurzun (2016) show how institutional weakness in Spain allowed banks to use board interlocks to consolidate power and limit economic competition.

Hence, despite different theoretical underpinnings, all theories suggest that stronger ties with financial firms will have a positive impact on borrowing in non-financial firms. Therefore, we hypothesise:

> ***Hypothesis 1:*** *The more a non-financial firm is interlocked with financial sector firms, the higher its level of borrowing.*

This hypothesis assumes a direct effect of finance–industry ties on firm-level finance patterns, ie borrowing is increased by a financier sitting on a firm's board or a person affiliated with the firm sitting on the financial firm's board. Yet, weak ties ('friend of a friend') may also have a more important impact by diffusing information or organisational practices via intermediaries (Granovetter, 1973), affecting behaviours related to mergers (Haunschild, 1993) or finance decisions (Mizruchi et al., 2006; Mizruchi & Stearns, 1994). This suggests a more general network effect than the one underlying Hypothesis 1, namely that even firms without direct banking ties may benefit from indirect ties with financial sector firms. In particular, the stronger a company's ties to firms that rely on debt, the more likely the company is to rely on debt financing as well (Mizruchi et al., 2006). We therefore hypothesise a more general network effect on borrowing patterns:

> ***Hypothesis 2:*** *The higher the use of debt among a firm's connections, the stronger the use of debt by the focal firm.*

The literature also suggests that both the structure and the function of finance–industry networks change over time. Changing corporate finance strategies and changing lending strategies of financial firms may affect the network structure via their propensity to interlock with each other. Evidence from the US in the 1980–1990s suggests that changes in board links with industrial firms followed a strategic reorientation of American banks from interest-based towards fees-based activities (Davis & Mizruchi, 1999). Similar effects have been found in other countries and periods, including the financial crisis of the 1920s leading Dutch banks to refocus their strategy from industry lending to trade finance, with a corresponding decline in network density (Westerhuis, 2014).

Much less studied, but theoretically just as important, is the changing impact of finance–industry links. Evidence for the US suggests that increasing professionalisation of banking and of the corporate finance function within firms has made personal relationships less important in recent decades (Mizruchi et al., 2006). A similar phenomenon may be observed in Britain, where the main financial centre – the City of London – has shifted from a distinctly informal, relationship, and trust-based form of 'gentlemanly capitalism' towards a highly professionalised global industry (Thompson, 1997). As we discuss in more detail in Section 3, the 1986 'big bang' financial market reforms led to British banks moving away from commercial lending while fostering new corporate strategies – such as shareholder value management – that privilege market-based approaches to financing over relationship-based ones (Deeg et al., 2016; Froud et al., 2006; van der Zwan, 2014). These trends imply a decline in the importance of relationships for corporate finance, leading us to hypothesise that finance–industry ties should matter more strongly before the 'big bang' reforms than thereafter:

> ***Hypothesis 3:*** *Network effects on corporate borrowing are stronger before the 1986 reforms than after.*

3. Historical context: key features of the British banking system

The City of London started to emerge as the dominant force in British banking towards the end of the nineteenth century after a wave of mergers created large joint stock banks with nationwide reach. While the larger resources and branch networks of these banking houses enabled a national market for short-term business finance, the centralisation of power in the London headquarters also eroded links with local business (Collins, 1995). Although the banks saw it as part of their function to provide funding to private enterprise (Cassis, 1985), they generally did so at a lower level and at shorter terms than their American, German, and Japanese counterparts (Kennedy, 1987). British commercial banks also stayed almost completely out of the investment banking business, avoiding taking long-term equity positions in industrial firms, which may also constitute a source of 'patient capital' for firms (Deeg et al., 2016). The sector was thus highly specialised, despite universal banking being allowed (Fohlin, 2012). Board-level interlocks between finance and industry were rare in this period, with only 9% of directors from the country's leading banks also sitting on industrial boards (Collins, 1995).

The lack of deep and long-term engagement with industry can be largely attributed to the historical development of British industry. As the first industrialising nation, the UK not only developed well-capitalised stock markets early on to provide funding to industry, but the success and size of British industrial firms of the time also allowed them to self-finance much of their activities (Gerschenkron, 1962). Universal banking with strong ties to industry is usually seen to have developed in late-industrialising countries as a means of accelerating industrial development (Chandler, 1990; Gerschenkron, 1962). Consequently, the British financial sector developed an outward orientation early on. By the inter-war era, 'gentlemanly capitalism' of the City of London – while reliant on informal relationships for its domestic business – was predominantly focused on overseas business, with merchant banks getting accused of being 'better informed on conditions in Latin America than in Lancashire or Scotland' (Cain & Hopkins, 1993, p. 19).

3.1. Turning inward: 1945–1980

World War II marked the beginning of a reorientation towards domestic activity, both in lending and stock market finance. Wartime capital export controls, sales of British overseas assets, and continued capital issue restrictions hastened the decline of London as a leading financial centre and depressed international demand for the City's services. By the late 1940s, about 90% of securities listed on the London stock exchange were domestic, compared with 8% in 1913 (Thomas, 1978). Merchant banks began to participate more fully in those issues and stock exchange reforms increased financial disclosure requirements for listed firms, making the City a more important provider of industry finance in the post-World War II era (Morgan & Thomas, 1962).

Bank lending to industry also expanded in scale and scope in this period. While bank borrowing accounted for just over half of all externally raised finance at the beginning of the 1960s, this proportion rose to almost two-thirds in the 1970s (Committee of London Clearing Bankers, 1978). This expansion occurred on the back of two factors. First, 1971 saw the relaxation of some credit controls that, until then, had aimed to reign in recurring inflation through restrictive macro-economic policy (Pollard, 1992). Although firms rarely used more than two-thirds of their short-term credit facilities (Thomas, 1978), the partial lifting of credit controls enabled more flexible and expansive approaches for lending.

The increased reliance of British industrial firms on bank borrowing may also reveal a trend that has been observed in the US, where slowing growth from the mid-1960s onwards reduced retained earnings and made companies more reliant on banks loans, leading to a stronger influence of American banks on industry (Davis & Mizruchi, 1999; Stearns, 1986). A similar process may have unfolded in the UK.

A second driver of increasing lending to industry was that the scope of bank lending expanded from providing little more than overdraft facilities and 'cash on call' to include medium-term credit alongside new services such as leasing and factoring. Leasing developed particularly rapidly in this time, with clearing banks emerging as the pre-eminent suppliers of these services by the mid-1970s (Committee of London Clearing Bankers, 1978). Indeed, contemporaneous sources suggest that there were few limits on bank lending in this period; if anything, the economic difficulties of the 1970s limited the take-up of widely available credit (Committee of London Clearing Bankers, 1978). Importantly, however, British banks still did not engage in the kind of long-term lending so common among their American, German, and Japanese counterparts.

Historical accounts suggest that the inward turn of British finance went together with a deepening of board-level links to industry. Some sources suggest that in 1976, 32 directors on the boards of the 50 largest industrial firms represented clearing banks (Utton, 1982), with others suggesting that 94 directors among those companies had ties to the City even if not necessarily representing a bank (Stanworth & Giddens, 1975). The expansion of board interlocks in this period arguably shows how City bankers on industrial boards 'were pivotal points in loose groupings of industrial, trading and financial enterprises ... act[ing], in effect, as proxies for the wider financial community; they act as the guardians of the interests of the hegemonic financials' (Scott, 1987, p. 60). These sources would therefore suggest that the deepening relationship between British finance and industry started to resemble the 'finance capital' (Hilferding, 1968) model in this post-war period.

3.2. Global reorientation: post-1980

After its election in 1979, the new Conservative government under Margaret Thatcher began a far-reaching programme of reforms and privatisations. It soon set its sights on liberalisation of financial markets, which were still subject to some of the restrictions put in place in the first half of the twentieth century. Financial market reform became a cornerstone of Thatcher's government programme, seeking to restore the City of London as the world's premier financial centre. This reform package came to be known as the 'big bang', as it went into effect in one fell swoop in 1986 and contained a number of significant changes. The London Stock Exchange (LSE) became one of the first major stock exchanges to move from 'open outcry' to computerised trading. Fixed minimum commissions were abolished, along with the 'single capacity rule' that had strictly separated the roles of brokers, acting as agents for investors, and jobbers, who made markets and provided liquidity by holding stocks (Konzelmann, Fovargue-Davies, & Schnyder, 2012; Lawson, 2006). It also removed access barriers, allowing non-member firms of the LSE – banks, insurance firms, and foreign investment banks – to trade directly.

Despite its primary aim of easing securities trading, the 'big bang' had knock-on effects on the wider British financial market. The late 1980s marked the end of the historically developed, yet never legally mandated, separation of deposit and merchant banking. While merchant banks had traditionally been highly risk-averse in their investments, made with their own funds, their behaviour changed dramatically after merging with retail banks as they now had access to larger deposits. British banks were also thrust into an increasingly globalised financial system, with American banks in particular emerging as competitors in Europe (Battilossi & Cassis, 2002; Sylla, 2002). Competitive pressure together with the computerisation of banking transformed European and British banks' strategic direction. In continental Europe, this meant a pronounced shift away from the historically deep relationship with domestic industry towards global engagement, investment banking, and generally higher levels of risk-taking (Larson, Schnyder, Westerhuis, & Wilson, 2011).

British banks followed suit, putting an end to the post-war engagement with domestic industry and returning to their historically rooted global orientation. As they moved away from commercial banking activities into fees-based and investment banking, small and medium-sized businesses bore the brunt of the retreat from industrial lending. This was particularly pronounced during the global financial crisis of 2008–2009, when the government went as far as committing the nation's five largest banks to a 'neo-corporatist bargain' (Financial Times, 2012; Jones & Cohen, 2012) aimed at expanding lending to businesses.

For large non-financial companies, on the other hand, the reforms of the 1980s and changing bank strategies presented less of a challenge. With changing corporate finance strategies in that period, large businesses became less dependent on bank financing.

Financial reforms as well as the 'financialisation' of the economy more generally (Froud et al., 2006; van der Zwan, 2014) meant that stock markets gained an entirely new significance for firms, exposing them to new pressures but also offering new opportunities for corporate finance – even 'financial engineering' (Froud et al., 2006; Lazonick & O'Sullivan, 2010).

Taken together, these trends transformed the financial landscape in Britain, reducing both the supply and demand of intermediated finance. Whereas British banks reluctantly turned towards domestic markets and industrial financing when left without choice in the war and post-war period, they were quick to abandon these markets as soon as regulatory constraints were removed and global competition intensified. In parallel, financial globalisation and innovation made large non-financial companies less and less dependent on financial intermediation to access sources of funding.

4. Data and methodology

We use a mixed methods approach that recognises the historically contingent nature of finance–industry relationships while also offering statistically robust evidence of the impact of board interlocks on corporate finance patterns. We investigate the relationships between non-financial companies and companies active in the financial sector, including banks and insurance companies as well as other financial services providers. This is because banks are not the only financial service firms providing non-financial firms with access to finance (eg Mizruchi et al., 2006). Insurance companies, for instance, have traditionally played an important – albeit in the UK limited – role in corporate finance through facilitating private placements of corporate bonds (Slaughter & May, 2014).

We focus on the period from 1950 to 2010, combining social network and regression analysis to investigate the impact of network interlocks between financial sector and non-financial firms on corporate borrowing. Our data set consists of the board composition of the 50 largest financial[2] and 200 largest non-financial firms by total assets in Britain in eight benchmark years across the period (1950, 1958, 1976, 1983, 1993, 1997, 2003, and 2010).[3]

To create the sample, we relied on *The Times 1000* list of the largest companies in the UK, lists compiled by other scholars (Fiedler & Gospel, 2010), and the *Thomson Reuters Datastream* database. We then used existing data sets on board composition (Conyon & Muldoon, 2006; Scott, 1987; Windolf & Nollert, 2001), which we supplemented with data from the *BoardEx* database and hand-collected data from the *Stock Exchange Official Yearbook (Macmillan)*.

In order to describe and interpret the corporate network topography we used exploratory social network analysis (de Nooy, Mrvar, & Batagelj, 2011). We calculated a series of network measures using the 'igraph' package for the *R* statistical software program, following the approach of David and Westerhuis (2014) in calculating various measures of network structure, cohesion, density, and firm-level network position. To describe the basic network structure and its cohesiveness we calculated the number of isolated firms (those without network ties), the number of marginal firms (with only one or two ties), and the size of the 'major component', ie the largest connected sub-graph in the network. We measured network density using the average degree measure, which is calculated as the number of ties divided by the number of firms in the network (Wasserman & Faust, 1994). We also calculated 'network distance' as a measure of the ease with which information or practices can flow across the network along network ties (de Nooy et al., 2011; Wasserman & Faust, 1994). This is defined as the average length (number of edges) of the shortest path between any two vertices (firms) in the network. Low values indicate a network in which information and practices flow quickly between different nodes. These measures of network topography are presented in Table 1.

We then computed various measures of firm centrality in the network including Freeman degree centrality, closeness centrality, and betweenness centrality in order to assess the position of different firms in the network. The centrality rankings, reported in Tables 2 and 5, are substantively the same using the three measures in so far as the sectoral composition of the top 10 companies does not substantially change. We therefore only report the results for the betweenness measure, which takes into account not only the focal company's connectedness and local centrality, but also its position in the network. Betweenness counts the number of times a node is on the shortest path between any pair of other nodes in the network. As such, it is often interpreted as a measure of brokerage and information control power (de Nooy et al., 2011).

4.1. Regression analysis: variables and models

To complement the descriptive, network-mapping part, we formally test our three hypotheses about the impact of network ties on borrowing by non-financial companies using regression analysis. To this effect, we specified the following variables and models.

4.1.1. Independent variables

To assess the impact of connectedness of non-financial firms to financial sector firms, we calculated a measure based on a company's proximity in the network to financial sector firms. This measure is based on the above-mentioned insight that having bankers or other financial sector executives on the board or, conversely, sending people affiliated with the company to sit on the board of a financial sector firm will facilitate access to finance through loans or bond issues. Yet, financial sector–industry ties do not need to be direct to have an impact on corporate finance, because even intermediated links will increase the ease with which loans can be obtained or debt issued (Granovetter, 1973; Mizruchi et al., 2006). Rather than measuring direct ties with financial companies, we calculate a measure of the sum of the distance (shortest path) of every non-financial firm in our sample from every financial firm. This is based on the distance matrix for each year, with higher values indicating larger distance from financial sector companies. We normalised this measure to vary between 0 and 1; its mean across all years is 0.27.[4]

To test our second hypothesis about the general network diffusion effect, we ran a network autoregressive model as suggested by Mizruchi et al. (2006) (see below). We replicated their independent variable, which is a measure of the network effect. This variable is calculated based on the normalised distance matrices for each yearly network. We then multiply the normalised distance score for each firm with the dependent variable, namely the level of

Table 1. Main measures of network topography.

	1950	1958	1976	1983	1993	1997	2000	2010
Isolated firms (% of total sample)	58.52	29.15	24.90	29.48	19.60	10.00	12.80	9.20
Marginal firms (%)	19.35	28.64	21.69	25.10	26.40	25.20	35.20	24.00
Firms in main component (%)	36.41	65.83	73.49	69.72	78.40	89.20	82.00	87.60
Average degree	1.29	3.73	4.15	3.04	3.63	4.25	3.39	3.90
Average distance	3.92	3.13	3.33	3.72	3.97	3.86	4.40	4.15

debt. This gives us a weighted debt measure, which consists essentially of the 'sum of the level of borrowing engaged in by each of a firm's network partners, weighted by the strength of the relations between the focal firm and the partners' (Mizruchi et al., 2006, p. 320). Mizruchi et al. (2006) carried out two additional transformations on the distance matrix, which we refrained from. First, they capped the maximum distance between two vertices at three. They justify this transformation by the fact that their data contained few observations of distances of greater than three and that the distribution of distances was skewed after three (Mizruchi et al., 2006, p. 321). Our data do not show this pattern. Indeed, quite a large number of distance scores are greater than three and the distances for each year before normalisation are approximately normally distributed with an average greater than three in each year. Therefore, we concluded that truncating would distort the real nature of our data. Similarly, Mizruchi et al. (2006) use the inverted values of the distance matrices (namely 1, 0.5, and 0.33 instead of 1, 2, 3) to facilitate interpretation of the coefficient. We prefer to keep the original values.

We assess the third hypothesis on the declining impact of network ties on corporate borrowing over time using the same models as above. If our expectations are correct, we would expect to find no or only weakly statistically significant relationships between network embedding and borrowing behaviour of non-financial firms in the post-1986 benchmark years.

4.1.2. Dependent variable and controls

Our hypotheses concern borrowing patterns of non-financial firms and in particular the extent to which they rely on long-term debt (as opposed to equity or retained earnings) to finance their operations. Given the longitudinal and historical nature of the study – and challenges arising from changes in accounting practices and data availability – we had to rely on simple measures. We used as our main dependent variable the amount of long-term debt divided by total assets. This variable corresponds with the most commonly used measure in similar studies, except that we use absolute levels instead of yearly changes as our data consist of benchmark years, not yearly data (cf. Mizruchi et al., 2006, p. 319). It is important to note that our dependent variable includes not only long-term loans maturing in more than one year's time, but also bond debentures. It excludes short-term loans. As such, it cannot be interpreted as a direct measure of bank lending, but rather as a measure of the extent of corporate debt finance, as opposed to equity or self-finance. This is in line with the focus in the comparative capitalism literature, which distinguishes debt finance-based from equity finance-based systems (Deeg et al., 2016; Hall & Soskice, 2001). We therefore consider this measure to be appropriate for the questions at hand.

We include the most commonly used control variables in similar studies (Kroszner & Strahan, 2001; Marquis, 2003; Mizruchi et al., 2006; Mizruchi & Stearns, 1994). We include industry dummies because debt levels may vary depending on an industry's fixed capital requirements and other industry-level factors (Talberg et al., 2008). Firm size, as measured by total assets, serves as a control because larger firms tend to have more collaterals and therefore an advantage in obtaining bank loans or issuing bonds. We also control for the ability to finance operations internally. As retained earnings are not reported for most years in our study, we use current assets as an approximation of a company's ability to generate cash via its working capital, of which current assets are an important part. Finally, we control for the extent of equity finance measured as nominal issued capital.

Similar studies use several additional controls, including a measure of financial health (eg interest coverage ratio), firm performance, number of employees, short-term debt (Kroszner &

Strahan, 2001), the type of ownership and control (Mizruchi & Stearns, 1994), and percentage of financial directors on the board (Mizruchi et al., 2006). We do not include any of these controls in our models given that most of these measures are either not available at all, or only in vastly inconsistent form over time, from the publicly available sources used. The limited sample size also meant that we refrained from estimating overly complex models. Descriptive statistics for our variables for all eight years are reported in the Appendix.

4.1.3. Statistical models

We first ran a simple linear regression model on the logged dependent variable to reduce heteroscedasticity problems:

$$Y = \boldsymbol{X}\beta + \varepsilon$$

where *Y* is our dependent variable (long-term debt divided by total assets), ***X*** is a vector of independent and control variables, β is the regression coefficient, and ε an error term.[5]

We also ran the autoregressive network linear model suggested by Mizruchi et al. (2006) to test our second hypothesis regarding a more general diffusion effect of finance practices:

$$Y = \rho WY + \boldsymbol{X}\beta + \varepsilon$$

where *Y* is the dependent variable as previously defined, ρ is the network effect coefficient, *W* is the square matrix of distances between firms, ***X*** is the matrix of independent variables, β is the vector of regression coefficients, and ε is an error term.

We estimated this model following Mizruchi et al. (2006, p. 325) by treating *WY* as a separate variable that is included in the matrix **X** on which we then ran ordinary least squares (OLS). This model constitutes an autoregressive model in the sense that the calculation of the **WY** matrix includes the dependent variable. While such a 'spatial OLS' (Franzese & Hays, 2004) approach has certain limitations regarding the independence of error terms, it has been shown that the estimates are not systematically biased due to the endogeneity issues compared with maximum likelihood estimations of the same model (see, for a discussion, Mizruchi et al., 2006).

5. Results and discussion

Historical research suggests that the post-war period was marked by a deepening relationship between British finance and industry, even beginning to take the shape of Continental-European-style 'finance capital' (Hilferding, 1968). Our own data on the network topography broadly support this view (see Table 1). The first three post-war decades from 1950 to 1976 were a phase of increasing network integration, which peaked sometime in the 1970s. Indeed, our census year 1976 is the one where all our network cohesion and centrality measures indicate the densest network during the period studied, and indeed for the entire twentieth century (cf. Schnyder & Wilson, 2014; Wilson et al., 2017).

The evolution of the basic network structure illustrates the increasing cohesiveness of the network, as illustrated by the decline of isolated and marginal firms (Table 1). Consequently, the size of the network of connected firms (major component) (from only 36% of firms in 1950 to about two-thirds thereafter) as well as its density, ie number of ties, increased throughout the period. The average degree of the network increased from a low level of 1.29 in 1950 to the highest observed level in 1976 (4.15), before dropping back to 3.04 in 1983. Similarly, network distance – the average length of the shortest path between two companies – is at its lowest in this period (3.13 in 1958). Our network measures also indicated that the second half of the 1970s marked the high watermark of the UK interlocks network. Indeed, between 1976 and 1983 the number of isolated firms increased again from 25% in 1976 to 29% in 1983 and the mean degree dropped from 4.15 in 1976 to 3.04 in 1983. The size of the main component declined from 73.49% to below 69.72%.

Concerning firms' position in the network, the key development during this period is the increasing centrality of banks and other financial sector firms. As Table 2 shows, seven out of the ten most central companies by betweenness centrality in 1950 were financial sector firms. This number rose to nine out of ten in 1958 and 1976. Our network data therefore support the notion that the City began to play a more important role in British industry in the post-war period, underpinned by more extensive board interlocks (Scott, 1987; Scott & Griff, 1985).

These descriptive results of network integration and their comparison with previous studies of the UK network (Schnyder & Wilson, 2014; Scott, 1987; Scott & Griff, 1985; Wilson et al., 2017; Windolf & Nollert, 2001) indicate that the UK company network was at its most cohesive and densest sometime during the period from the early 1950s to the mid-1970s.

Interpreting the increasing number of inter-company relations as an indicator of an increasingly well-integrated British business elite and a more relationship-based way of doing business, we would expect the impact of network ties on firm-level practices – such as patterns of corporate finance – to be strongest during this phase. We formally test this expectation by investigating whether there is a link between a given firm's interlocking patterns and its borrowing behaviour.

Table 3 summarises the results from the OLS estimation for our first period using the average distance of the focal firm from financial sector firms as independent variable. The results partly confirm our expectations, showing the expected and significant impact of the network embedding of a firm on its borrowing behaviour in 1976 when network density peaked. The significant and negative coefficient indicates that the further a company is from financial sector firms in terms of interlocks, the lower its level of debt will be. No such effect exists in 1958, when the network was still emerging, or in 1983, when it had started to decline again. The effect was even positive, albeit only very marginally significant (at the 0.1 level), in 1950. This lends support to the view that over the period 1950–1976 network ties became more important.[6]

Table 4 reports the results for the autoregressive network model investigating the network effect on firm debt levels.[7] For 1958, 1976, and 1983 the network effect is significant and shows the expected negative sign. These results suggest that a firm's financing practices are shaped by other companies it is connected to through its network. This effect is weaker the further removed the connected firms are, as the negative sign on the network coefficient suggests.

Interpreting these results substantively – how the network effect affects borrowing – is difficult, however, as being connected to a company that borrows much (little) does not necessarily have to mean that the focal firm borrows much (little) too. Rather, the network effect may have to do with financial expertise, which may mean that being connected to a firm with such expertise leads the focal firm to choose the 'right' level of debt for its particular circumstances, rather than simply emulating the other's financial choices (see Mizruchi et al., 2006). Therefore, the important point with these results is not so much whether connections lead to more or less borrowing, but that the position in the network does influence companies' borrowing behaviour for the two post-war benchmarks 1958 and 1976 and that the strength of the association increased between the 1950s and the 1970s.

The election of the Thatcher government in 1979 and the 'big bang' reforms in 1986 marked the beginning of a new phase in British banking and of new corporate finance

Table 2. Top 10 companies by betweenness centrality 1950–1983.

1950		1958		1976		1983	
Company	Sector	Company	Sector	Company	Sector	Company	Sector
William Cory & Son	Energy	Bank of London & South America Ltd	Financials (banking)	British Petroleum plc	Energy	Midland Bank	Financials (banking)
British Aluminium Company	Materials	National Commercial Bank of Scotland Ltd	Financials (banking)	Imperial Chemical Industries	Industrials	Hill Samuel Group	Financials (other)
Vickers	Industrials	P&O Steam Navigation Company	Transport	Guardian Royal Exchange Company	Financials (insurance)	Standard Chartered Bank	Financials (banking)
District Bank Ltd	Financials (banking)	District Bank Ltd	Financials (banking)	Hill Samuel Group	Financials (other)	National Westminster Bank	Financials (banking)
Glyn, Mills and Co.	Financials (banking)	Barclays Bank Ltd	Financials (banking)	Commercial Union	Financials (insurance)	Sun Alliance & London Insurance	Financials (insurance)
Alexander's Discount Company	Financials (other)	Royal Insurance Company	Financials (insurance)	Tube Investments	Financials (other)	Royal Insurance	Financials (insurance)
Lloyds Bank Ltd	Financials (banking)	Royal Exchange Assurance	Financials (insurance)	Midland Bank	Financials (banking)	Imperial Chemical Industries	Industrials
Guardian Assurance Company Ltd	Financials (insurance)	Lloyds Bank Ltd	Financials (banking)	Barclay's Bank	Financials (banking)	Rio Tinto-Zinc Corporation	Materials
Midland Bank Ltd	Financials (banking)	National Provincial Bank Ltd	Financials (banking)	NatWest Bank	Financials (banking)	Lloyds Bank	Financials (banking)
National Provincial Bank Ltd	Financials (banking)	Midland Bank Ltd	Financials (banking)	Lloyds Bank	Financials (banking)	Barclays Bank	Financials (banking)

Table 3. OLS estimates for corporate borrowing, 1950–1983.

Variables	1950	1958	1976	1983
Distance from financial company	0.539 (1.86)†	−0.172 (.28)	−0.369 (−2.28)*	0.017 (0.08)
Total assets	0.003 (0.18)*	0.007 (1.21)	0.001 (2.30)*	0.001 (2.43)*
Current assets	−0.018 (−1.73)†	−0.007 (−1.19)	−0.001 (−2.00)*	−0.001 (−1.72)†
Nominal capital	0.031 (0.71)	0.000 (−0.86)	0.000 (0.78)	
Manufacturing industry dummy	−0.550 (−0.51)	−2.018 (−1.72)†	−0.269 (−0.77)	0.592 (1.47)
Primary industry dummy	−1.066 (−0.70)	−3.141 (−2.19)*	0.105 0(.24)	0.996 (1.93)†
Service industry dummy	−0.86 (−0.78)	−2.477 (−2.08)*	−0.431 (−1.18)	0.402 (0.95)
Constant	−2.27 (−2.07)*	−0.570 (−0.48)	−1.768 (−5.14)***	−3.001 (−7.55)***
N	67	92	148	132
Adjusted R^2	0.07	0.03	0.11	0.05

Note: Data in parentheses are *t*-values.
†$p < .1$, *$p < .05$, **$p < .01$, ***$p < .001$.

Table 4. Spatial regression estimates of debt levels, 1958–1983.

Variables	1958	1976	1983
Network effect	−16.382 (−2.60)*	−102.192 (−2.93)**	−17.890 (−3.51)***
Total assets	0.008 (1.31)	0.001 (2.30)*	0.000 (1.81)†
Current assets	−0.006 (−0.94)	−0.001 (−2.18)*	−0.001 (−1.29)
Nominal capital	−0.013 (−1.03)	0.001 (0.81)	
Manufacturing industry dummy		0.054 (0.182)	0.863 (1.96)†
Primary industry dummy	−1.004 (−1.17)	0.231 (0.613)	1.18 (2.13)†
Service industry dummy	0.120 (0.23)	0.064 (0.20)	0.760 (1.63)
Constant	−1.743 (−4.14)***	8.470 (2.33)*	1.366 (2.67)**
N	67	111	104
Adjusted R^2	0.06	0.14	0.16

Note: Data in parentheses are *t*-values.
†$p < .1$, *$p < .05$, **$p < .01$, ***$p < .001$.

strategies. Our own results on the evolution of the corporate network support this notion. The four post-'big bang' benchmark years show a marked change in the network. Compared with 1983, the cohesiveness of the network bounced back over the next three decades, with a constant increase in the size of the main component, peaking at 89% in 1997 and remaining above 80% thereafter. The UK interlocks network thus remained encompassing throughout the period analysed. This is reflected in the mean degree, which had dropped from a maximum of 4.15 in 1976 to 3.04 in 1983, but increased again to above 3.00 for the 1990s and 2000s.

One explanation for the relatively encompassing network during the 1990s and 2000s may have to do with emerging corporate governance norms and in particular minimum quotas for independent directors and targets for women on boards. Evidence from other countries has shown how such quotas create constrained markets for directors, boosting networks and creating a new wave of 'big linkers' (Huse, 2016). This may lead to the creation of new ties in the network, without necessarily implying a similar functionality as in 'traditional' company networks (Ferraro, Schnyder, Heemskerk, Corrado, & Del Vecchio, 2012). Given that the UK has been at the forefront of the corporate governance movement since the 1990s, it is very likely that a similar process explains the features we observe.

Despite this relative stability in the basic network cohesion, the network's structure changed in important ways that may have affected its conduciveness to information flows and thus hide a considerable change in its functionality.

Thus, the mean distance – measuring conduciveness for information flows – increased to just under 4.00 in the 1990s and over 4.00 in the 2000s. Importantly, for our purpose, the role of financial firms seems to have changed significantly in the network, shifting from cornerstones of the network to becoming virtually irrelevant for network cohesion by 2010

Table 5. Top 10 companies by betweenness centrality, 1993–2010.

1993		1997		2000		2010	
Company	Sector	Company	Sector	Company	Sector	Company	Sector
Trafalgar House plc	Real estate	Bank of Scotland plc	Financials (banking)	Standard Chartered plc	Financials (banking)	Standard Chartered plc	Financials (banking)
Smithkline Beecham plc	Industrials	Intercontinental Hotels Group plc	Consumer services	Lloyds Banking Group plc	Financials (banking)	Johnson Matthey plc	Industrials
De La Rue plc	Industrials	Diageo plc	Consumer staples	Cable & Wireless Communications plc	Telecom	Segro plc	Real estate
English China Clays plc	Industrials	National Westminster Bank plc	Financials (banking)	Bank of Scotland plc	Financials (banking)	Experian plc	Financials (other)
Sainsbury plc	Retail	Marks & Spencer Group plc	Retail	Rolls-Royce Holdings plc	Industrials	Sainsbury plc	Retail
Rio Tinto plc	Materials	RSA Insurance Group plc	Financials (insurance)	Barclays plc	Financials (banking)	WM Morrison Supermarket plc	Retail
BAA Airports Ltd	Transport	Marconi plc	Telecom	Invensys plc	Telecom	Bank of Scotland plc	Financials (banking)
Abbey National plc	Financials (banking)	Barclays plc	Financials (banking)	British Airways plc	Transport	Tesco plc	Retail
Legal & General Group plc	Financials (insurance)	Alliance Boots plc	Retail	BT Group plc	Telecom	IMI plc	Industrials
Barclays plc	Financials (banking)	British Airways plc	Transport	Alliance Boots plc	Retail	National Grid plc	Utilities

(Table 5). While in 1983 still a large majority of the most central companies were active in the financial sector (eight out of ten), they were only a minority from the 1990s onwards (three or four out of ten). This trend, despite the relative resilience of other network features, may affect the impact of network ties on corporate borrowing.

To test this effect, we performed the same regression analyses for the second period. Table 6 summarises the OLS estimates with the distance from financial companies measure as independent variable and the debt by assets measure as dependent variable. While we found some evidence for an impact of distance for financial firms on corporate debt levels in 1950 and 1976, the results reported in Table 6 do not provide any evidence of such a relationship for the period 1993–2010. It would hence seem that the connections to financial sector firms do not play a major role during this period, supporting our third hypothesis.

Table 7 reports the results for our spatial regression, which tests for the broader network effect. The results show that the network effect became non-significant for the whole period (with the partial exception of 1997 where it is very marginally significant at the 0.1 level). These results suggest that after the 1980s the financing behaviour of connected firms stopped influencing the finance decisions of the focal firm. In other words, our results are consistent with Hypothesis 3 and the view that from the mid-1980s to date, networks stopped mattering altogether for corporate finance in the UK.

It is interesting to note that 1983 constitutes a year where the network had dropped considerably in cohesiveness and density, yet network ties still mattered, while they did not

Table 6. OLS estimates for corporate borrowing, 1993–2010.

Variables	1993	1997	2000	2010
Distance from financial company	−0.040 (−0.18)	−0.283 (−0.88)	0.112 (0.46)	−0.074 (−0.21)
Total assets	0.001 (0.03)	−0.001 (−1.42)	0.000 (0.97)	−0.000 (2.01)*
Current assets	0.001 (0.71)	0.001 (1.71)†	−0.000 (−0.77)	−0.001 (−2.51)*
Nominal capital	−0.001 (−0.13)	0.001 (0.40)	−0.001 (−3.89)***	0.001 (0.84)
Manufacturing industry dummy			5.84 (5.07)***	−1.88 (−1.70)†
Primary industry dummy	0.83 (1.92)†	0.417 (0.977)	6.000 (4.95)***	−2.00 (−1.73)†
Service industry dummy	−0.216 (−1.14)	0.468 (2.12)*	5.944 (5.14)***	−1.450 (−1.92)
Constant	−2.129 (−14.52)***	−2.228 (−12.65)***	−7.76 (−6.77)***	−0.334 (−0.30)
N	177	165	178	171
Adjusted R^2	0.03	0.01	0.17	0.03

Note: Data in parentheses are *t*-values.
†$p < .1$, *$p < .05$, **$p < .01$, ***$p < .001$.
For 1983 information on nominal capital was only sparsely available, which led us to remove it as a control.

Table 7. Spatial regression estimates of debt levels, 1993–2010.

Variables	1993	1997	2000	2010
Network effect	−17.473 (−1.56)	−30.354 (−1.90)†	−10.00 (−1.37)	3.371 (1.14)
Total assets	−0.000 (−0.10)	−0.000 (−1.29)	0.001 (2.12)*	0.000 (1.41)
Current assets	0.000 (0.69)	0.000 (1.67)†	−0.000 (−2.22)*	−0.001 (−1.77)†
Nominal capital	−0.000 (−0.10)	0.000 (0.39)	−0.001 (−3.76)***	0.000 (1.02)
Manufacturing industry dummy			5.66 (4.76)***	−1.63 (−1.00)
Primary industry dummy	0.842 (1.74)†	0.714 (1.44)	5.60 (4.43)***	−1.43 (−0.85)
Service industry dummy	−0.358 (−1.81)†	0.486 (2.06)*	5.49 (4.57)***	−1.09 (−0.66)
Constant	0.151 (0.11)	3.622 (1.17)	−5.52 (−3.02)**	−1.33 (−0.76)
N	141	145	156	155
Adjusted R^2	0.05	0.03	0.20	0.04

Note: Data in parentheses are *t*-values.
†$p < .1$, *$p < .05$, **$p < .01$, ***$p < .001$.
For 1983 information on nominal capital was only sparsely available, which led us to remove it as a control.

matter anymore in later years despite the network having 'rebounded' to some extent in terms of cohesion and density. This illustrates our point that structural features are not sufficient to understand network function. Considering the impact of ties on practices reveals that the function may remain constant despite structural changes (compare 1983 with 1976), or conversely, the function of the network may change despite some structural similarities of the network (compare 1958–1976 with 1993–2010).

6. Conclusions

This study constitutes, to our knowledge, the first systematic, direct, and longitudinal analysis of the impact of network ties on UK companies' finance patterns. Contrary to previous studies, we used a mixed methods approach combining the mapping of the network with a historical narrative and regression analysis.

Our study reveals that distinguishing the structure and the function of the network is important, because the two do not always evolve in synchronised fashion. Thus, while we found there was already a considerable decline in network ties from the mid-1970s to the early 1980s, we have shown that the functional impact of network ties on lending patterns only changed sometime during the 1980s. Similarly, while the network remained relatively stable and encompassing during the 1990s and 2000s, the position of financial institutions in it had changed and the impact of network ties on a company's financial practices had disappeared. Studies focusing solely on the structure of the network (eg Wilson et al., 2017) may hence miss important functional aspects of interlocking ties.

Our findings parallel those of Mizruchi et al. (2006) based on the US company network between 1973 and 1993. They found a declining network effect in the US from the 1970s similar to what we have observed in the UK. Mizruchi et al. (2006) explained this phenomenon with the professionalisation and internalisation of corporate finance. As companies build up increasing internal financial expertise and capabilities, they rely less on banks and other financial institutions to provide financial expertise and access to different types of finance, which may explain the declining impact of external network ties on corporate finance decisions. Our findings are consistent with such an evolution for the UK as well. Indeed, while direct evidence is scarce, the literature suggests that – just as in the US – large UK companies increasingly financialised their strategies from the 1980s, including substituting unmediated finance for mediated forms (Froud et al., 2006).

This should not, however, lead us to overlook the distinct aspects of the UK case. Unlike their American counterparts, British banks were never great providers of long-term debt to industry, the network was sparse even at its peak in the 1970s, and the impact of finance–industry ties on corporate finance was only significant during a relatively short period of time. Indeed, while the post-war era marked a domestic reorientation of British finance that was accompanied by the most extensive corporate networks the country has seen in its modern history, the City's inward turn occurred not on its own volition, but as a result of severe regulatory and economic constraints. It was thus somewhat reluctant, and the City did not engage as deeply as their American, German, or Japanese counterparts, refusing to extend long-term lines of credit. Nevertheless, we still find some evidence that during this period network ties played a role in corporate finance. However, as soon as the regulatory 'shackles' were removed during the 'big bang', British finance resumed its historically conditioned international orientation.

Notes

1. We are grateful to an anonymous reviewer for this point.
2. The share of banks in the financial sample declines from over half in the 1950s to about an eighth in the most recent benchmark year, reflecting the shifting composition of the British financial sector. More precisely, the share of banks in our financial sample is 56% in 1950 and 1958, 46% in 1976, 50% in 1983, 20% in 1993, 26% in 1997 and 2000, and 14% in 2010.
3. The historical and longitudinal nature of this project meant that data availability was an issue in particular for accounting information. This resulted in small sample sizes for analysis for some of our regression models due to missing values. However, this is not unusual for similar studies where samples considerably below 100 are common, even for much larger countries such as the US (Mizruchi et al., 2006, Table 2).
4. We ran robustness checks with two more limited measures, namely number of direct links with banks and number of direct links with financial services firms. The results are not substantively different, but the association between bank/finance–industry ties and borrowing is weaker even during the first period (1950–1978).
5. As a robustness test, we also estimated this relationship using a binomial logit model. The results are broadly consistent with our hypotheses and results from our linear regression models, in the sense that the only significant result across all benchmark years is in 1958 where the impact of our indebtedness measure (long-term debt by assets) on the likelihood of having a bank tie is weakly significant (0.1 level). This suggests that it is sometime during the 1950s and 1970s that borrowing behaviour and network ties were most strongly related, which is consistent with our OLS results. Given the limitations of the binomial logit model – it can only test the probability of direct ties with financial firms – we prefer the linear regression model. Results from this additional analysis are available from the authors on request.
6. The fact that we do not find any relationship corresponding to that in 1976 for 1958 and 1950 may also be due to the limitations of our data. Owing to restricted availability, the samples for analysis for these two years are smaller. However, this would lead us to underestimate the impact of network ties on borrowing during this period, which goes against our hypothesis.
7. Owing to inconsistent financial reporting in 1950, the number of observations is too low to provide meaningful results. We therefore do not report results for that year.

Acknowledgements

The data set the authors used for this study is the result of a multi-year collaborative effort that has been financed by funds from King's College London and Newcastle University Business School, which they acknowledge gratefully.

Disclosure statement

No potential conflict of interest was reported by the authors.

ORCID

Philipp Kern http://orcid.org/0000-0002-3793-7679
Gerhard Schnyder http://orcid.org/0000-0002-6681-6227

References

Battilossi, S., & Cassis, Y. (Eds.). (2002). *European Banks and the American Challenge*. Oxford: Oxford University Press.

Bordo, M., & Sylla, R. (Eds.). (1995). *Anglo-American financial systems: Institutions and markets in the twentieth century*. Burr Ridge, IL: Irwin.

Braggion, F. (2005). Credit market constraints and financial networks in Late Victorian Britain, Working Paper. http://www.bancaditalia.it/pubblicazioni/altri-atti-seminari/2005/BRAGGION_02_12_2005.pdf

Cain, P. J., & Hopkins, A. G. (1993). *British Imperialism*. London: Longman. doi:10.1086/ahr/99.5.1685

Cassis, Y. (1985). Bankers in English society in the late nineteenth century. *The Economic History Review, 38*(2), 210–229. doi:10.2307/2597144

Chandler, A. D. (1990). *Scale and scope*. Cambridge, MA: Harvard University Press.

Collins, M. (1995). *Banks and industrial finance in Britain, 1800–1939*. Cambridge: Cambridge University Press.

Committee of London Clearing Bankers. (1978). *The London clearing banks*. London: Committee of London Clearing Bankers.

Conyon, M. J., & Muldoon, M. R. (2006). The small world of corporate boards. *Journal of Business Finance & Accounting, 33*(9–10), 1321–1343. doi:10.1111/j.1468-5957.2006.00634.x

Cronin, B. (2011). Networks of corporate power revisited. *Procedia – social and behavioral sciences, 10*, 43–51. doi:10.1016/j.sbspro.2011.01.007

David, T., & Westerhuis, G. (Eds.). (2014). *The power of corporate networks*. London: Routledge.

Davis, G. F., & Mizruchi, M. S. (1999). The money center cannot hold: Commercial banks in the U.S. system of corporate governance. *Administrative Science Quarterly, 44*(2), 215. doi:10.2307/2666995

de Nooy, W., Mrvar, A., & Batagelj, V. (2011). *Exploratory social network analysis with Pajek*. Cambridge: Cambridge University Press.

Deeg, R., Hardie, I., & Maxfield, S. (2016). What is patient capital, and where does it exist? *Socio-Economic Review, 14*(4), 615–625. doi:10.1093/ser/mww030

Ferraro, F., Schnyder, G., Heemskerk, E. M., Corrado, R., & Del Vecchio, N. (2012). Structural breaks and governance networks in Western Europe. In B. M. Kogut (Ed.), *The small worlds of corporate governance*. Cambridge, MA: MIT Press.

Fiedler, M., & Gospel, H. (2010). The top 100 largest employers in UK and Germany in the twentieth century. Data (ca. 1907, 1935/38, 1955/57, 1972/73, 1992/95). Cologne Economic History Papers.

Financial Times. (2012). Misguided Merlin. Financial Times.

Fitch, R., & Oppenheimer, M. (1970). Who rules the corporations? *Socialist Revolution, 4*, 73–108.

Fohlin, C. (2007). *Finance capitalism and Germany's rise to industrial power*. Cambridge: Cambridge University Press.

Fohlin, C. (2012). *Mobilizing money*. Cambridge: Cambridge University Press.

Franzese, R. J., & Hays, J. C. (2004). Modeling international diffusion. WZB Markets and Political Economy Working Paper Series, 47.

Froud, J., Johal, S., Leaver, A., & Williams, K. (2006). *Finacialization and strategy. Narrative and numbers*. Oxon and New York: Routledge.

Gerschenkron, A. (1962). *Economic backwardness in historical perspective*. London: Belknap Press.

Granovetter, M. S. (1973). The strength of weak ties. *American Journal of Sociology, 78*(6), 1360–1380. doi:10.1086/225469

Hall, P. A., & Soskice, D. W. (Eds.). (2001). *Varieties of capitalism: The institutional foundations of comparative advantage*. Oxford: Oxford University Press.

Haunschild, P. R. (1993). Interorganizational imitation: The impact of interlocks on corporate acquisition activity. *Administrative Science Quarterly, 38*(4), 564. doi:10.2307/2393337

Hilferding, R. (1968). Das Finanzkapital. Europäische Verlagsanstalt.

Huse, M. (2016). *The 'Golden Skirts': Lessons from Norway about women on corporate boards of directors*. London: Routledge.

Jones, C., & Cohen, N. (2012). Lending conditions are worse than Merlin suggests. Financial Times.

Kennedy, W. P. (1987). *Industrial structure, capital markets and the origins of British Economic Decline*. Cambridge: Cambridge University Press. doi:10.1086/ahr/94.5.1380

Konzelmann, S., Fovargue-Davies, M., & Schnyder, G. (2012). The faces of liberal capitalism: Anglo-Saxon banking systems in crisis? *Cambridge Journal of Economics, 36*(2), 495–524. doi:10.1093/cje/ber049

Kotz, D. M. (1978). *Bank control of large corporations in the United States*. Berkeley, CA: University of California Press.

Kroszner, R., & Strahan, P. (2001). *Throwing good money after bad? Board connections and conflicts in bank lending* (pp. 1–40). Cambridge, MA: National Bureau of Economic Research.

La Porta, R., Lopez-de-Silanes, F., Shleifer, A., & Vishny, R. W. (1998). Law and finance. *Journal of Political Economy, 106*(6), 1–43.

Laeven, L. (2001). Insider lending and bank ownership: The case of Russia. *Journal of Comparative Economics, 29*(2), 207–229. doi:10.1006/jcec.2001.1708

Larson, M. J., Schnyder, G., Westerhuis, G., & Wilson, J. (2011). Strategic responses to global challenges: The case of European banking, 1973–2000. *Business History, 53*(1), 40–62. doi:10.1080/00076791.2011.546660

Lawson, N. (2006). Foreword. *Big bang 20 years on: New challenges facing the financial sector* (pp. i–v). London: Centre for Policy Studies.

Lazonick, W., & O'Sullivan, M. (2010). Maximizing shareholder value: a new ideology for corporate governance. *Economy and Society, 29*(1), 13–35. http://doi.org/10.1080/030851400360541.

Marquis, C. (2003). The pressure of the Past: Network imprinting in intercorporate communities. *Administrative Science Quarterly, 48*(4), 655–689. doi:10.2307/3556640

Mintz, B. A., & Schwartz, M. (1985a). *The power structure of American business*. Chicago, IL: University of Chicago Press.

Mintz, B. A., & Schwartz, M. (1985b). *The power structure of American business*. Chicago, IL: University of Chicago Press.

Mizruchi, M. S. (1996). What do interlocks do? An analysis, critique, and assessment of research on interlocking directorates. *Annual Review of Sociology, 22*(1), 271–298. doi:10.1146/annurev.soc.22.1.271

Mizruchi, M. S., & Stearns, L. B. (1988). A longitudinal study of the formation of interlocking directorates. *Administrative Science Quarterly, 33*(2), 194. doi:10.2307/2393055

Mizruchi, M. S., & Stearns, L. B. (1994). A longitudinal study of borrowing by Large American Corporations. *Administrative Science Quarterly, 39*(1), 118. doi:10.2307/2393496

Mizruchi, M. S., Stearns, L. B., & Marquis, C. (2006). The conditional nature of embeddedness: A study of borrowing by Large U.S. Firms, 1973–1994. *American Sociological Review, 71*(2), 310–333. doi:10.1177/000312240607100207

Morgan, E. V., & Thomas, W. A. (1962). *The stock exchange*. London: Elek Books.

Musacchio, A. (2009). Drawing links between corporate governance and networks: Bankers in the corporate networks of Brazil, Mexico, and the United States Circa 1910. *Entreprises Et Histoire, 54*(1), 16–36. doi:10.3917/eh.054.0016

Musacchio, A., & Read, I. (2007). Bankers, industrialists, and their cliques: Elite networks in Mexico and Brazil during early industrialization. *Enterprise & Society, 8*(4), 842–880. doi:10.1093/es/khm079

Pollard, S. (1992). *The development of the British economy, 1914–1990*. London: E. Arnold.

Rajan, R. G., & Zingales, L. (1998). Financial Dependence and Growth. *The American Economic Review, 88*(3), 559–586.

Ratcliff, R. E. (1980). Banks and corporate lending: An analysis of the impact of the internal structure of the capitalist class on the lending behavior of banks. *American Sociological Review, 45*(4), 553. doi:10.2307/2095008

Richardson, R. J. (1987). Directorship interlocks and corporate profitability. *Administrative Science Quarterly, 32*(3), 367. doi:10.2307/2392910

Rubio-Mondéjar, J. A., & Garrués-Irurzun, J. (2016). Economic and social power in Spain: Corporate networks of banks, utilities and other large companies (1917–2009). *Business History, 58*(6), 858–879. doi:10.1080/00076791.2015.1115483

Schnyder, G., & Wilson, J. (2014). The structure of networks: The transformation of UK Business 1904–2010. In T. David & G. Westerhuis (Eds.), *The power of corporate networks*. London: Routledge.

Scott, J. (1987). Intercorporate structure in Britain, the United States and Japan. *Shoken Keizai, 160*, 51–64.

Scott, J., & Griff, C. (1985). Bank spheres of influence in the British corporate network. In F. N. Stokman, R. Ziegler, & J. Scott (Eds.), *Networks of Corporate Power* (pp. 215–233). Cambridge: Polity Press.

Selznick, P. (1949). *TVA and the grass roots*. Berkeley, CA: University of California Press.
Slaughter & May. (2014). Breedon + 2 years: Where are we now? Current non-bank lending options for UK corporates. *Slaughter and May Briefing*, 1–8. https://www.slaughterandmay.com/media/2182575/breedon-plus-2-years-where-are-we-now.pdf
Stanworth, P., & Giddens, A. (1975). The modern corporate economy: Interlocking directorships in Britain, 1906–1970. *The Sociological Review*, *23*(1), 5–28. doi:10.1111/j.1467-954X.1975.tb00515.x
Stearns, L. B. (1986). Capital market effects on external control of corporations. *Theory and Society*, *15*(1–2), 47–75. doi:10.1007/BF00156927
Stearns, L. B., & Mizruchi, M. S. (1993). Board composition and corporate financing: The impact of financial institution representation on borrowing. *Academy of Management Journal*, *36*(3), 603–618. doi:10.2307/256594
Sylla, R. (2002). Financial systems and economic modernization. *The Journal of Economic History*, *62*(2), 277–292.
Talberg, M., Winge, C., Frydenberg, S., & Westgaard, S. (2008). Capital Structure Across Industries. *International Journal of the Economics of Business*, *15*(2), 181–200. http://doi.org/10.1080/13571510802134304
Thomas, W. A. (1978). *The finance of British industry, 1918–1976*. London: Routledge.
Thompson, P. (1997). The pyrrhic victory of gentlemanly capitalism: The financial elite of the city of London, 1945–90, Part 2. *Journal of Contemporary History*, *32*(4), 427–440. doi:10.1177/002200949703200401
Utton, M. A. (1982). *The political economy of big business*. Fremont, CA: M. Robertson.
van der Zwan, N. (2014). Making sense of financialization. *Socio-Economic Review*, *12*(1), 99–129. doi:10.1093/ser/mwt020
Vasta, M., & Baccini, A. (1997). Banks and industry in Italy, 1911–36: New evidence using the interlocking directorates technique. *Financial History Review*, *4*(2), 139–159. doi:10.1017/S0968565000000937
Vasta, M., Drago, C., Ricciuti, R., & Rinaldi, A. (2017). Reassessing the bank–industry relationship in Italy, 1913–1936: A counterfactual analysis. *Cliometrica*, *11*(2), 183–216. doi:10.1007/s11698-016-0142-9
Wasserman, S., & Faust, K. (1994). *Social network analysis*. Cambridge: Cambridge University Press.
Westerhuis, G. (2014). The dutch corporate network: Considering its persistence. In T. David & G. Westerhuis (Eds.), *The power of corporate networks*. London: Routledge.
Whitley, R. (2007). *Business systems and organizational capabilities*. Oxford: Oxford University Press.
Wilson, J. F., Buchnea, E., & Tilba, A. (2017). The British corporate network, 1904–1976: Revisiting the finance–industry relationship. *Business History*, *3*(1), 1–28.
Windolf, P. (2009). Coordination and Control in Corporate Networks: United States and Germany in Comparison, 1896–1938. *European Sociological Review*, *25*(4), 443–457.
Windolf, P., & Nollert, M. (2001). Institutions, Interests, and corporate networks. A comparative analysis. *Politische Vierteljahresschrift*, *42*(1), 51–78. doi:10.1007/s11615-001-0004-2

Appendix. Descriptive statistics

	Debt/ assets	Long-term debt	Total assets	Current assets	Nominal cap	Distance from FIRE	No FIRE neighbours	No bank neighbours	Network effect (ρ)
1950									
Min	0.01	0.20	1.30	0.10	0.60	0.00	0.00	0.00	0.03
Max	0.65	17.75	1707.50	277.00	1259.40	1.00	5.00	1.00	0.15
Mean	0.12	3.61	79.36	24.53	26.55	0.63	0.59	0.25	0.04
Std dev.	0.11	4.31	242.40	41.76	130.63	0.48	1.10	0.43	0.02
1958									
Min	0.00	0.20	2.20	0.00	0.17	0.00	0.00	0.00	0.01
Max	0.58	63.68	2613.50	310.50	1165.81	1.00	11.00	1.00	0.25
Mean	0.11	9.99	164.84	37.51	23.91	0.34	1.77	0.56	0.06
Std dev.	0.10	15.28	360.64	52.20	90.29	0.47	2.35	0.50	0.02
1976									
Min	0.00	2.75	2.80	1.60	0.41	0.00	0.00	0.00	0.01
Max	0.76	542.40	19,320.00	6685.00	1714.31	1.00	9.00	1.00	0.11
Mean	0.17	99.42	1112.94	319.56	65.41	0.26	1.61	0.44	0.10
Std dev.	0.12	142.07	2507.85	700.99	157.62	0.44	2.01	0.50	0.01
1983									
Min	0.00	3.42	6.50	4.10	14.80	0.00	0.00	0.00	0.07
Max	0.36	307.77	59,046.00	10,764.00	500.00	1.00	6.00	1.00	0.09
Mean	0.13	87.70	2346.37	436.74	84.35	0.30	1.01	0.33	0.08
Std dev.	0.08	88.10	7417.31	943.74	104.82	0.46	1.30	0.47	0.00
1993									
Min	0.00	5.94	313.39	10.50	0.00	0.00	0.00	0.00	0.06
Max	0.97	1746.44	206,007.00	30,441.00	29,830.53	1.00	5.00	1.00	0.18
Mean	0.18	382.32	6885.03	1078.69	386.04	0.22	0.88	0.30	0.13
Std dev.	0.14	475.74	21,737.25	2633.55	2576.29	0.41	1.12	0.46	0.01
1997									
Min	0.00	9.20	443.39	19.00	0.24	0.00	0.00	0.00	0.05
Max	6.32	2452.00	286,333.00	10,752.00	51,000.20	1.00	6.00	1.00	0.25
Mean	0.25	522.01	10,150.63	1035.70	471.51	0.11	0.92	0.30	0.18
Std dev.	0.50	625.86	32,186.29	1401.87	3457.34	0.31	1.11	0.46	0.01
2000									
Min	0.00	0.96	464.18	13.09	0.00	0.00	0.00	0.00	0.00
Max	0.91	5238.80	450,849.70	30,773.10	52,304.50	1.00	4.00	1.00	0.41
Mean	0.21	907.65	14,492.79	1398.76	437.45	0.18	0.76	0.29	0.18
Std dev.	0.16	1342.36	50,857.78	3211.11	3393.94	0.38	1.01	0.45	0.02
2010									
Min	0.00	0.00	575.07	32.05	0.00	0.00	0.00	0.00	0.15
Max	3.65	10,027.00	1,568,546.28	84,617.60	8843.08	1.00	4.00	1.00	0.54
Mean	0.23	1719.07	37,692.06	3142.46	222.09	0.12	0.73	0.28	0.20
Std dev.	0.29	2786.17	179,869.14	9682.97	824.22	0.33	0.88	0.45	0.03

The banking-industry relationship in Italy: Large national banks and small local banks compared (1913–1936)

Alberto Rinaldi and Anna Spadavecchia

ABSTRACT
Using a large dataset of Italian joint-stock companies, this article analyses the networks of corporate interlocks of the major universal banks and 20 most 'central' local banks in a critical period of Italian industrialisation. The networks of the two types of banks were largely independent, with universal banks being affiliated principally to larger concerns in electricity, transport and storage, and financials; and local banks to riskier, younger and smaller firms in light manufacturing. The article then explores whether the bank-industry relationship in Italy reflected the hegemony of banks and followed a bank-control model. Our analysis does not support that view. It rather indicates that interlocking directorates were driven principally by a convergence of interests between banks (monitoring customers) and industrial firms (interested in tapping capital and credit flows), with the latter exerting a slightly higher influence over the former. This significantly differentiates Italy from Germany and the USA, where banks had a more dominant position in the corporate system.

1. Introduction

Italy occupies an important place in the literature of the bank-industry relationship. In his path-breaking contribution, Gerschenkron (1962) argued that banks played a pivotal role in industrialisation for 'moderately backward' countries where they acted as a substitute for financial markets in their bid to catch up with the early industrialiser, Great Britain. As a result, Italy became a well-known case of a bank-oriented financial system, a group often associated with France, Germany, and Japan (Lescure, 2008; Rajan & Zingales, 2003).

Gerschenkron singled out the main universal banks, founded in the 1890s with German capital, as the major driver of Italy's 'big spurt' in the years prior to World War I. These banks functioned as a 'substitution factor' that prompted Italy's economic growth by providing financial support and managerial advice to the major industrial companies, especially in modern capital-intensive sectors such as steel, heavy engineering, electricity, and shipping. According to Gerschenkron, universal banks exerted considerable influence and control over industrial firms through three major channels: capital participation, sharing of board members, and monitoring of day-to-day financial affairs. However, the role of universal banks has been reconsidered by a more recent 'revisionist' historiography. In particular, Fohlin (1998, 1999) found evidence that these banks had a limited impact on capital mobilisation, industrial investment and economic growth. Furthermore, she highlighted that universal banks tended to establish their networks with large well-established companies instead of trying to create connections with promising, but risky, small firms, which needed venture capital.

Despite the relevance of the relationship between banks and industry, only a few studies have analysed interlocking directorates between Italian banks and industrial companies in the pre-World War II period. Cohen (1967) and Fohlin (1999) found that universal banks were at the centre of an entangled network with large firms in modern capital-intensive sectors such as electric power, chemicals, iron and steel, and shipyards. However, Vasta & Baccini (1997) argued that the Italian corporate network was not characterised by such a strong centrality of banks. The location of banks at the centre of the network could be detected in 1911 and even more in 1927, but this was no longer the case in 1936, after the collapse of the universal banks. Moreover, Vasta, Drago, Ricciuti, and Rinaldi (2017) argued that Italian capitalism is structured to a remarkable extent on a sizeable and stable system of corporate interlocks that existed in parallel to that centred on the universal banks. They also showed that the influence, at least in Lombardy and some other areas of the North, was exerted by local banks that in turn developed a dense web of ties with industrial firms in both capital-intensive and labour-intensive industries.

None of these previous studies analysed the directionality of interlocks, however, and whether these were an instrument for banks to exert an influence on industry or *vice versa*. To date, two alternative views have been proposed in the literature. The 'bank control' model places banks at the top of the decision-making hierarchy within a group of companies, using this power in their own interest; control of credit flows and, more rarely, part of the firm's equity enables banks to determine industrial firms' strategies. Or, in a less radical view, bank control can be interpreted as ensuring efficient monitoring of resources provided by banks to industrial concerns. The use of interlocking directorates plays a central role in this respect. In fact, the presence of bank fiduciaries on company boards serves as a major instrument to enforce this control and indicates the pre-eminence of banks over industrial firms (Kotz, 1978).

Conversely, 'resource dependence' models argue that restrictions on resources, information, or markets stimulate firms to create business groups, whose presence can be detected through the existence of interlocking directorates. The hypothesis is that companies use the sharing of board members as means to co-opt or absorb, partially or completely, other organisations with which they are interdependent (Aldrich & Pfeffer, 1976; Pfeffer, 1988; Pfeffer & Salancik, 1978). In the case of the bank-industry relationship, interlocking directorates are not an instrument for banks to exert control over industry, but are driven by a convergence of interests between banks (monitoring customers) and industrial firms (participating in decisions about capital and credit allocation). Moreover, for an individual firm, corporate interlocks provide business scan – i.e. access to information about other sectors of the economy – and, because of their unique role in the economy, banks are privileged in the types of information to which they have access (Useem, 1984). Thus, banks have been uniquely successful in recruiting outside directors from heavily interlocked firms because bank board membership provides information about capital flows as well as information about many other sectors (Mintz & Schwartz, 1985).

This article adds to previous literature by exploring these two hypotheses in the context of the bank-industry relationship in Italy during the first third of the twentieth century when universal banking was in place there. The core issue of the directionality of the banking-industry relationship is investigated for large universal banks and small local banks in a comparative perspective in three benchmark years: 1913, 1927, and 1936. The comparative analysis is justified by the fact that Italy had a segmented banking system, i.e. very few large banks and a multitude of local banks with mostly local clienteles (Carnevali, 2005). Thus, for each of these years, we selected the major German-style universal banks – defined as the largest universal banks that had branch networks which covered most of the peninsula – and the 20 most 'central' local banks in the whole Italian corporate network.

2. The dataset

The source we used for this work is *Imita.db*, a large database of Italian joint-stock companies.[1] We selected the largest nation-wide German-style universal banks – *Banca Commerciale Italiana* (henceforth Comit), *Credito Italiano* (henceforth Credit), *Banco di Roma* (henceforth BdR), *Banca Nazionale di Credito* (henceforth BNC), and *Società Bancaria Italiana* (henceforth SBI)[2] – and the 20 most 'central' local banks by nBetweenness centrality.[3] As for the directors, we only used data for members of a board of directors, excluding members of *Collegi sindacali*.[4]

Network analysis presumes that central actors have better access to information, better opportunities to spread information, and some 'power' to coordinate the whole network. Degree centrality is the most straightforward measure of actor centrality and is based on the total number of direct ties between a given company and all others. An alternative is closeness centrality, based on the distance between nodes. Central actors are defined as having 'minimum steps' between themselves and other actors. Thus, the closeness centrality of a node is calculated as the reciprocal of the sum of the length of the shortest paths between the node and all other nodes. Different from degree centrality, closeness centrality considers also indirect ties between nodes. However, the nodes to which an actor relates can still be at the periphery of the network. This shortcoming is overcome by nBetweenness centrality. This measure is based on the idea that a firm is more central if it is more important as an intermediary in the communication network: it calculates the number of shortest paths between any pairs of actors in the network that pass through any given actor (De Nooy, Mrvar, & Batagelj, 2011). Thus, we resort to this latter indicator to select the top 20 local banks whose networks are analysed in this paper. The underlying assumption is that the top 20 by nBetweenness had better access to information, better opportunities to spread information, and were in a better position to coordinate the whole network than the remaining local banks.

By 1913, three of the four major universal banks were well placed among the most central firms in the Italian corporate network – SBI and Comit in the top five and Credit thirteenth – and their degrees were sizeable as well, with only BdR lagging behind.[5] By that time several local banks, despite their smaller size, had also developed their web of interlocks and one of them, *Banca Bergamasca di Depositi e Conti Correnti* had an even higher nBetweenness and the same degree as Credit. Overall, we found six local banks in the highest decile of nBetweenness.

In subsequent years, the major universal banks further strengthened their central position in the ranking. The year 1927 represents the apex of the role of these banks: Comit ranked first and the remaining three among the top six. The top 20 local banks, despite the high churning in the group, improved their position in the ranking of most central firms as now all of them were in the highest decile of nBetweenness; their average degree also rose to 52.4 and was three times as high as in 1913 (detailed statistical information is included in the on-line Appendix).

When the Great Depression struck, the three major universal banks and their industrial clients were baled out by the newly created big state-owned holding *IRI* (*Istituto per la Ricostruzione Industriale* or Institute for Industrial Recovery). In 1936, a new Banking Law imposed the end of universal banking in Italy. Banks were allowed to practise only short-term credit, while their share participation in non-financial firms was strictly limited. At the same time, industrial credit was entrusted to newly created specialised institutions, many of them state-owned (La Francesca, 2004).

These changes had profound effects on the structure of the Italian corporate network and in 1936 the three major universal banks lost their pre-eminent position. Conversely, local banks' networks seem to have better withstood the Great Depression. In 1936 all the top 20 local banks were once again in the highest decile of nBetweenness and above all, their average nBetweenness dropped much less (25%) than that of the major universal banks (56%). Similarly, the number of interlocks also diminished proportionally less for the top 20 local banks (35%) than for the major universal banks (55%).

3. A comparison of the major universal banks' and twenty local banks' networks

In all benchmark years most of the top 20 local banks (between 60 and 75% overall) were headquartered in Lombardy and in the other regions of the North-West, i.e. in the area with the longest history of industrialisation. The North-East and Centre accounted for between 25 and 35% of the top 20. Networks of Southern local banks were instead nearly absent, with just one occurrence in 1913 and 1927 and none in 1936. Figure 1 below displays the regions of Italy.

Three of the four major universal banks were headquartered in Milan, with only one, BdR, located in the capital city. As Tables 1 and 2 show, the geographical distribution of universal banks' and local banks' networks of interlocked businesses was concentrated to a great extent (40% and above) in the banks' own provinces throughout the period. Both groups of banks had broadened the geographical scope of their networks by the second benchmark year. However, while the expansion towards the national dimension continued until 1936 for the universal banks, this was not the case for the local banks that, instead, retrenched in their own macro-regions between 1927 and 1936.

The increase in national scope of the universal banks' network, observable in 1936, was led by BdR and Comit. The latter, in particular, was taken over by *IRI* in 1933 which led the bank to severing its links with many firms in the North-West and creating new ties with both state-owned and private enterprises located in Rome where *IRI* was headquartered.[6] In fact, the government drastically downsized Comit's board of directors from 44 (1927) to 19 (1936) and appointed representatives of the new controlling shareholder, i.e. *IRI*.[7] Also Credit's

Figure 1. Italian macro regions.

Macro-regions are: North-West (includes the regions Piemonte, Liguria, and Lombardia); North-East (includes the regions Venezia, Venezia Tridentina, Venezia Giulia, and Emilia-Romagna); Centre (includes the region Toscana, Lazio, Umbria and Marche); and South and Islands (includes regions Abruzzo e Molise, Campania, Puglie, Basilicata, Calabria, Sicilia and Sardegna).

Table 1. Major universal banks' networks by geographical distribution of interlocked firms (%).

	1913			1927			1936		
HQ of interlocked firms	Min.	Median	Max.	Min.	Median	Max.	Min.	Median	Max.
Same province	41.7	43.5	77.3	19.7	41.8	46.2	34.3	40.2	40.3
Same region	44.0	50.1	77.3	19.7	45.3	52.8	34.3	41.1	43.1
Same macro-region	66.7	69.8	77.3	30.3	63.2	75.4	39.4	51.9	77.5
Other macro-region	22.7	30.2	33.0	24.6	36.8	69.7	22.6	48.1	60.6

Table 2. Top twenty local banks' networks by geographical distribution of interlocked firms (%).

	1913			1927			1936		
HQ of interlocked firms	Min.	Median	Max.	Min.	Median	Max.	Min.	Median	Max.
Same province	8.3	42.3	100	4.7	40	84	3.9	45.4	92.9
Same region	25	76.2	100	9.7	69.2	92	8.3	83.9	100
Same macro-region	25	84.2	100	9.6	77.9	94	8.3	87.2	100
Other macro-region	0	15.8	75	6	22.1	90.3	0	12.8	91.7

board of directors was downsized from 34 to 14, but it retained some major private industrialists based in the North-West, including Giovanni Agnelli (owner and president of FIAT), Giacinto Motta (president of Edison, Italy's largest electricity company), and Lorenzo Bruzzo (a Genovese industrialist with concerns in the steel, shipping, chemicals, and sugar-refinery industries). By contrast, BdR's board was reduced only from 18 to 16, but retained Antonio Pesenti, president of the nation's largest cement producer Italcementi.

Table 2 shows the geographical distribution of the networks of the top 20 local banks. The differences among these networks were huge as indicated by the immense gap between their minimum and maximum values. In fact, Lombard banks in particular had a high propensity to generate interlocks on the local level, whereas banks headquartered outside the North-West tended to create links not only with their local firms but also with firms located in other macro-regions, in particular the most industrialised macro-region the North-West.

The median value of affiliated firms located in other macro-regions rose from 16 to 22% between 1913 and 1927, to plummet to 12.8% in the last benchmark year. The geographical expansion of many local banks' networks occurred in the context of the unprecedented wildcat boom of the banking industry in the early 1920s, a time when Italian banks were subject to the Commercial Code of 1882 that did not distinguish between banking and other business activities – and was fostered by the expansionary monetary policy of the post-World War I years. As a result, between 1919 and 1926 the number of banks increased by 30% and that of bank branches nearly doubled (Toniolo, 1995).

However, the Great Depression caused many local banks' networks to lose most of their national scope and to retrench to the local and regional level, hence the sharp decrease of the median value in 1936. The change was also prompted by the reform of the banking sector of 1931–1938, generally known as the 1936 Banking Reform Law, which gave the Bank of Italy increased regulatory powers over the banking sector (Battilossi, Gigliobianco, & Marinelli, 2013). The three universal banks rescued by *IRI*, i.e. Credit, Comit, and BdR, were entitled to operate throughout the country. The banks included in our group of the 'Top 20 local banks' belonged to the institutional group of 'ordinary credit banks' and 'cooperative banks'. These types of banks could operate only at a regional or provincial level.[8] Therefore, on the one hand the reshaping of the banking structure regulated competition and established clearer geographical boundaries between banks, thus ensuring supply of credit to regional economies (Carnevali, 2005); on the other hand, it reduced local banks' scope for generating networks beyond the local level.

The sectoral distribution of banks' interlocks is a debated topic in the literature on Italian industrialisation. Table 3 examines such distribution for the two groups of banks in each benchmark year. More detailed information on the sectoral distribution of the networks is included in the on-line statistical appendix.[9]

Table 3. Sectoral distribution of interlocked firms.

	1913						1927						1936					
	Major Univ. Banks			Top 20 Local Banks			Major Univ. Banks			Top 20 Local Banks			Major Univ. Banks			Top 20 Local Banks		
Sector	% Firms	% Assets	Mean assets*	% Firms	% Assets	Mean assets*	% Firms	% Assets	Mean assets*	% Firms	% Assets	Mean assets*	% Firms	% Assets	Mean assets*	% Firms	% Assets	Mean assets*
Agriculture, forestry and fishing	2.2	1.8	13.0	1.3	2.1	15.9	2.7	1.1	32.6	5.2	2.3	24.1	1.9	1.0	104.3	4.0	1.4	33.5
Mining and quarrying	3.9	1.7	6.6	1.7	0.5	2.7	4.4	1.9	34.0	3.1	0.8	14.2	3.1	0.4	23.1	1.7	0.4	25.0
Manufacturing	47.0	36.7	12.2	62.0	51.9	8.2	42.4	34.0	63.8	45.9	31.5	38.0	37.6	17.9	93.8	50.5	24.1	44.9
- Light industry	*21.1*	*12.4*	*9.2*	*33.8*	*24.6*	*7.1*	*19.2*	*8.4*	*34.6*	*27.4*	*11.8*	*23.8*	*9.7*	*2.0*	*40.9*	*30.7*	*7.5*	*23.1*
- Heavy industry	*25.9*	*24.3*	*14.6*	*28.3*	*27.3*	*9.4*	*23.2*	*25.6*	*87.9*	*18.4*	*19.7*	*59.1*	*27.9*	*15.9*	*112.1*	*19.8*	*16.5*	*78.7*
Electricity, gas and water supply	14.0	19.0	21.1	8.0	12.4	15.1	18.1	28.8	126.4	9.9	26.0	145.3	16.3	29.5	356.9	15.4	41.1	250.9
Construction	3.5	2.9	12.7	3.0	1.9	6.3	2.9	0.8	22.9	3.1	0.9	16.3	4.3	1.5	69.2	2.1	1.6	71.6
Trade	6.6	1.2	2.9	5.9	2.6	4.3	5.7	3.2	44.9	9.4	3.4	19.9	6.6	0.8	24.3	7.5	1.2	14.8
Transport and storage	15.4	23.0	23.3	10.5	9.2	8.5	11.0	9.8	71.3	9.3	10.0	59.5	8.1	2.8	68.7	5.8	4.1	66.4
Telecommunications				0.8	0.2	1.8	0.8	1.7	174.3	1.0	2.7	143.8	1.6	4.1	516.2	0.6	0.7	109.4
Financials	5.3	13.4	39.5	3.4	18.5	53.6	10.0	18.0	143.8	10.3	21.6	115.3	19.0	41.7	431.7	10.2	25.2	232.8
Public administration, health and social service	1.8	0.4	3.6	3.4	1.0	2.8	2.1	0.5	20.2	2.5	0.7	15.0	1.6	0.2	31.4	1.7	0.2	8.7
Total	100.0	100.0	15.6	100.0	100.0	9.8	100.0	100.0	79.5	100.0	100.0	55.3	100.0	100.0	196.7	100.0	100.0	94.3

Key: * = Million Lire.

Similarly to Fohlin's (2007) findings for Germany, local banks were connected to nearly every sector of the corporate economy. However, Italian local banks had a higher proportion of affiliated firms in manufacturing. Thus, in 1913, manufacturing accounted for 62.0% of firms interlocked to the top 20 local banks, compared with 47.0% of firms affiliated to the major universal banks. Due to their smaller average size, the proportion of manufacturing firms on total assets of network membership is lower, but the bias in favour of local banks remains substantial (51.9% versus 36.7%).

In addition to manufacturing, two sectors stood out in the major universal banks' networks: electricity, gas and water supply; transport and storage (these banks were interlocked to Italy's largest railway and passenger shipping companies).

In 1927 we find a convergence in the sectoral distribution of affiliated firms between the major universal banks and the top 20 local banks. Heavy industry and electrical-commercial companies were now only slightly more represented among the former and light industry among the latter.

In 1936 we observed a new divergence between networks. Major universal banks' networks now differed remarkably one from another with Comit's network concentrated to an unprecedented proportion on finance companies, Credit focused more on large electrical commercial firms, and BdR in between.[10] By contrast, local banks' networks hinged principally on manufacturing and electricity companies. In particular, the latter had jumped to 15.4% of firms and 41.1% of total assets, highlighting a change in the investment pattern of local banks towards less risky activities as local utilities.

An interesting feature is the presence of financials – both insurance and finance companies – in the networks of larger universal banks as well as some local banks. This raises the issue of the extent to which the large universal banks and the local banks were interlocked. A more detailed analysis highlights that in 1913 only two of the four major universal banks had interlocks with other banks: SBI with four, and BdR with one. Out of the 20 local banks, four were linked to major universal banks, of which two were linked also to *Banca d'Italia*, Italy's largest bank of issue. The situation changed in 1927, when all the major universal banks had developed a dense web of banking interlocks mainly with local banks. Conversely, the propensity of local banks to be networked to other banks also reached its apex in that benchmark year, with 17 of them being linked to at least another bank, eight of which were networked to a universal bank. The number of bank connections fell dramatically in 1936 particularly for the universal banks. These dropped to three for Comit, two for BdR, and one for Credit. Also the 20 local banks' connections with the universal banks declined significantly, whereas their links with other local banks and central institutes of local banks increased.

These links between universal and local banks probably existed for the larger banks to have access to the funds collected in peripheral areas by the smaller banks. However, the majority of the top 20 local banks were disconnected from the large national banks: three had no banking interlocks and eight were connected only to other local banks. We can argue, therefore, that the extent to which local banks were linked to major universal banks – and therefore might function as branches of the latter – varied over time but was never the preponderant trait of local banking in Italy.

We can observe from Table 3 that size appears as a major difference between firms attached to the larger universal banks and firms attached to local banks. In all benchmark years we find the firms linked to the former were significantly larger than those linked to the latter. The bias of the larger universal banks' relationship towards largest firms was present – with some exceptions – in all sectors.

A focus on telecommunications can shed some light on the propensity of the various types of banks to establish ties with firms in well-established industries or instead with small firms in new fast-growing industries. In 1913 no large universal bank was connected to any telecommunication firms, whereas two small telecommunication firms were linked to as many local banks, even if the former accounted for a very low share of the total assets of the latter's affiliated firms. In 1927 the share of telecommunications was still higher in the networks of local banks, but the situation reversed in 1936. Thus, the impression is that small firms operating in the infant stage of their industries tended more often to be connected to small local banks but once they grew in size and became well-established companies, they moved to the networks of the larger universal banks that could more properly satisfy their increased financial needs.

The sectoral analysis above highlights that large universal banks were mainly connected with established industries whereas emerging industries, characterised by smaller average size were mainly connected with local banks. To investigate further we compared the age of businesses in the two networks and their level of risk, measuring the variability of profits, which is one of the standard indicators of risks (Brealey & Myers, 2003).

Table 4 shows that overall the top 20 local banks were interlocked to younger, riskier, and less profitable firms. The coefficient of variation (C.V.), indicator of risk, is consistently higher than the counterpart figures for the major universal banks and the differences are highly statistically significant. An exception is the mean profit in the first benchmark year, for which the values are very close and their difference is not statistically significant.

Overall, Table 4 confirms that a more geographically concentrated network of the local banks also meant that less profitable and riskier industrial concerns could benefit from external finance and business advice. This is consistent with the approach by Stiglitz & Weiss (1981 and 1990) who emphasised that screening and assessing the credit-worthiness of loan applicants is one important function performed by banks, which will endeavour to select low-risk borrowers and will follow up by monitoring them. These are costly functions due to the opacity of the credit market and information asymmetries. However, the embeddedness of banks and borrowers in the same economic and social fabric lowers information asymmetries through less costly direct and informal knowledge, which in turn enables an assessment of the credit-worthiness of borrowers based not merely on financial criteria, thus enabling SMEs perceived as riskier on the basis of their accounts to access credit (Carnevali, 1996; Conti & Ferri, 1997). Therefore, the top 20 local banks performed an important role

Table 4. Profitability and age of interlocked firms.

	Major Universal Banks				Top twenty local banks			
	Profit/losses (mean, 000 lire)	C.V.	Age (Mean)	Obs	Profit/losses (mean, 000 lire)	C.V.	Age (Mean)	Obs
1913	0.6	2.4	15.8	269	0.6	5.20***	12.7***	310
1927	3.5	3.7	16.7	810	2.5***	4.74***	14.8**	852
1936	5.3	2.6	22.1	295	3.6***	3.19***	21.5	582

Notes: we have used coefficients of variation (C.V.), rather than standard deviations, as the coefficient of variation seems more appropriate to compare different samples; We tested whether the differences between the two groups of interlocked firms are statistically significant: ***$p<0.01$,. **$p<0.05$,. *$p<0.1$.

in interlocking with businesses that other financial institutions may not have considered credit-worthy and that were nevertheless important for the Italian economy.

The major universal banks demonstrate a cautious stance by interlocking with less risky concerns than those of the top 20 local banks. A more risk-prone approach is suggested by the 1927 figures, which might be explained by a wave of new industrial concerns being established in the fast growth years between 1922 and 1925, which ended with a sharp fall in the stock market (Toniolo, 1995). The level of risk decreased, and the age increased considerably, in the last benchmark year, suggesting a widespread risk aversion following the Great Depression and the subsequent salvaging of banks and industrial concerns by the state. Both the Great Depression and state intervention reshaped the industrial structure of the country and the state-controlled system of industrial credit reduced the instability in both the industrial and banking systems.

4. Directionality of interlocks

An analysis of the directionality of interlocks provides some further insights about the nature of the relationship between banks and industry. This assumes that the direction of the interlock goes from the company in which a director holds a more important position to that in which his position is of a lesser importance. As a result, the interlock becomes an instrument for the former company to exert an influence on the latter (Pennings, 1980; Wasserman & Faust, 1994). We have defined the following hierarchy of the importance of board positions in Italian joint-stock companies to identify the directionality of interlocks:

$$\text{President} = \text{CEO} \rightarrow \text{Executive Manager} \rightarrow \text{Vice-President} \rightarrow \text{Secretary of the Board} \rightarrow \text{Direct}$$

According to this methodology, in the case of the links between banks and industry, two types of directed interlocks can be detected: those that go from the bank to the industrial firm and those that go in the opposite direction. We refer to the former as to the 'outdegree', which is an indicator for the influence banks had on industry; and *vice versa* to the latter as to the 'indegree' that expresses the influence of industry on banks.[11] Thus, following Windolf (2009, 2010), we have computed the 'outdegree/indegree' ratio: the higher this indicator, the more dominant banks are over industry, and *vice versa*.

Table 5 shows that in all benchmark years, directed interlocks account for a higher proportion of total interlocks with industrial firms for the major universal banks than is the case for the top 20 local banks.[12] For the former, the proportion of directed interlocks increased between 1913 and 1927 but then it slightly decreased in 1936, whereas for the latter the

Table 5. Directionality of interlocks.

	Large universal banks			Top twenty local banks		
	1913	1927	1936	1913	1927	1936
Total number of interlocks with industrial firms (1)	343	1041	276	349	1025	709
Directed interlocks with industrial firms [% of (1)]	54.8	59.8	59.4	46.4	52.0	55.3
Number of outdegrees (2)	85	295	37	63	231	129
Outdegrees per bank	21.2	73.8	12.3	3.2	11.6	6.4
Number of indegrees (3)	103	327	127	99	302	162
Indegrees per bank	25.8	81.8	42.3	5.0	15.1	8.1
Outdegree / Indegree ratio [(2)/(3)]	0.8	0.9	0.3	0.6	0.8	0.8
Total number of industrial firms interlocked (4)	225	627	233	237	670	513
Industrials firms receiving banks' outdegrees [% of (4)]	32.4	32.9	15.0	20.7	27.8	23.6

Great Depression seems to have had an opposite effect and the proportion of directed interlocks rose to its highest value in 1936.

As we move on to the direction of interlocks, we observe that throughout the period investigated both large universal banks and small local banks had on average more 'indegrees' than 'outdegrees'.[13] Thus, the ratio 'outdegree/indegree' is always <1. In 1913 and 1927 this ratio is higher – even if slightly – for universal banks, but in 1936, after these had been taken over by *IRI*, it drops to its lowest value (0.3) and now the ratio is higher for the top 20 local banks for which it remains stable at the same level as in 1927 (0.8). Thus, the Great Depression and the 1930s restructuring of the banking system seem to have affected the relationship with industry much more for the major universal banks than was the case for local banks.

As we have anticipated, this ratio can be interpreted as an indicator for bank hegemony. In our case, as this ratio is always <1, but with values often not much lower than 1, we can infer that the relationship between banks and industry in Italy was fundamentally one of mutual dependency, with a slightly higher influence of industry over banks, a situation which makes Italy more in line to the 'resource dependence' model than to the 'bank control' model.

The high proportion of 'indegrees' in the structure of Italian banks' interlocks posed a problem. In fact, such a circumstance increased the risk of bankruptcy among banks because of the influence the actual or potential debtors were able to exert on the creditor banks. And this was probably one of the causes of the high instability of the Italian banking system until the 1930s.

Figure 2 shows that, in comparative perspective, the 'outdegree/indegree' ratio of Italian banks was significantly lower than that in other countries. Even though the samples of the various countries reported in Figure 2 were selected using different methodologies, and therefore are not exactly comparable, the differences in the orders of magnitude are striking.[14] The 'outdegree/indegree' ratio was particularly high in Germany, where banks had a more dominant position in the corporate system, but was also significantly higher in the USA. Instead, in France the ratio was much more similar to Italy's and this indicates a more reciprocal relationship between banks and industry within these two countries.

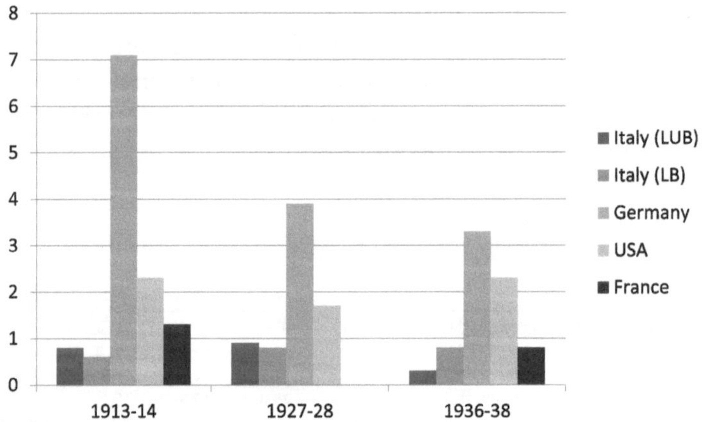

Figure 2. Outdegree/Indegree ratio in some selected countries. Keys: LUB = Large universal banks; LB = Top 20 local banks.

Source: For Germany, USA and France: Windolf (2009, 2010); for Italy: Imita.db

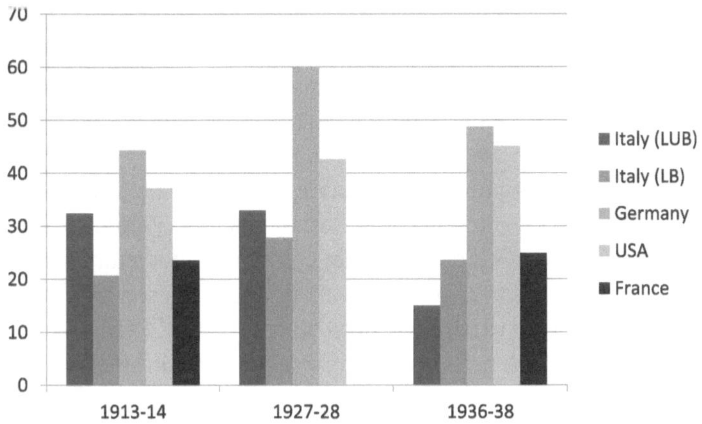

Figure 3. Industrial firms receiving banks' outdegrees (%). Keys: LUB = Large universal banks; LB = Top 20 local banks.

Source: For Germany, USA and France: Windolf (2009, 2010); for Italy: Imita.db

In examining bank influence over industry, we must also investigate the proportion of industrial firms that received 'outdegrees' from banks. The last row in Table 5 shows that the figure for industrial firms linked to large universal banks is about one-third in 1913 and 1927, but then it dramatically drops to 15% in 1936. Conversely, the corresponding figure for the top 20 local banks is lower in the first two benchmark years, but then in 1936 the situation reverses and in that year local banks sent 'outdegrees' to a higher proportion of industrial firms (23.6%) to which they interlocked than was the case for larger universal banks.

Nonetheless, as is shown in Figure 3, this indicator is also much lower than for Germany and the USA, to further underscore the higher influence of banks over industry in these two countries. Once again, the figures of Italy are much more in line with those of France, which had a more similar proportion of industrial firms receiving 'outdegrees' from banks.

Thus, our overall picture on the directionality of interlocks provides no evidence in favour of the 'bank-control' model. It is rather in line with the 'resource dependence' model. This insight is further corroborated by the high proportion of undirected interlocks between banks and industry. Thus, interlocking directorates seem to be driven principally by a convergence of interests between banks (monitoring customers) and industrial firms (interested in tapping capital and credit flows), with the latter exerting a slightly higher influence over the former.

5. Case studies

The two case studies below provide insights into the networks of interlocking directorates of local banks. From the four local banks ranked among the 'Top 20 local banks' in all the three benchmark years, i.e. the Banca Lombarda di Depositi e Conti Correnti, Banco Lariano, Banca di Legnano, and Credito Commerciale all located in the region of Lombardy, we selected two banks for which some literature is available in addition to the reports on inspections conducted by the Banca d'Italia between 1926 and 1936.

The Banca Lombarda di Depositi e Conti Correnti (henceforth Banca Lombarda) was established in Milan in 1870 with a share capital of 6 million lire and was the first joint-stock bank in the region of Lombardy (Cafaro, 2000). In 1913 it was interlocked to 33 firms, which rose to 53 in 1927. By 1932 it had reached a share capital of 24 million and had established various branches in the region.[15] The Banca Lombarda's directors were representatives of the local industrial elite. At the time of the Banca d'Italia's 1932 inspection report, the Banca Lombarda's president, Luigi Bellini, was also president of the Banca per il Commercio Serico (Bank for the Commerce of Silk) and president of a firm specialised in the ageing of silk (Società Anonima Stagionatura Seta). The Banca Lombarda's vice-president, Andrea Pedroni, was also the owner of an industrial concern in the silk industry. Banca Lombarda's board of directors was mainly made of industrialists in the silk and textile industries, and to a lesser extent in the steel and electricity industries, in addition to bankers and aristocrats some of whom were also involved in industry and banking. For instance, one of the directors, Mauriziano Piantanida, was also the manager of the Banca d'Italia's branch in Milan; Darvino Salmoiraghi was also a director at the Credito Commerciale in Cremona (Lombardy); and Polidoro Redaelli was also a syndic at the Credito Commerciale di Verona (Veneto) and had previously been managing director at the Banca Popolare in Milan. In 1936 the Banca Lombarda was interlocked to 36 firms.

The Banca d'Italia's scrutiny of the loans and commercial papers extended by the Banca Lombarda indicates its great involvement in a range of industries, including steel (Società Anonima Acciaierie e Ferriere Lombarde Falk), electricity and telephones (E.L.T.E – Società Elettro Telefonica), automobile industry (Alfa Romeo and Società Anonima Italiana Pirelli), and mechanical engineering (Società Anonima E. Marelli & C. Magneti), in addition to textiles and silk. The report identified some bad loans and some excessive loans considering the financial situation of the borrowers, nevertheless the report states that the financial situation of the Banca Lombarda was solid. Furthermore, the report identifies some irregularities and infringements of rules in extending loans and poor book-keeping, and interpreted these as a result of the relationship between the bank and its clientele based on personal knowledge and trust, as well as the bank's paternalistic approach to extending credit in the local economy.[16]

The Banca di Legnano (henceforth BdL) was established in 1887 with the aim of collecting the abundant local savings and making them available to industrial and commercial enterprises operating in the area, essentially the Northern part of the Milan province. In 1913, BdL had interlocks with 19 firms, which jumped to 74 in 1927 but then halved to 37 in 1936. By 1932, BdL was particularly involved with textile and mechanical engineering enterprises and, with its seven branches, was considered one of the major credit institutions in the area.[17] The local involvement dominated the operations of the BdL in the first decade of its life. Following the economic crisis of the early 1890s and the demise of the Italian Crédit Mobilier, large local industrialists became interested in their 'local bank' as opposed to large banks, the management of which was more difficult to influence. Furthermore, the management of the ambitious CEO Angelo Pogliani directed the BdL towards high-finance operations (Cafaro, 2000; De Luca, 2005). Some prominent local industrialists were members of BdL's board of directors, thus for instance Baron Eugenio Cantoni was its first president and Eugenio Tosi chaired the board from 1913 until 1930. These gentlemen were also the owners and presidents of two among the largest firms in the area, the Cantoni (textiles) and Franco Tosi & Co. (mechanical engineering), which employed 3,000 and 1,500 workers, respectively.[18] Eugenio Cantoni was a strong supporter of the presence of industrialists in banking institutions and had been on the board of other banks in Northern Italy (Cafaro, 2000). Moreover, the textile industrialist Carlo Dell'Acqua was a director both in the BdL and Credito Varesino.

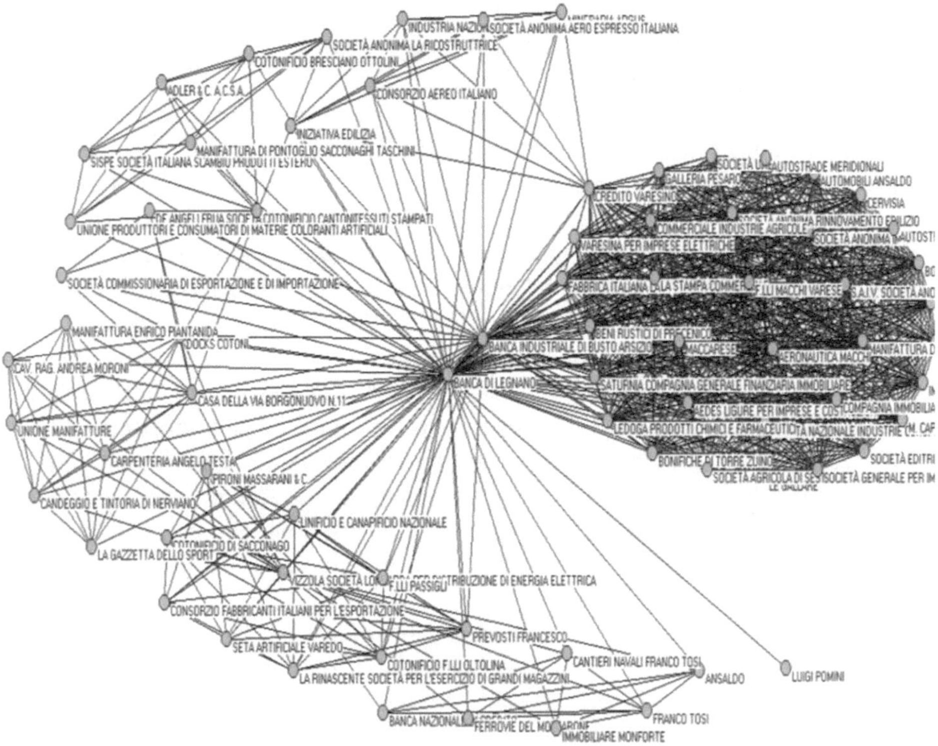

Figure 4. The Banca di Legnano network of interlocking directorates, 1927.

Banca d'Italia's 1932 inspection report mentioned the involvement of local industrialists as a factor contributing to the solid financial position of BdL as they provided an insider's knowledge of the credit-worthiness of borrowers.[19] Furthermore, BdL's embeddedness in the local economy meant that financial transactions were supported by personal relationships and trust. In some cases, this allowed small concerns to overcome the hurdle of lack of collaterals (De Luca, 2005). Figure 4 below shows the dense network of interlocks developed by the BdL by 1927. Some enterprises that played a significant role in Italian history can be recognised in the network, such as the engineering enterprise Ansaldo and the department-store chain la Rinascente.

The presence of large enterprises among BdL's customers meant that it had to resort to interbank lending to meet the financial requirements of its clientele and the second largest universal bank (Credit) was a major source of interbank lending (Piluso, 2009). Credit also supported BdL in 1915, when it was badly affected by the bankruptcy of a bicycle manufacturer that had considerable debts with the bank. In 1921, Credit bought shares in the BdL for 4.5 million lire, a large fraction of BdL's share capital which amounted to 20 million lire in 1932.[20]

6. Conclusions

This article examined some important and previously unexplored facets of the banking-industry relationships in a critical period of Italian industrialisation. We investigated the differences between the interlock networks of the major universal banks and a sample of local banks, before moving on to the central question, never investigated in the Italian case, of the directionality of the relationship.

Important differences between the two networks emerged. The bias of the major universal banks' relationship with largest firms could be detected throughout the three benchmark years and – with some exceptions – in all sectors. Firms in manufacturing, especially in light industry, had a greater weight in the networks of local banks, whereas industries such as electricity, transport and storage, and financials were more represented in the networks of universal banks. Local banks' networks were more structured on the local level, with a higher proportion of interlocked firms located in the same province and region as the bank. Lastly, we found that local banks were interlocked to riskier and less profitable firms. This confirms that more geographically concentrated networks of local banks also meant that less profitable and riskier industrial concerns could benefit from external finance and business advice. Thus, local banks performed an important role in interlocking with businesses that other financial institutions may have not considered credit-worthy but were nevertheless important for the Italian economy. This supports the argument by Stiglitz and Weiss conferring local banks an advantage in screening and monitoring small businesses.

A central question in our analysis is whether the industry-banking relationship in Italy reflected the hegemony of banks and followed a 'bank-control' model. The insights provided by our quantitative analysis and case studies of local banks do not support that view. They rather indicate that, both in the case of universal banks and small local banks, interlocking directorates were driven principally by a convergence of interests between banks (monitoring customers) and industrial firms (interested in tapping capital and credit flows), with the latter exerting a slightly higher influence over the former. This significantly differentiates Italy from Germany and the United States, where banks had a more dominant position in the corporate system.

We have also shown that the creation of interlocks with other banks was a common practice for local banks already before World War I. The extent to which they were linked to large national banks – and therefore might function as branches of the latter – varied over time but was never the preponderant trait of local banking in Italy, the majority of their interlocks being with other local banks. Thus, our evidence seems to confirm that local banks were largely part of a system of interlocks that existed independently of the one centred on the larger universal banks and that only in part redressed the segmentation of the Italian banking system.

Overall, our results challenge Gerschenkron's claim that Italian industrialisation was fundamentally prompted by two great banks, which were both financial intermediaries and the main industrial policy players of the nation. Our evidence suggests that, although his thesis was mainly related to the new capital-intensive sectors of the second industrial revolution, Gerschenkron seems to have underestimated the resource mobilisation occurring in the regional economies and the role played by local banks in financing small firms especially in light-industry sectors. Our evidence is instead to some extent in line with Fohlin's findings that downplay the role of universal banks as the latter tended to establish their networks on large well-established companies instead of trying to create connections with promising, but risky, small firms, which needed venture capital.

Acknowledgements

We would like to thank Alberto Baffigi and the Archivio Storico at Banca d'Italia, the participants to the session 'Banks, State and Industry' of the European Business Hitory Association 22nd Annual Congress (Ancona, 6-8 September 2018), the participants to the Henley Business School Workshop (University of Reading, 15 November 2018), and two anonymous referees for their helpful comments. This work has relied on the use of Imita.db, a large database funded by Miur, the Italian Ministry for University and Scientific Research. The usual disclaimer applies.

Disclosure statement

No potential conflict of interest was reported by the authors.

Notes

1. The database is available online: http://imitadb.unisi.it. For the details of *Imita.db*, see Vasta (2006).
2. Bankruptcies and mergers changed over time the landscape of universal banks in Italy: BdR was founded in 1880, Comit in 1894, Credit in 1895, and SBI in 1904. SBI merged in 1914 with the *Società Italiana di Credito Provinciale*, establishing the *Banca Italiana di Sconto* which bankrupted in 1921. What remained of the latter gave rise to the BNC, which in 1930 merged with Credit.
3. We considered as local banks the totality of banks included in *Imita.db* except the major universal banks; the banks of issues (*Banca d'Italia* and, until 1926, *Banco di Napoli* and *Banco di Sicilia*); the 'public law banks' according to the Banking Law of 1936 (*Banca Nazionale del Lavoro, Monte dei Paschi di Siena, Istituto Bancario San Paolo di Torino, Banco di Napoli and Banco di Sicilia*); and the central institutes of the cooperative banks and the savings banks.
4. During the period investigated in this article, the 1882 Commercial Code regulated corporate governance in Italy. This had designed a two-board system of corporate administration in which the assembly of the shareholders appointed the two following boards: (1) the board of directors (*Consiglio di amministrazione*), which was the executive body of the assembly of the shareholders. This usually included both inside and outside directors; (2) the board of syndics (*Collegio sindacale*), which monitored the financial probity of the firm and whose function did not coincide with that of the supervisory board in the German system (Teti, 1999). Thus, similarly to what was done in the two major international research projects on corporate networks in comparative perspective (David & Westerhuis, 2014; Stokman, Ziegler, & Scott, 1985), for our analysis we have selected only members of the board of directors.
5. In network analysis, the degree of a node is the number of edges connected to it (De Nooy, Mrvar, & Batagelj, 2011).
6. The cut of ID links, however, did not necessarily imply a shift in the geographical specialisation of Comit's credit relationships.
7. Among the state-owned enterprises located in Rome and now interlocked with Comit, stood out ANIC (chemicals); Finmare (IRI's sub-holding in charge of the shipping industry); IMI (Italy's largest industrial credit institute); INA (Italy's monopolist in life insurance) and IRI itself. At the same time Comit became connected with several private enterprises headquartered in Rome, operating in real estate, construction, insurance, public transport and utilities.

8. Only banks with deposits amounting to more than 300 billion lire could operate in the regions where their head offices were located. Banks with deposits below that threshold could operate in the whole province if their head office was located in the provincial capital, otherwise in the municipalities where the head office and branches were located (Battilossi et al., 2013).
9. We decided to separate the banking sector because the assets of banks are usually much higher than those of firms in other industries. Thus, addressing the sectoral distribution of banks' interlocks by including simultaneously all sectors in the analysis would have blurred the differences between network membership in industries other than banking. We also excluded real estate because of the large number of missing data in this sector.
10. Thus, in 1936 finance companies accounted for 41.5% of the assets of affiliated companies for Comit, 33.0% for BdR, and 17.9% for Credit. By contrast, the share of electrical commercial firms was 19.7% for Comit, 23.1% for BdR, and 36.2% for Credit.
11. Our methodology differs from the one used by Windolf (2009, 2010) for Germany, France and the USA. For Germany, where there is a two-board system of corporate governance, he defines *outdegrees* of the banks the interlocks in which members of banks' executive boards were sent to industrial companies' supervisory boards and, *vice versa indegrees* the interlocks in which members of industrial companies' executive boards sat on banks' supervisory boards. For France and the USA, which similarly to Italy have a one-board system, he establishes that if an executive manager of firm A sits on the board of directors of firm B as a non-executive or an external director, this person creates a directed interlock. In the case of Italy, we think that our procedure can be preferred as it has the advantage to give a directionality to a higher number of interlocks and thereby it provides a more comprehensive picture of the ties between banks and industry.
12. We define industrial firms as all firms operating outside the financial sector.
13. The most important exception was Comit – the largest universal bank – in 1913, whose outdegree/indegree ratio was 1.7. However, after World War One the ratio plummeted below 1 also for this bank, its values being 0.9 in 1927 and 0.3 in 1926.
14. Data on Germany, France and the USA are drawn from Windolf (2010). For each of these countries, the sample selection was based on published lists of the largest corporations in some benchmark years and its size varies over time. Thus, for Germany the sample consists of the top 346 companies (45 banks) in 1914; the top 377 companies (51 banks) in 1928, and the top 361 companies (40 banks) in 1938. For the USA: the top 242 companies (36 banks) in 1914; the top 369 companies (46 banks) in 1928; the top 409 companies (53 banks) in 1938. For France: the top 292 companies (32 banks) in 1914; and the top 274 companies (31 banks) in 1938.
15. Archivio Storico della Banca d'Italia (ASBI), *Vigilanza sulle Aziende*, Pratiche, n.1302.0, fascicolo1, Rapporto sull'ispezione eseguita dal capo ufficio f.f. Vladimiro Liguori alla Banca Lombarda di Depositi e Conti Correnti in Milano, 14 Giugno 1932.
16. Ibid.
17. ASBI, *Vigilanza sulle Aziende*, Pratiche, n.1864.0, fascicolo1. Banca di Legnano – Legnano – Rapporto sulla visita ispettiva, 15 Ottobre 1932.
18. Ibid.
19. Ibid.
20. Ibid.

References

Aldrich, H., & Pfeffer, J. (1976). Environments of organizations. *Annual Review of Sociology, 2*(1), 79–105. doi:10.1146/annurev.so.02.080176.000455

Battilossi, S., Gigliobianco, A., & Marinelli, G. (2013). Resource allocation by the banking system. In G. Toniolo (Ed.), *The Oxford handbook of the Italian economy since unification* (pp. 485–515). Oxford: Oxford University Press.

Brealey, R. A., & Myers, S. C. (2003). *Principles of corporate finance*. Boston, MA: McGraw-Hill/Irwin.

Cafaro, P. (2000). Alle origini del sistema bancario in Lombardia: Casse di risparmio e banchieri privati. In G. Conti & S. La Francesca (Eds.), *Banche e Reti di Banche nell'Italia Postunitaria* (pp. 437–502). Bologna: Il Mulino.

Carnevali, F. (1996). Between markets and networks: Regional banks in Italy. *Business History, 38*(3), 83–100.

Carnevali, F. (2005). *Europe's advantage: Banks and small firms in Britain, France, Germany, and Italy since 1918*. Oxford: Oxford University Press.

Cohen, J. (1967). Financing industrialization in Italy, 1894–1914: The partial transformation of a late-comer. *The Journal of Economic History, 27*(03), 363–382. doi:10.1017/S0022050700068959

Conti, G., & Ferri, G. (1997). Banche locali e sviluppo economico decentrato. In F. Barca (Ed.). *Storia del capitalismo italiano dal dopoguerra a oggi* (pp. 429–465). Rome: Donzelli.

David, T., & Westerhuis, G. (Eds.). (2014). *The power of corporate networks. A comparative and historical perspective*. New York, NY: Routledge.

De Luca, G. (2005). *La Costruzione della Fiducia. La Banca di Legnano, le Imprese e il Territorio tra Miracolo Economico e Globalizzazione*. Legnano: Banca di Legnano.

De Nooy, W., Mrvar, A., & Batagelj, V. (2011). *Explanatory social network analysis with Pajek*. New York, NY: Cambridge University Press.

Fohlin, C. (1998). Fiduciari and firm liquidity constraint: the Italian experience with German-style universal banking. *Explorations in Economic History, 35*(1), 83–107. doi:10.1006/exeh.1997.0690

Fohlin, C. (1999). Capital mobilisation and utilisation in latecomer economies: Germany and Italy compared. *European Review of Economic History, 3*(2), 139–174. doi:10.1017/S1361491699000088

Fohlin, C. (2007). *Finance capitalism and Germany's rise to industrial power*. New York, NY: Cambridge University Press.

Gerschenkron, A. (1962). *Economic backwardness in historical perspective*. Cambridge, MA: Cambridge University Press.

Kotz, D. (1978). *Bank control of large corporations in the United States*. Berkeley, CA: University of California Press.

La Francesca, S. (2004). *Storia del Sistema bancario italiano*. Bologna: Il Mulino.

Lescure, M. (2008). Banking and finance. In G. Jones & J. Zeitlin (Eds.), *The Oxford handbook of business history* (pp. 319–346). Oxford: Oxford University Press.

Mintz, B., & Schwartz, M. (1985). *The power structure of American business*. Chicago, IL: University of Chicago Press.

Pennings, J. M. (1980). *Interlocking directorates: Origins and consequences of connections among organizations' boards of directors*. San Francisco, CA: Jossey-Bass.

Pfeffer, J. (1988). A resource dependence perspective on intercorporate relations. In M. Mizruchi & M. Schwartz (Eds.). *Intercorporate relations: The structural analysis of business* (pp. 25–55). Cambridge: Cambridge University Press.

Pfeffer, J., & Salancik, G. R. (1978). *The external control of organizations: A resource dependence perspective*. New York, NY: Harper & Row.

Piluso, G. (2009). Le banche locali in Italia: Pluralità e segmentazione. In G. Conti, O. Feiertag, & R. Scatamacchia (Eds.). *Credito e nazione in Francia e in Italia (XIX-XX secolo)* (pp. 245–267). Pisa: Pisa University Press.

Rajan, R., & Zingales, L. (2003). The great reversals: The politics of financial development in the twentieth century. *Journal of Financial Economics, 69*(1), 5–50. doi:10.1016/S0304-405X(03)00125-9

Stiglitz, J. E., & Weiss, A. (1981). Credit rationing in markets with imperfect information. *The American Economic Review, 71*(3), 393–410.

Stiglitz, J. E., & Weiss, A. (1990). Banks as social accountants and screening devices for the allocation of credit [supplemental material]. *Greek Economic Review, 12*, 85–118.

Stokman, F.S., Ziegler, R. & Scott, J. (Eds.). (1985). *Networks of corporate power. A comparative analysis of ten countries*. Cambridge: Polity.

Teti, R. (1999). Imprese, imprenditori e diritto. In F. Amatori, D. Bigazzi, R. Giannetti, & L. Segreto (Eds), *Storia d'Italia. Annali 15: L'industria* (pp. 1211–1303). Turin: Einaudi.

Toniolo, G. (1995). Italian banking, 1919–1936. In C. H. Feinstein (Ed.). *Banking, currency, and finance in Europe between the wars* (pp. 296–314). Oxford: Clarendon Press.

Useem, M. (1984). *The inner circle*. New York, NY: Oxford University Press.

Vasta, M. (2006). Appendix: The source and the Imita.db dataset. In R. Giannetti & M. Vasta (Eds.), *Evolution of Italian enterprises in the 20th century* (pp. 269–273). Heidelberg: Physica Verlag. [The database is available online: http://imitadb.unisi.it]

Vasta, M., & Baccini, A. (1997). Bank and industry and Italy 1911–1936: New evidence using interlocking directorates technique. *Financial History Review*, *4*(2), 139–159.

Vasta, M., Drago, C., Ricciuti, R., & Rinaldi, A. (2017). Reassessing the bank-industry relationship in Italy, 1913-1936: A counterfactual analysis. *Cliometrica*, *20*(2), 183–216. doi:10.1007/s11698-016-0142-9

Wasserman, S., & Faust, K. (Eds.). (1994). *Social network analysis. Methods and applications*. Cambridge: Cambridge University Press.

Windolf, P. (2009). Coordination and control in corporate networks: United States and Germany in comparison, 1896-1938. *European Sociological Review*, *25*(4), 443–457. doi:10.1093/esr/jcn059

Windolf, P. (2010). *Germany, France and the US: A statistical network analysis (1900-1938)*. Paper presented at the International Workshop 'Corporate Networks in Europe during the 20th Century'. Utrecht, November 12-13.

Index

Page numbers in **bold** refer to tables and those in *italic* font refer to figures.